Banks fail, but banks are not designed to be secured. The recent collapses of Signature Bank and Silicon Valley Bank (SVB) in March 2023 are, *inter alia*, showing that some banks are less secure despite all regulations. Although SVB parked many of its deposits in extremely safe assets, mainly long-term bonds issued by the US government and government-backed agencies, with increasing interest rates, the bank failed. Although the issues facing the US economy in 2023 are very different from those it faced in its last crisis, in 2008, one notes that since the year 2000, there have been 562 American bank failures (https://www.businessinsider.com/personal-finance/list-of-bank-failures). In the never-ending debate between systemic risk and regulation, this edited collection *Alternative Acquisition Models and Financial Innovation: Special Purpose Acquisition Companies in Europe, and the Italian Legal Framework* by Daniele D'Alvia, Ettore Maria Lombardi, and my former student Yochanan Shachmurove, is reminding us that the rise of non-banks can leverage new uninsurable risks: Special Purpose Acquisition Companies (SPACs) are a case in point. Law too has its regulatory limits, and we must never be complacent in our assumptions that we can simply regulate all market dangers away. Thus, rules are necessary rather than discretion.

Finn Kydland (Nobel Laureate), *Professor of Economics, University of California, Santa Barbara, California*

In concrete settings, the authors study how to 'regulate the regulators' in the face of possibly conflicting regulatory purposes and constituencies, model uncertainty, and consequent unintended consequences. The cases studied illustrate practical limits of available theories and tools.

Thomas J. Sargent (Nobel Laureate), *William R. Berkley Professor of Economics and Business, Leonard N. Stern School of Business, New York University*

This useful volume contains contributions from eminent legal scholars, particularly in Italy, to examine the legal framework for SPACs in the EU and Italy. A one-stop shop for everything one needs to know about how SPACs are set up, governed, regulated and subject to tax. A must-have for practitioners, the industry and corporate law researchers.

Iris H. Chiu, *Professor of Corporate Law and Financial Regulation, University College London*

Alternative Acquisition Models and Financial Innovation is a comprehensive analysis of Special Purpose Acquisition Companies (SPACs) in Europe, with a focus on the Italian legal framework. The book provides valuable insights into SPACs' financial regulation, corporate governance structure, and tax legal framework. The contributors are renowned scholars and practitioners in the field and the book is of great interest to anyone interested in financial innovation and securities law.

Luca Enriques, *Professor of Corporate Law, University of Oxford*

Special Purpose Acquisition Companies (SPACs) have become increasingly popular outside the United States. For practitioners and academics wishing to learn about their regulation in Italy and other non-US jurisdictions, I highly recommend this book.

Jesse M. Fried, *Professor of Law, Harvard Law School*

Businesses need new finance to be competitive on global markets. Even before the hard blows recorded in the banking world, not only overseas and not only for banks that operate in particularly innovative areas (example start-ups), but also in Germany and even in the Swiss stronghold, the banks have shown that they have lost the institutional function of reallocation of the collection in favor of their corporate clients. It is enough to examine their balance sheets to have proof of this. Today Funds and not always 'vultures', but also 'Angel Fund' and 'venture capitals', perform this function, but normally, have very high costs. SPACs can provide a good answer to this financial need, make assisted companies grow adequately and accompany them towards listing on the stock exchange. Certainly SPACs and their sponsors, if credible and worthy of trust, can constitute an important tool for economic and social development to achieve higher and more competitive business and corporate objectives.

Lucio Ghia, *Avvocato in Rome*

The book edited by D'Alvia, Lombardi and Shachmurove can be considered a milestone in the practical and theoretical comprehension of an institution that can be rightly considered a bright toolbox to use to solve relevant issues in the present and future of both private and commercial law.

Bruno Inzitari, *Professore di diritto civile, Dipartimento di Giurisprudenza, Università degli Studi di 'Milano-Bicocca'*

I had already the opportunity to appreciate the volume by Daniele D'Alvia, *Mergers, Acquisitions and International Financial Regulation*, published last year. This collective work constitutes, at the same time, its development and completion. The work offers a complete and convincing reconstruction of the discipline of SPACs in the European context, with particular focus on the Italian experience. The authors are able to offer an exhaustive picture of the first applications of these alternative structures of access to the capital market, which are gaining interesting spaces also in our country. The multidisciplinary analysis and the attention, on the one hand, to the theoretical-systematic reconstruction and, on the other, to practical themes make it a unique work in the literary panorama of the sector. The reader – both scholar and the practitioner – will find many suggestions and many answers, placed in the peculiar context of Italian corporate law, with specific reference to the delicate issues of corporate governance. In particular, we can appreciate the analysis dedicated to the use of shareholders' agreements within these structures, and the original insights on the phenomenon of the so-called shadow banking.

Raffaele Lener, *Professore di diritto dei mercati finanziari e di diritto commerciale, Universita di Roma 'Tor Vergata'*

Alternative Acquisition Models and Financial Innovation

This is the first book in English on Special Purpose Acquisition Companies (SPACs) in the context of European and Italian financial law, introducing the topic with a general overview at the European level. It is also the first book on the European financial regulation of SPACs. As such, it is a groundbreaking reference book for SPAC studies at the international level.

Alternative Acquisition Models and Financial Innovation: Special Purpose Acquisition Companies in Europe, and the Italian Legal Framework offers the most comprehensive overview of the current international financial regulation of SPACs in the EU and the UK against the main legal system where SPACs originate: the US. This edited book is focused on finding a European legal framework for SPACs by discovering whether the Alternative Investment Fund Managers Directive (AIFMD) or the Undertakings for the Collective Investment in Transferable Securities Directive (UCITS) are applicable to them or not, and why; and identifying the objectives of financial regulation of SPACs in the EU, the US and the UK.

Essentially, the edited collection explores soft law and self-regulation instances against the state-based Westphalian approaches that are centred on hard law instances; describes practical examples of SPACs in Italy and Europe; and analyses the limits and perspectives of such investment vehicles on the Italian capital market as well as their possible uses as forms of shadow banking and venture companies at the international level.

Daniele D'Alvia is Lecturer in Banking and Finance Law at CCLS – Queen Mary University of London, an associate research fellow at the Institute of Advanced Legal Studies in London and an associate researcher at the European Banking Institute in Frankfurt.

Ettore Maria Lombardi is Professor of Private Law and International Business Law at the University of Florence School of Law and of counsel at Lombardi and Hage-Chahine Law Firm.

Yochanan Shachmurove is Professor of Economics and Business at the City College and the Graduate Center of the City University of New York (CUNY), affiliated with the Department of Economics at New York University, US, and is the Economic MA Program Director at the City College of CUNY.

Routledge International Studies in Money and Banking

For more information about this series, please visit: www.routledge.com/Routledge-International-Studies-in-Money-and-Banking/book-series/SE0403

Alternative Acquisition Models and Financial Innovation

Special Purpose Acquisition Companies in Europe, and the Italian Legal Framework

Edited by
Daniele D'Alvia, Ettore Maria Lombardi
and Yochanan Shachmurove

LONDON AND NEW YORK

First published 2024
by Routledge
4 Park Square, Milton Park, Abingdon, Oxon OX14 4RN

and by Routledge
605 Third Avenue, New York, NY 10158

Routledge is an imprint of the Taylor & Francis Group, an informa business

British Library Cataloguing-in-Publication Data
A catalogue record for this book is available from the British Library

Library of Congress Cataloging-in-Publication Data
Names: D'Alvia, Daniele, editor. | Lombardi, Ettore Maria, editor. |
    Shachmurove, Yochanan, editor.
Title: Alternative acquisition models and financial innovation : special
    purpose acquisition companies in Europe, and the Italian legal
    framework / edited by Daniele D'Alvia, Ettore Maria Lombardi and
    Yochanan Shachmurove.
Description: Abingdon, Oxon [UK] ; New York, NY : Routledge,
    2023. | Includes bibliographical references and index.
Identifiers: LCCN 2023018693 (print) | LCCN 2023018694 (ebook) |
    ISBN 9780367769314 (hardback) | ISBN 9780367769321 (paperback) |
    ISBN 9781003169079 (ebook)
Subjects: LCSH: Special purpose acquisition companies—Europe. |
    Consolidation and merger of corporations—Law and legislation—
    Europe. | Going public (Securities)—Law and legislation—Europe. |
    Tender offers (Securities)—Law and legislation—Europe. | Financial
    institutions, International—Law and legislation—Europe. | Financial
    services industry—Law and legislation—Europe.
Classification: LCC KJC2628 .A94 2023 (print) | LCC KJC2628
    (ebook) | DDC 346.4/06626—dc23/eng/20230808
LC record available at https://lccn.loc.gov/2023018693
LC ebook record available at https://lccn.loc.gov/2023018694

ISBN: 978-0-367-76931-4 (hbk)
ISBN: 978-0-367-76932-1 (pbk)
ISBN: 978-1-003-16907-9 (ebk)

DOI: 10.4324/9781003169079

Typeset in Sabon LT Pro
by Apex CoVantage, LLC

Contents

Figures

Tables

About the Editors

Daniele D'Alvia is Lecturer in Banking and Finance Law at CCLS – Queen Mary University of London, an associate research fellow at the Institute of Advanced Legal Studies in London and an associate researcher at the European Banking Institute in Frankfurt. Prior to joining Queen Mary University of London, he was the Ronnie Warrington Scholar in Comparative Law at Birkbeck College, University of London, and he was the Module Convener of Business Law at Bayes Business School, City University of London, former Cass.

He is an internationally recognised expert on SPACs, corporate finance law, M&As law, investment banking, international finance and international financial regulation. He is a pioneer in SPAC studies in law, author of the first book on SPACs ever published by Routledge in 2021, and award winner of the Colin B. Picker Prize by the American Society of Comparative Law.

He has authored law review articles, books and edited collections addressing issues ranging from payment systems, mobile payments and CBDC to financial stability treats stemming from fintech and mutual or pension funds. His research is eclectic, and it takes into account issues concerning financial history as well as sociology and comparative law methodologies.

He is frequently mentioned in financial newspapers or interviewed on matters related to financial regulation, private equity and SPACs. He is also a Bloomberg Contributor in New York City.

He is an Italian Qualified Lawyer, and he has worked at international law firms such as Bonelli Erede, Dewey&Leboeuf LLP and Deloitte LLP, where he assisted clients in relation to M&As transactions, bond issuance and initial public offerings (IPOs). He has also worked for the Financial Conduct Authority in London in the Criminal Investigation Unit, and he has acted as a consultant at the European Bank for Reconstruction and Development.

He has been a visiting researcher in leading universities and institutions such as the Commercial Law Centre at Harris Manchester College University of Oxford, the International Chamber of Commerce and the Max Planck Institute for Comparative and International Private Law.

 **Ettore Maria Lombardi** is Professor of Private Law and International Business Law at the University of Florence School of Law and of counsel at Lombardi & Hage-Chahine Law Firm. From an academic perspective, he is co-director (alongside Prof. Rodrigo Olivares-Caminal) of the Executive Course on Alternative Investment, which is organised by the Queen Mary University of London (Centre for Commercial Law Studies – CCLS), and co-director (alongside Prof. Marc-André Renold and Prof. Eike Schmidt) of the Executive Course on Art & Law, which is co-organised by the University of Florence School of Law, the Université de Genève and the Gallerie degli Uffizi.

He holds an LLB (University of Florence), a JCL (Pontifical University of Lateran), an LLM (Harvard Law School), a PhD (University of Florence), an advanced certificate in AI (Oxford Saïd Business School), an advanced certificate in Business Sustainability Management (University of Cambridge) and an advanced certificate in Sustainable Finance (University of Cambridge).

He is a visiting professor at Birkbeck College – University of London (London, UK), visiting scholar in dispute resolution at the Carey Center for Dispute Resolution, St. John's Law School (New York, US), research fellow at BRICS Competition Law and Policy Center of the National Research Higher School of Economics (Moscow, Russia), visiting fellow of the Institute for Global Law, Economics and Finance (IGLEF) at the Centre for Commercial Law Studies, Queen Mary University of London (London, UK), senior visiting fellow of private international law at UCLan Cyprus – School of Law (Pyla, Cyprus), and research associate at the University College London Centre for Blockchain Technologies – UCL CBT (London, UK).

From a professional perspective, prior to joining Hage-Chahine & Lombardi Law Firm (Beirut Florence Rome) as of counsel, Dr. Lombardi was of counsel at DLA Piper (Rome Milan).

He is a member of the Arbitro Bancario Finanziario by appointment of Bank of Italy (Bologna, Italy) and president of the Supervisory Board on "231 Model" at Nuovo Pignone Holding S.p.A. (global holding of the Baker Hughes Company) (Florence, Italy).

He has been teaching and researching at the most prestigious American, British and German universities, and he received various academic awards from distinguished and renowned universities and institutions. He is a lawyer in Italy and a member of various international legal associations, and among these, he is an event officer of the Harvard Law School

Association of Europe, member of the Association Henry Capitant (Paris, France) and The London Centre for Commercial and Financial Law – LCF (London, UK).

Dr. Lombardi has published four books *Warranty and Liability in the Sale of Consumer Goods*, Giuffré, Milano, 2010, p. XVI ff.; *The Financial Authorities' "Responsibilization": Models and Functions*, ESI, Napoli, 2016, p. 1 ff.; *The Impact of Digitalization on the Property: The* Copyleft, ESI, Napoli, 2020, p. 1 ff.; and *Person, Consciousness and Freedom, or the Contractual Autopoiesis*, Giuffré, Milano, 2022, p. 1 ff.). Also, he has published more than 50 articles published in nationally and internationally renowned law reviews.

Yochanan Shachmurove is Professor of Economics and Business at the City College and the Graduate Center of the City University of New York (CUNY), and affiliated with the Department of Economics at New York University, US. He is the Economic MA Program Director at the City College of CUNY. For more than 25 years, he was affiliated with the University of Pennsylvania. Dr. Shachmurove has worked with the Harvard Institute for International Development advising the government of Ukraine with regard to its macroeconomic policies, including fiscal policy, energy and natural resources issues. He has served as a guest editor for three special issues of the *International Journal of Business*, two of them dealing with financial markets of the Middle East, and one co-edited with Nobel Laureate Professor Lawrence Klein about the BRICS (Brazilian, Russian, Indian, Chinese and South African) economies. Additionally, he has served as a guest editor for two issues of the *Journal of Entrepreneurial Finance and Business Ventures*. He is the editor of the Proceedings of the Academy of Entrepreneurial Finance, 2002.

He has been on the board of many journals, including *Montenegrin Journal of Ecology, Studia Historiae Oeconomicae, The Journal of Adam Mickiewicz University, Poznan University of Economics Review, Economics and Economy* and *Interdisciplinary Journal of Economics and Business Law*.

Prof. Shachmurove has taught at leading institutions of higher learning in five continents and has been awarded four Fulbright Senior Specialist awards in Shanghai, China in 2004, in Lodz, Poland in 2003–2004, in Warsaw, Poland in 2010–2011 and in Kiev, Ukraine in 2014.

Dr. Shachmurove has published extensively in the areas of economics, finance and management with more than 150 refereed papers and more than 200 papers accepted for presentation at professional meetings throughout the world, travelling to numerous numbers of countries. His papers are published in journals, including, among others, *Kyklos, Public Choice, The*

Manchester Journal, Review of International Economics, Review of Development Economics and The World Economy.

Prof. Shachmurove has been awarded grants from, among others, the Kauffman Foundation; the US State Department; The Institute for International Education Research; The Eurasia Foundation; and University of Pennsylvania, Institute for Economic Research.

Main research interests of his include applied econometrics (including vector auto regressions, Bayesian vector auto regressions, emulative neural networks, non-linear deterministic systems and chaos), international economics, international finance, economic growth, industrial organization, entrepreneurial finance, law and economics and futures and options.

Prof. Shachmurove likes to read, write, sing, enjoy music and run regressions.

Contributors

Filippo Annunziata is Professor of Financial Markets Law at Bocconi University, Milan. He is the author and co-author of a long list of publications in the fields of financial markets legislation, banking legislation and EU Law. Before Bocconi University, he taught at the University of Bologna, where he held courses in financial law, banking law and antitrust law. He is the founder of AC Group, a network of professionals based in Italy that covers the entire range of services for the financial industry. Prof. Annunziata also holds a PhD in musicology and teaches at the Università Statale of Milan. He is the author of several articles and books on music, and in particular on opera and law.

Giuseppe Cavallaro graduated in law from the University of Rome Tor Vergata, where he obtained a PhD in legal protection of rights, businesses and administrations, and is qualified to practice law and legal representation before the Supreme Court of Justice in Italy. He is a contract professor, among other positions, and holds additional teaching contracts for the Chairs of Financial Market Law and Commercial Law at the University of Rome LUISS Guido Carli, where he is a lecturer in banking and finance law. He is also the director of the master in listed companies and the master in NPLs at the Tutela dei diritti association in Rome.

Anna Chiara Chisari graduated in law from Bocconi University (Italy) with an executive master in finance from SDA Bocconi. She specialises in financial markets with a focus on economic and legal/regulatory issues of structured products (certificates, bonds, derivatives) and funds under EU (Luxembourg and Italy) and Swiss law. Currently, she is the legal counsel at Heritage Holdings and teaching assistant at Bocconi University, supporting teaching and research activities in the field of financial markets, including fintech space.

Giorgio Tosetti Dardanelli holds a dual Italian and French law degree from Universities of Turin (Italy) and Nice-Sophia Antipolis (France) and is a dual qualified Italian lawyer and solicitor in England and Wales. In 2010, he obtained an LLM in banking law and financial regulation from the

London School of Economics and Political Science, defending a dissertation on hedge fund regulation under the supervision of Prof. Niamh Moloney. He has extensive experience in legal, compliance, regulatory and corporate matters related to the banking, financial and payment services industries. Dardanelli is currently the general counsel and Corporte Secretary of Banca Profilo, a boutique private bank listed on the Milan Stock Exchange, which is also very active in investment banking and payments and holds subsidiaries in Switzerland and Luxembourg.

Maria Lucia Passador is an academic fellow in corporate law and financial markets at Bocconi University. She is also a research associate at the University College London Centre for Blockchain Technologies. She works as a law clerk for Davis Polk and Wardwell LLP advising corporate, financial institution and private equity clients on a wide range of cross-border capital markets, corporate finance and M&A transactions. These include cross-border IPOs, SPACs, private placements, investment-grade, high-yield, convertible and regulatory capital debt offerings as well as liability management transactions.

Raimondo Premonte has over 25 years' experience in advising multinational corporations, investment banks and private equity funds in cross-border M&A transactions, public tender offers and other stock exchange transactions, complex restructures and equity capital raisings. He joined Gianni Origoni and Partners in 1995, and from 1998–2000, he served as general counsel of a corporation listed on the Milan Stock Exchange. From 2000–2003, Mr. Premonte was a senior associate of the firm, with the New York offices of Linklaters. During those years he was also a sessional lecturer in corporate law at the New York University. He became partner of the firm in 2005. He led the public M&A department of the firm, and from 2011, he became responsible for the London office, coordinating the international M&A activities.

Donato Romano is of counsel of Gianni Origoni Grippo and Partners specialising in M&A, corporate and commercial law, and providing legal assistance primarily in connection with acquisition transactions, including transfer of stock and businesses, drafting and negotiating joint ventures agreements, shareholders agreements and commercial agreements. He joined the firm in 2009. Mr. Romano graduated in law from the University of Rome in 2004 and obtained from there a PhD in 2006. He obtained an LLM with merit from the University College of London in 2008. In 2014, he was an academic visitor at the University of Oxford. He is the author of several legal publications in corporate law and bankruptcy law.

Giovanni Romano is a senior researcher in business law in the Department of Business and Law (University of Siena), where he teaches business law (basic) and insolvency law. Graduating cum laude from the University of Perugia, he received a PhD in banking and financial market law from the

University of Siena, where he then worked as a research fellow in business law. His research mainly focuses on company and banking law, with special attention to company director duties and cooperative banks; the law and regulation of financial contracts and collective investment schemes; and insolvency law. He is a member of the editorial boards of the reviews 'Ianus' (the on-line review of the Department of Business and Law – University of Siena) and 'Diritto della Banca e del mercato finanziario'.

Luisa Scarcella is Global Policy Lead of Taxation at the International Chamber of Commerce in Paris. She received her PhD in tax and fiscal law in 2020 from the Karl-Franzens University of Graz (Austria), where she was a research and teaching assistant from 2016–2020. She is a research fellow at University College London (UCL Centre for Blockchain Technologies), and during her PhD, she worked as a research associate at Cambridge Centre for Alternative Finance. Dr. Scarcella received her LLM from the University of Udine (Italy) in 2015. Before starting her PhD, she interned at the European Investment Bank (Luxembourg) in 2013 and at the European Central Bank (Frankfurt am Main) in 2015. Her research interests include international and European tax law, comparative tax law, law and technology.

Foreword

In the hearings related to the Securities Enforcement Remedies and Penny Stock Reform Act of 1990, the US Attorney for the District of Utah stated regarding blank check companies' (BCCs) initial public offering (IPO):

> [We] find no evidence that these offerings provide any benefit to the U.S. economy or capital formation.

After more than thirty years, between 2020 and 2022, this sentence has been remarkably reversed. Special Purpose Acquisition Companies (SPACs) are not BCCs. Indeed, as opposed to BCCs and notwithstanding the Securities and Exchange Commission efforts to bring SPACs down, the majority of 2020–2022 SPACs gained a remarkable new reputation. For the first time, important underwriters were acting as bookrunners and co-managers (including Citigroup, UBS Investment Bank, JP Morgan etc.). Furthermore, there was a shift in the quality of the teams that were sponsoring SPACs (e.g. Bill Ackman, Goldman Sachs, Michael Klein, Douglas Braunstein and Chamath Palihapitiya) and there was a higher quality of investors in terms of important hedge funds and private equity firms. Beyond critiques, it is clear that SPACs are a remarkable form of capitalism: they are a form of financing, and so far they represent a unique alternative acquisition model as well as an alternative path to traditional IPOs.

I believe that SPACs constitute also one of the most important grand experiments that have ever been conducted so far in the financial history of US securities law since the enactment by Congress of the Securities Act of 1933. In 2023, after one hundred years, the SPAC has the unique chance to re-write the future of securities law in the United States. The SPACs are the reverse of the normal IPO procedure. Instead of the operating company seeking investors, investors seek an operating company. This is undeniably reforming the future of underwriters which in the case of SPACs – as opposed to traditional IPO – are re-framing their original role as gate-keepers of public markets. Indeed, in SPACs, an underwriter will perform more the role of an advisor and broker rather than a gate-keeper of public markets. This is because SPACs are non-operating companies (namely, they are cash-shell vehicles) without previous balance sheets or financial information to scrutinise apart from the verification of the track-record of the sponsor management team. It is undeniable that in the years to come, the management team shall keep and increase in quality because this is the only valuable asset that a potential public investor as well as an underwriter can evaluate.

It is against this background that this edited collection represents a very important effort in financial literacy in Europe and the US. Daniele D'Alvia of Queen Mary University of London has already been known for writing the first book on SPACs ever in comparative law titled *Mergers, Acquisitions, and International Financial Regulation: Analysing Special Purpose Acquisition Companies* (Routledge 2021). This time he writes and co-edits this collection of chapters on European SPACs together with Ettore Maria Lombardi of University of Florence and Yochanan Shachmurove of the Graduate College of the City University of New York.

The edited collection highlights that in Europe, SPACs are still a growing market because of four main features:

I. A diversification of corporate law provisions in relation to redemption rights that may vary from Member State to Member State
II. Different investment cultures by which European investors are more risk-averse
III. The variegated structures of the promote, namely founders' shares that in Europe take the form of preference shares
IV. The different structure of units that in the case of Europe are not necessarily implying shares and warrants, but might concern only the issuance of preference shares to public investors (think of 2MX Organic listed on Euronext Paris in December 2020 with the admission to trading and direct listing of 30,000,0000 preference shares and 30,000,000 stock warrants)

The authors analyse limits and perspectives both from a financial regulation point of view and from a company law perspective with also a specific focus on the Italian legal system in Parts I and II of this edited collection. Indeed, in Europe, there is not a harmonised legal framework for SPACs or a better uniform European secondary legislation such a Directive or Regulation focused on SPACs, as this edited collection by D'Alvia, Lombardi and Shachmurove is claiming numerous times. The same is true for SPAC listing requirements that are not enshrined in any European Exchange's market rules, with the very recent exception of the London Stock Exchange in late 2021, and the Italian AIM since 2018.

SPACs are targeting growing companies. Hence, they are definitely an important tool of progression and an instrument of wealth in economic terms. Indeed, as this edited collection highlights, SPACs are also useful investment vehicles capable of attracting new capital inflows into economies. Furthermore, SPACs generally increase liquidity in financial markets, something that today is desperately needed, following the numerous systemic liquidity crises both in the United States and in Europe at the banking level. Indeed, SPAC's units composed of shares and warrants are separately tradable securities from a few days after the closing of the IPO phase, and redemption rights are an undeniable means of liquidity for public investors that are exercisable until the moment of the completion of the business combination. This is why SPACs are defined as risk-free investments until the de-SPAC phase, namely the business combination. Nonetheless, in the face of many potential macro-economic benefits, SPACs may present a series of micro-economic shortcomings such as information asymmetry and moral hazard on the side of managers. Those economic issues are prominently addressed in this edited collection. Disclosures are the way forward, although in the case of SPACs, such disclosures at the IPO phase can only be illustrative rather than definitive. In fact, at the pre-IPO and IPO phases of the SPAC, it is impossible to determine the structure of the business combination because the identity of the target company is not known. To this end, the edited collection shows how the Italian legal framework might constitute a rare exception with the definition of 'instant-SPACs', namely SPACs that have already identified a target company pre-IPO and, therefore, are able to announce the business combination only a few months completing the IPO phase. Finally, the SPAC sponsor needs to be creative. This is the main instruction of this edited collection. Beyond regulatory concerns the future of SPACs is based on avoiding an excessive dilution of public investors post-business combination. This can only be possible through innovative sponsorship structures where the management concedes and shares the creation of value post-business combination with the public investors that sustained and supported the SPAC during the listing process.

This is a very well-written and magisterially supervised work that surely will constitute a point of reference for lawyers, SPAC sponsors, public investors, target companies, and financial regulators world-wide.

Prof. Milos Vulanovic (EDHEC Business School)

Paris, 25 March 2023

Foreword

I.   Sono molteplici e profondi i cambiamenti che, soprattutto nell'ultimo decennio, stanno incidendo sulla struttura del mercato e, in particolare, sulle dinamiche concorrenziali tra gli operatori, impegnati a confrontarsi in modalità innovative riconducibili al passaggio dall'analogico al digitale. L'attenzione dei giuristi – nell'intento di ricercare formule tecnico/organizzative idonee a fluidificare lo svolgimento dei rapporti negoziali – non si limita all'analisi dell'impatto della cibernetica sulla realtà economico finanziaria in osservazione; si riscontra, infatti, un crescente interesse alla riscoperta di modelli, già sperimentati nel passato, oggi rivisitati in una logica coerente con l'istanza alla realizzazione di un intenso programma di riforme.

In tale contesto si colloca il volume sulla SPAC (*Special Purpose Acquisition Company*), curato da Daniele D'Alvia, Ettore Maria Lombardi e Yochanan Shachmurove, nel quale si analizzano detti veicoli di investimento costituiti specificatamente per raccogliere capitale al fine di effettuare operazioni di fusione e/o acquisizione di un'azienda c.d. *target*. L'espresso riferimento, formulato nel titolo dell'opera, a "modelli di acquisizione alternativa", riporta l'indagine in un ambito di finanza innovativa, affiancando la costituzione delle SPAC alle moderne strumentazioni di apporto di capitali per finanziare la gestione operativa e le spese correnti fino alla data dell'offerta pubblica iniziale (IPO) di titoli azionari con cui una società provvede alla loro collocazione sul mercato borsistico, offrendoli al pubblico degli investitori.

L'indagine ha riguardo all'impianto sistemico dello schema organizzativo che trae origine dalle "*blank check companies*", società che iniziarono ad operare sul mercato statunitense all'inizio degli anni ottanta del secolo scorso, il cui modello è stato ampiamente analizzato in letteratura con valutazioni non sempre positive, come quella del commissario della SEC Schapiro che ne evidenziò i profili di pericolosità.

Nello specifico, le principali fasi della 'vita sociale' della SPAC si articolano nella ricerca e nella acquisizione di una società *target* non quotata – che presenti significative prospettive di crescita – ad opera di alcuni promotori, soggetti dotati di riconosciute capacità imprenditoriali e gestionali, nonché di capacità di *scouting* nel settore in grado di vantare un esteso *network* di contatti. I promotori svolgono un compito particolarmente delicato, per il quale non ricevono un compenso, né una commissione calcolata sulla massa del capitale gestito *(*il c.d. *management fee)*; essi sono, infatti, remunerati solo al momento della *business combination* attraverso il conferimento di *warrant* di sottoscrizione di azioni ordinarie a condizioni particolarmente vantaggiose, o azioni speciali, con rapporti di conversione premianti. La società *target* da essi individuata deve presentare le caratteristiche indicate nella "politica di investimento" adottata dalla SPAC al fine di consentire la sottoposizione dell'operazione alla approvazione dell'assemblea dei soci, con piena *disclosure* delle caratteristiche della società *target*, ivi incluse le informazioni relative al *business* di quest'ultima e allo specifico settore in cui essa opera.

Si è in presenza di una costruzione nella quale è consentito agli investitori di controllare le modalità con cui il denaro investito viene utilizzato dai *manager* della SPAC, mitigando quindi i principali rischi insiti nell'investimento. Segnatamente rileva l'impossibilità per un potenziale investitore di fare affidamento sul *track record* della società; infatti, in assemblea gli azionisti della SPAC possono votare a favore o contro il perfezionamento della *business combination*.

L'investimento nella società *target* può essere realizzato in differenti modalità, sebbene la prassi di mercato prevalente abbia evidenziato una scelta preferenziale per l'incorporazione da parte della SPAC, con la conseguenza che la società acquisita assume automaticamente lo *status* di società quotata. E' possibile anche che sia la società *target* ad incorporare la SPAC, con il risultato che i soci di quest'ultima riceveranno in concambio azioni della prima (tenuta, nel frattempo, ad avviare e completare il processo di quotazione, sì da consentire ai soci della SPAC di ricevere azioni quotate senza soluzione di continuità). Da ultimo, lo *Special Purpose* in parola potrebbe limitarsi ad acquistare una partecipazione sociale nella società bersaglio senza procedere ad un'ulteriore forma di integrazione, per cui assumerebbe la natura di una *holding* di partecipazioni.

II. E' evidente come il meccanismo posto a fondamento della complessa formula operativa dianzi delineata si presti ad un'interessante analisi giuridica in relazione ai molteplici aspetti di 'diritto societario' che ne caratterizzano i contenuti.

Al riguardo, si fa presente che appare problematico lo stesso accordo di investimento stipulato tra gli *sponsor*; donde talune perplessità riguardanti il procedimento da cui trae origine la costituzione della *newco* alla quale vengono conferiti i capitali iniziali per dar corso all'operazione. A ben considerare, infatti, si è in presenza di un *iter* negoziale che sembra riconducibile a quello a base della configurazione di un *Club Deal,* rappresentativo di un 'gruppo selezionato' che si prefigge la realizzazione di investimenti col proprio patrimonio, contribuendo allo sviluppo dell'economia reale; ciò avendo di mira l'obiettivo di rinvenire, per tal via, una valida soluzione al finanziamento delle *start up* o imprese innovative e ad elevato potenziale di crescita.

In altri termini, di fronte alla realtà che si individua nella SPAC, ci si deve chiedere se detta formula operativa non abbia una valida – e forse più *semplice* misura sostitutiva – nell'*agere* finanziario che si compendia nel *crowdfunding,* anch'essa tecnica di finanza alternativa alla strumentazione tradizionale utilizzata per sovvenire alle esigenze delle piccole e medie imprese. Di certo, sul piano teleologico, nella fattispecie in esame ricorrono i medesimi presupposti che connotano la misura da ultimo nominata, come è dato desumere dal fatto che anche alle SPAC è stato dato ampio sviluppo a seguito della crisi degli anni 2007 e seguenti, allorché si è dovuto affrontare il problema di superare le difficoltà derivanti, soprattutto alle piccole e medie imprese, da una diffusa restrizione del credito bancario.

Consegue la necessità di approfondire il sottoinsieme delle relazioni negoziali attraverso le quali persone fisiche, investitori istituzionali e professionali, mediante innovative modalità d'incontro, aderiscono alla richiesta di risorse avanzata dai promotori (*rectius*: soggetti collegati a imprese di ridotte dimensioni) delle SPAC che intendono realizzare un progetto comune. E' ben vero che gli *editors*, Daniele D'Alvia ed Ettore Maria Lombardi, analizzando la regolazione in materia (vigente nell'EU e nel Regno Unito) sottolineano che gli *sponsor* in questione si impegnano attivamente con i propri investitori una volta identificato un obiettivo che presenti interesse economico; ciò, tuttavia, non è sufficiente ad assicurare un alto tasso di probabilità di successo dell'operazione, in quanto non viene eliminato (ma solo ridotto) il rischio sotteso alle iniziative di cui trattasi, le quali evidenziano un'alea analoga a quella che caratterizza le attività rivolte *ad incertam personam* e, dunque, sottratte a compiute valutazioni di razionalità economica.

A ciò si aggiunga che i rischi in parola appaiono significativamente elevati ove si abbia riguardo alle asimmetrie informative che per solito contraddistinguono il mercato, nonché alla mancanza di garanzie in ordine agli esiti di tale investimento; fattori d'indagine che inducono a ravvisare ampi profili di pericolosità nella posizione del finanziatore il quale, divenuto partecipe delle sorti dell'impresa, è esposto senza limitazione alcuna alle intemperie di un possibile *default* di quest'ultima, ipotizzabile specie nella fase di avvio della gestione. Di ciò è conferma la crescente attenzione dedicata dalla SEC statunitense alla forma di investimento in questione, orientamento del quale si dà atto nel volume richiamando le prime 'linee guida' sulle SPAC emanate da detta autorità di controllo; del pari ne è riprova la considerazione formulata dagli *editors* del volume secondo cui 'le acquisizioni effettuate tramite SPAC possono essere più costose dal punto di vista del venditore rispetto a una tradizionale IPO'.

Ed ancora, non possono trascurarsi le perplessità correlate alle modalità di adozione delle delibere da parte dell'assemblea dei soci di una SPAC; ciò ove si faccia riferimento vuoi alla identificazione delle maggioranze previste dalla legge, vuoi all'esercizio del diritto di recesso, fermo restando che per solito gli statuti condizionano al mancato esercizio del diritto di recesso l'efficacia delle delibere funzionali alla realizzazione della *business combination*. Va da sé come, in tale contesto, si delinei la proposizione di ulteriori dubbi in ordine alle prospettive di una facile operatività riservata dalla regolazione ai modelli societari che fanno ricorso al mercato del capitale di rischio, ponendosi al di fuori degli schemi tradizionali; dubbi che si acuiscono in base alla considerazione secondo cui, alla scadenza del termine di durata della società, le entità soggettive che non riescono a realizzare l'oggetto sociale vanno messe in liquidazione.

Non a caso in alcuni contributi di questo volume (v. Filippo Annunziata – Anna Chiara Chisari – Maria Lucia Passador) si segnala che il rapporto tra la struttura delle SPAC e la legislazione sui mercati finanziari non risulta lineare; ipotesi ricostruttiva che sembra condivisibile sulla base delle considerazioni poste a fondamento della stessa. Ci si riferisce all'assunto secondo cui alcune aree della regolamentazione finanziaria non si applicano alle SPAC, nonché alla considerazione che queste ultime talora non rientrano nell'ambito di alcuni settori della legislazione dei mercati dei capitali, mentre tal altra beneficiano di specifiche esenzioni da alcune disposizioni ovvero possono essere interamente assoggettate a determinati tipi di regolazione.

III. Dalle brevi considerazioni che precedono si evince che la strategia di investimento delle SPAC presenta una connotazione idonea a farle conseguire un *appeal* nel mercato, donde il successo riscontrato in taluni paesi (come l'Italia). Nello specifico, rileva il vantaggio di beneficiare della accelerazione del processo di quotazione della società *target,* evitando situazioni (*in primis* la volatilità dei mercati) che non consentono un'adeguata valorizzazione del titolo portato in quotazione. Inoltre, va ascritto peculiare rilievo alla circostanza che la valutazione della società *target* (in termini di rapporti di concambio, ecc.) viene stabilita in maniera autonoma dalle parti indipendentemente dalle condizioni dei mercati (evitando il meccanismo del *bookbuilding*).

Non può trascurarsi di osservare, tuttavia, che la vigente regolamentazione non elimina alcune discrasie riscontrabili in sede applicativa, per cui si individua la possibile evenienza di rischi con riguardo a specifici aspetti del procedimento costitutivo ovvero alla effettiva resa dell'investimento. Ciò ridimensiona i menzionati vantaggi della operazione, ai quali deve aggiungersi anche quello – cui si fa riferimento in alcuni contributi del volume – relativo alla mitigazione del rischio di molti riscatti riveniente dal *Private Investment in Public Equity* (PIPE); infatti, nel caso in cui scende il prezzo di mercato al di sotto di determinate soglie, la società potrebbe essere costretta ad emettere azioni aggiuntive ad un prezzo ridotto, con l'ovvia conseguenza di causare una riduzione del valore degli investimenti degli azionisti.

Per concludere può dirsi che il veicolo societario in osservazione grazie alla sua particolare funzione – vale a dire l'acquisizione di società, da effettuare tramite una raccolta di fondi tra investitori interessati alla tipologia di operazione dianzi delineata – si presta ad una larga diffusione, che può decretarne il successo. Ne consegue che la struttura della *Special purpose acquisition company* deve ritenersi idonea alla promozione di affari nel mercato azionario, bypassando il classico *iter* d'ingresso in tale mercato e facilitando l'apertura del medesimo verso settori operativi che diversamente ne sarebbero rimasti al di fuori.

Restano fermi i limiti che derivano dalla natura di 'scatola vuota' ascrivibile, sul piano delle concretezze, alla Spac; donde le possibili conseguenze negative di cui si è detto, le quali potrebbero essere ulteriormente aggravate da ipotizzabili elusioni delle forme di controllo che le normative domestiche ed europea pongono a tutela degli investitori.

Professor Francesco Capriglione
Roma, 4 Aprile 2023

Acknowledgements

Writing on Special Purpose Acquisition Companies (SPACs) today is a challenging activity, but surely one that is worth it because SPACs represent the new alternative acquisition models of the future, especially following the collapse of Silicon Valley Bank in March 2023. In other words, SPACs might act as late-stage venture capital financing. However, since 2022, the Securities and Exchange Commission (SEC) has remarkably influenced and dominated the SPAC debate with a negative prospective. This new approach has surely had a negative effect both on SPAC sponsors and on public investors alike in the United States. By contrast, in the European Union and the UK, the financial regulators have adopted a principle of technical neutrality by establishing a regulation by objectives. In doing so, we would like to firmly argue that a regulation by enforcement is simply a *de facto* regulation that is mainly punitive, and it hardly respects the supreme and universal principles of the rule of law that US Founding Fathers wished to recognise, protect and respect. In other words, it shall not be the role of a financial regulator or supervisor to pick 'winners' and 'losers' in the SPAC market. This function should be left to the market itself. Regulatory steps that are taken beyond the fulfilment of the principle of the rule of law shall worry us. This is one of the main teachings we have learnt from writing and supervising this edited collection.

During the long gestations of this co-edited book on SPACs, we have benefitted and would like to thank our research assistants, Teona Andonovska and Yansong Zhang, from New York University, and Jennifer V. Lavayen, Sidie S. Sisay, Cassidy Drummond and Tanmay M. Thomas from the City College of the City University of New York.

We would like also to thank friends and colleagues who have shared with us precious insights. We thank Ferdinand Mason of White&Case (London office); Esther Warburg and Victor Artola Recolons of Ontier (Madrid Office); Axel Wittmann and George Hacket of Clifford Chance (Frankfurt Office); Dewi Habraken of JTC Group (Amsterdam Office); and Douglas Ellenoff of Ellenoff Grossman & Schole LLP in New York.

Professor Shachmurove thanks the Schwager Fund from the City College of the City University of New York, and the Professional Staff Congress of the City University of New York (PSC-CUNY) award # 65419–00 53 for the financial support to this project.

London, 24 March 2023

Abbreviations

ABS	Asset-Backed Securities
AIFMD	European Directive 2011/61/EU on the Alternative Investment Fund Manager
AIM	Alternative Investment Market or Euronext Growth Market since October 2021 in Italy, whereas in the UK the name 'AIM' is still retained under the London Stock Exchange
AMEX	American Stock Exchange
AQSE	Aquis Stock Exchange in London
Banca D'Italia	Bank of Italy (the Italian Central Bank)
Borsa Italiana or Borsa Italiana S.p.A.	The Italian Exchange in Milan, which is part of the Euronext Group
BV	*besloten vennootschap*
CCP	Central Counterparty
CDO	Collateralized Debt Obligation
CFIML	Captive Financial Institution and Money Lender
CNMV	*Comisión Nacional del Mercado de Valores* (National Securities Market Commission)
CONSOB	the *Commissione Nazionale per la Società e la Borsa*, namely the Italian public authority responsible for regulating the Italian financial markets (i.e. the Italian Financial Regulator)
CoVaR	Conditional Value-at-Risk
CP	Commercial Paper
de-SPAC	The transactional phase of the SPAC where the public investor funds either deposited in the escrow account or held on trust are used to complete the business combination
EBITDA	Earnings before interest, taxes, depreciation, and amortisation
ESG	Environmental, Social and Corporate Governance
ESMA	European Securities and Markets Authority
EU	European Union

FCA	Financial Conduct Authority
FDIC	Federal Deposit Insurance Corporation
Fintech	Financial Technology
FSMA	Financial Services and Markets Authority
FTSE	The Financial Times Stock Exchange 100 Index, also called the FTSE 100 Index, FTSE 100, FTSE or informally the 'Footsie'. It is a share index of the 100 companies listed on the London Stock Exchange with the highest market capitalisation
GAAP	Generally Accepted Accounting Principles
GBP	British Pound Sterling
GDP	Gross Domestic Product
GSE	Government-Sponsored Enterprise
ICC	Italian Civil Code
IMF	International Monetary Fund
IPO	Initial Public Offering
IRA	Italian Revenue Agency
LSE	London Stock Exchange
M&A	Merger and Acquisition
MIV	Market for Investment Vehicles
MLBO	Merger Leveraged Buy-Out
MMF	Money Market Fund
MSB	Money Services Businesses
MTA	*Mercato Telematico Azionario*
NASDAQ	National Association of Securities Dealers Automated Quotations
NBFI	Non-Bank Financial Intermediary
NV	*Naamloze vennootschap*
NYSE	New York Stock Exchange
OECD	Organisation for Economic Co-operation and Development
OFI	Other Financial Intermediary
OTC	Over-the-Counter
PBC	People's Bank of China
Prospectus Regulation	Regulation (EU) 2017/1129 of the European Parliament and the Council of 14 June 2017 on the Prospectus to be published when securities are offered to the public or admitted to trading on a regulated market, and repleading Directive 2003/71/EC
PSM	Penny Stock Market
SICAF	*Société d'investissement à capital fixe* or *Società di investimento a capitale fisso*
SICAV	*Société d'investissement à capital variable* or *Società di investimento a capitale variabile*

SIV	Special Investment Vehicle
SME	Small-Medium Enterprise
SOE	State-Owned Enterprise
SPAC/s	Special Purpose Acquisition Company/ies
SPV	Special Purpose Vehicle
SRL	*Société à responsabilité limitée*
TUF	Legislative Decree n. 58/1998 (Italy), the Italian Consolidated Law on Financial Intermediation
UCI	Undertakings for Collective Investment
UCITS	Undertakings for the Collective Investment in Transferable Securities
UK	United Kingdom
US	United States
WMP	Wealth Management Product
WRDS	Wharton Research Data Services

Introduction

This edited collection focuses on Special Purpose Acquisition Companies (SPACs) in Europe. It offers the most comprehensive overview of the current international financial regulation of SPACs in the European Union and the United Kingdom (U.K.) against the main legal system where SPAC originates: the United States (US).

The SPAC has come a long way from the obscure legal innovation of the 1980s era to a celebrity status symbol in 2020–2021.[1]

SPACs are born as blank check companies first listed on the Penny Stock Market (PSM) in the 1980s, performing mostly notorious 'pump-and-dump' schemes. While movies like *Wall Street* and *Barbarians at the Gate* evoke cultural images of the 1980s-era leveraged buyouts, *Boiler Room* and *Wolf of Wall Street* evince what was happening off-exchange with blank check penny stock schemes and outright scams. For instance, in 1988, Mary L. Shapiro, Commissioner of the US Securities and Exchange Commission defined the PSM and its investment vehicles as a dangerous tool in the following terms:

> Many penny stocks represent legitimate investment opportunities, and the market for these stocks is an honest one. However, experience has shown that many other penny stocks are used in a fraudulent schemes which involve 'shell' companies with no operating history, few employees, few assets, no legitimate prospects for business success, and markets that are manipulated to the benefit of the promoters of the companies and/or the market professionals involved.[2]

As it can be seen, the SEC Commissioner Schapiro illustrated a negative image of the PSM as a primary example of market venue where illegal activities of blank check companies might flourish. This includes pre-arranged trading, nominee accounts, and securities fraud. Furthermore, the North America Securities Administrators Association strongly argued a year later, in 1989, that the blank check companies were a *per se* fraudulent investment tool:

> Blank check blind pool offerings are inherently defective because of failure to disclose material facts concerning the offering and issuer, and

DOI: 10.4324/9781003169079-1

such offerings have been subject of pervasive, recurrent abusive and fraudulent practices in the sale of securities . . . the Association declares that the sales of blank check blind pool securities *per se* constitute fraudulent business practices.[3]

It is clear that by the end of the 1980s, the PSM was dominated by fraud and manipulation of asset prices, which had a negative influence on trading practices in penny stocks offerings, because the primary capital market was basically not regulated, and broker firms were usually unscrupulous as we said.

Blank check companies were listed on the PSM, which was a nonexchange venue. Hence, it did not impose pre-trade transparency or basic listing requirements on the issuers of securities. This made the market a fertile playground for the cash-shell companies' game.

The main purpose of a blank check company was to be listed on the PSM to raise funds, through an initial public offering (IPO), and complete a business combination with an unidentified target company. In particular, at the IPO stage, the management of the blank check companies did not sell their securities directly to retail investors, but condescending brokerage firms. Subsequently, the brokers misled the investors about a possible imminent acquisition or just circulated official statements, according to which the blank check company had merged with an important operating company with profitable turnovers. This circumstance contributed to exaggerate the price of the issued securities and attracted new retail investors. At that point, the managers of the blank check company and the brokers sold their securities and caused a collapse of the market in relation to the price of equity and to the value of the firm with high returns for their investment portfolios. In other words, they committed fraud against investors who did not possess enough information to assess their financial risk, and who just trusted the information provided by the broker firms.

This is highlighting two different risk factors for public investors. On the one hand, an economic issue, which is defined as information asymmetry and related to the legal nature of these investment companies (i.e. cash-shell companies); and, on the other hand, the uncertainty of the legal framework, which did not provide public investors and in particular retail investors with any form of protection. Indeed, in the 1980s, there were neither legal instruments nor a sophisticated legal framework to protect investors from the frauds that were often perpetrated by blank check companies.

Thus, the US Congress enacted the Securities Enforcement Remedies and Penny Stock Reform Act (PSRA) on 20 July 1990. The PSRA 1990 (U.S.) was passed to protect investors, and definitively regulate the PSM.

The PSRA 1990 (U.S.) read for the first time a definition of penny stocks under Section 3 (a) of Securities Exchange Act 1934 (U.S.) (SEA 1934), which was further implemented by virtue of Rule 3a51–1 of the Securities and Exchange Commission (SEC).[4] Specifically, a company would be entitled to issue equity securities (i.e. penny stocks) if – *inter alia* – they had an authorized share capital value not exceeding $5 million, and the company had no less than three-year financial history with a minimum net income of $750,000. Thus, the scope of the PSRA 1990 (U.S.) was to define the content of penny stocks, the legal nature of the companies operating on the PSM, and to fix a minimum cap in relation to the authorized share capital. Additionally, the PSRA 1990 (U.S.) amended, inter alia, Section 7 of the Securities Act 1933[5] (U.S.) entitling the SEC to enact different rules in order to impose restrictions and disclosure duties to the blank check companies.

The SEC adopted the famous Rule 419,[6] by which blank check companies that were issuing penny stocks as defined in Rule 3a51–1 of the SEC, were, inter alia, compelled to fulfil three main obligations:

I. First, all of the securities and proceeds raised during the IPO should have been deposited in an escrow account or held on trust, and the interests or dividends earned on the deposit funds could not be distributed until an acquisition was completed.
II. The acquisition should have been carried out within a very short period (i.e. eighteen months), and the funds held on trust should have been released – in the measure of at least 80% – in the case of completion of a business combination, otherwise the funds should have been returned in full to investors.
III. Shareholders should have expressed their consent to the proposed acquisition, providing that those who dissented had the right to rescind from their shareholders position and receive funds, interests, or dividends of a pro rata aggregate amount of the securities held on trust (i.e. conversion right).

As a result, in the late 1990s, the blank check companies slowly disappeared due to the onerous conditions imposed by the SEC in Rule 419 and on the basis that cash-shell companies without any form of financial data were definitively forbidden from listing on the PSM (indeed, the SEA required at least one or two years of net incomes of at least $750,000). However, this was not the end but rather the beginning of SPACs. In fact, following the PSRA 1990 (U.S.), and the sharp fall of blank check offerings; a new phoenix arose from the ashes with the name of Special Purpose Acquisition Company.

SPACs were exempted from the application of Rule 419 because they started to issue securities through IPOs, which did not fit into the definition of penny stocks, and – since 2003 – they started to be listed on capital markets, which required less strict requirements such as the Over-the-Counter Bulletin Board (OTC Bulletin Board) and the American Stock Exchange (AMEX). Hence, they were subject to common provisions, which generally governed the IPO in the United States. However, SPACs voluntarily complied with the conditions set forth in Rule 419 in order to prioritize the confidence of investors. For instance, SPACs were used to deposit the securities and proceeds of the IPO in an escrow account until the acquisition was completed and to use at least 80% of funds held on trust to finance the acquisition, and they provided public investors with a conversion right (namely, the right to convert securities into cash if the shareholders voted against the proposed acquisition). This was an example of 'self-imposed' SPAC restrictions. This approach is credited to Mr David Nussbaum (chairman of the GKN Securities). This evolution of a modern conception of SPACs that are run by well-known managers and that they tend to secure investment through a trust is known as SPAC 2.0. Furthermore, new 'self-imposed' features were implemented:

I.   Important and well-known managers were used to direct SPACs.
II. The equity securities could be traded even before the completion of a business combination (i.e. this feature provided public investors and retail investors in particular with liquidity and with a specific form of way-out from the investment).
III. The time frame to carry out an acquisition was extended to twenty-four months (i.e. usually eighteen months to announce a business combination and to sign a possible letter of intent, in addition to six months for the closing).
IV. The articles of association pre-established the potential sectors and industries of the target companies to be acquired.

Hence, the voluntary compliance with Rule 419 and the implementation of new features made SPACs an attractive investment tool. This historical event also contributed – as we said – to the development of a modern conception of SPACs, which were different from blank check companies based on fraudulent practices. This circumstance created a new SPAC identity in relation to their corporate structure that would have been adopted with slightly modifications by other US capital markets regulations. In fact, in 2008, the National Association of Securities Dealers Automated Quotations (NASDAQ) and New York Stock Exchange (NYSE) issued a proposal to allow the listing of SPACs on their exchanges. Until then, SPACs were not listed on those regulated capital markets, but only on the OTC Bulletin Board and the AMEX (namely, capital markets with less strict and generic listing requirements). In the end, the SEC approved the proposals and the SPACs started then to be listed on the NASDAQ (Rule IM-5101–2 of the NASDAQ listing rules) and the NYSE (Rule 102.6 of the Listing Company Manual). Finally, the NYSE American (formerly known as AMEX) and more recently as NYSE MKT adopted in November 2010 similar listing rules in relation to SPACs. The NYSE AMEX underlines that the exchange does not contemplate the possibility of listing a cash-shell company unless specific conditions set out in the NYSE MKT Company Guide are fulfilled under Section 119 of the 'Listing of companies whose business plan is to complete one or more acquisitions'. In particular, a listing company must also comply with the corporate governance requirement of part 8 of the NYSE MKT Company Guide.

This clearly shows that the US capital markets have evolved since the blank check companies' phenomenon in the 1980s. The main regulated markets such as NYSE, NASDAQ, and NYSE MKT have adopted strict and specific listing requirements in order to list SPACs as we have exhaustively outlined in the previous paragraphs.

Furthermore, the market rules clearly indicate that an SPAC must fulfil specific conditions before its listing. However, those conditions are only minimum mandatory requirements which do not prevent any exchange to exercise its unlimited discretion in order to delist the SPAC even when all the listing requirements are met, because the SPAC might constitute a threat against the public interest and the protection of investors' interests. This servers as a continuous reminder of the possible financial risks that were generated by blank check offerings, although modern SPACs have implemented more corporate safeguards for investors (see Chapters 1 and 2 of this edited collection).

The US regulation of SPACs is remarkable and truly constitutes the first real attempt to provide a legal framework for SPACs. However, as we said, an SPAC that does follow these listing requirements will not automatically be guaranteed a listing. A case-by-case assessment is always exercised by each exchange. Nonetheless, it is useful to say that NYSE and NASDAQ are highly pro-market, and they will always try to work out an ideal balance between sponsors' and investors' interests. For example, they will try to protect an issuer if a business combination is not found within the agreed timeframe, they might allow sponsors to avoid a delisting of the SPAC if certain guarantees are in place for public investors and if the prospect of closing a deal is realistic, and so on.

Now that the listing requirements of SPACs have been analysed from a historical financial prospective, it is clearer to discuss the company law mechanisms that have highly influenced the evolution of SPACs in the United States.

One of the main concerns in SPACs from a company law prospective has always been the issue of 'controlling' dissenting minorities. This is, for example, a current issue in Italy that in recent SPAC listings has also contributed to the unfortunate liquidation of several SPACs in the country (see Part I, Part II, and the conclusions of this edited collection).

Historically, in the United States, the threshold to stop an acquisition in SPACs was 20% of the share capital because SPAC mergers generally required an 80% approval threshold. Hence, this gave significant leverage to the 20% of the share capital holdout.

Today this percentage has been increased up to 95% of the share capital. Indeed, at the time of the SPAC 2.0, this issue was not solved. In fact, a public investor or SPAC shareholder could redeem shares only if he had previously expressed a negative vote in opposition to a proposed business combination. Hence, potentially and in practice, a group of investors could 'greenmail' a deal with only 20% of the share capital. Specifically, hedge funds figured out the potential to use various greenmail tactics against sponsors eager to close acquisitions and realize their 'promote' (the 20% sponsor equity or founders shares). Because SPACs are time-constrained by design, the eighteen- to twenty-four-month window to consummate a deal made the failure of a shareholder vote very likely to result in the SPAC's liquidation. For sponsors who need to consummate a deal to receive the sponsor promote, the incentive to pay greenmail was high. However, the incentive for public investors was not the traditional activist approach seeking to force changes in management or strategy. Instead, the interest in SPACs seemed to be based on the dynamics of the structure itself. Hedge funds were not interested in being long-term investors, or even they were not particularly interested in what the target company was identified for acquisition. To defeat the greenmail tactics used in the shareholder votes, NASDAQ proposed allowing SPACs to launch tender offers to allow shareholders who were unhappy with the acquisition to tender their shares back to the SPAC. Eventually, SPACs used their tender offer structure to dispense with shareholder approval, but exchange listing standards remained an obstacle to abandoning the vote. The first to use the tender only structure was 57th Street General Acquisition Corp. filed its S-1 in November 2009.

Today, many SPACs prefer to cap the possibility to redeem shares by which shareholders that possess more than 15% of the share capital cannot redeem their shares without the previous consent of the issuer. For example, K Road Acquisition Corp. had a 40% threshold or Trian Acquisition I Corp. capped the amount of shares an investor could convert in cash after voting against the acquisition (i.e. the conversion right) or the management as founder shareholders can step in and buy the shares of investors in a tender offer to complete the acquisition. Nonetheless, this can be costly for the sponsors or underwriters, who may incur expenses like offering fees or proxy solicitation. However, this can also show how terms have become more investors-friendly and less favourable to sponsors. In this evolution lies a part of the SPACs' success in 2020.

Furthermore, as this edited collection also will show in Chapter 1, in 2015, the issue of vote and redemption right has been further addressed by virtue of de-coupling the right to vote from the right to redeem shares. In other words, this means that today in such as SPAC in the United States, a shareholder can still vote in favour of the business combination, but does keep the possibility to redeem its shares and to keep warrants. This is an SPAC 3.0 model. In fact, it is not by chance that in 2015, nineteen SPACs completed IPOs, raising £3.6 billion in a 120% increase over the amount raised in SPAC IPOs in 2014, and seven more in registration (e.g. Double Eagle Acquisition Corp. completed an IPO that raised $480 million and Pace Holdings Corp completed an IPO that raised $400 million).

In 2019, Conyers Park II Acquisition Corp. tried to put in place the model of SPAC 3.5. Here the units were composed of common shares and warrants. However, in relation to warrants, the SPAC adopted a fraction of one warrant structure. It means that each whole one warrant entitles the holders to purchase one common share and each unit is composed of one share and ¼ of one warrant. This is an incentive to buy shares to be entitled to have one warrant and an extra share. It is a consolidation of the share capital of the SPAC. The same trend has been followed recently during the 'SPAC boom' in 2020 where SPACs issued many times ½ of one warrant.

Those company law mechanisms from the de-coupling of voting rights and redemption rights until the fractional warrant structure and tender offers are quintessential in the success of SPACs nowadays, and to some extent, it might be said that those financial innovations have contributed to the rise of SPACs in the US at least from a legal prospective.

SPACs used to be outside the mainstream, and by the end of 2020, they became a novel and unique financial product of Wall Street. This is justified, as we said, not only from a legal historical prospective, but from clear economic data that have created the basis for the surge of SPAC offerings. Specifically, three main triggers can be identified:

I. Supply and demand: the number of public companies has gone down dramatically over the last twenty to thirty years, dropping from 8,000 to just over 4,000 in 2019–2020, but the amount of money flowing into the public markets has simultaneously been increasing. Because the stock exchanges make their money by bringing on new companies, they have pushed to bring more SPACs into the market.

II. The private equity market: there has been a huge increase in the amount of capital invested in private equity (over $2 trillion today), but the number of exits has seen a decline. Private equity-backed portfolios are always looking for opportunities to exit and make a return, so they are supportive of the SPAC model.

III. The SEC become more involved in regulating SPACs, which has proven to boost their reputation in the investment world. They have stepped in to set a fixed price for each IPO, as well as regulate voting and redemption rights to the benefit of all parties involved, although since 2022, the SEC seems to have lost its progressive approach.

Those are some of the reasons by which 2020 became the 'Year of the SPAC' with more than 240 SPACs listed in the US (on NASDAQ or the NYSE), which raised a record $83 billion.[7] SPACs overtook 2020's record in 2021 with over $115.16 billion raised via more than 400 SPACs.[8] However, in the first quarter of 2022, the SPAC market saw fifty-four SPACs raised only $9.9 billion in proceeds,[9] which is 90% less than a year earlier, but still an increase in proceeds by 82% raised from the IPO market in the United States.[10]

From those data, one question seems inevitable: why a company may want to participate in an SPAC deal rather than taking private equity investment or going public with a traditional IPO? The answers are diversified and still today we do not have a final answer. We have tried to come up with some simple suggestions based on reasonable assumptions that not necessarily need to be interpreted as an absolute and dogmatic truth:

I. Valuation: public companies trade at higher multiples than private companies, so SPACs offer an opportunity for higher valuation;

II. control: while business owners lose some control when taking on private equity, SPACs allow a sponsor to maintain a significant stake in the company (it has been the case why several family offices preferred SPACs in 2020 and 2021);

III. liquidity: SPACs offer security in liquidity through the cash raised in the IPO;

IV. time: traditional IPOs can take up two to three years to finalize, but SPACs are typically completed in two to three months;

V. cost: unlike traditional IPOs that are very expensive to execute, SPACs typically pay for most of the costs, saving a significant amount of money for the target company unless otherwise agreed (namely, when the target company agrees to pay investment banks and underwriters as a part of the discounted fees are passed from the SPAC to the target company);

VI. certainty: SPAC deals are identified ahead of time, and the valuation is agreed upon by both parties. Rather than 'hoping the window is open', the target company can be certain that the transaction will occur, and that it will be for a value it is on board with.

This is a direct evidence that nowadays many commentators tend to be worried about SPACs being on public markets or helping private companies to tap public markets. Those doubters they do not usually take into account first the reason of existence of the same SPAC mechanism, namely the inefficiencies of traditional IPO. In other words, if traditional IPOs could be more efficient, indeed, we agree there would have not been much room for SPACs at least at the beginning.

Between 2020 and 2023, SPACs have surely confirmed that they can constitute a path to public markets for high-growth companies. However, this trend is not always successful, and it has given rise to current litigation. Looking forward, evaluating would-be SPAC partners is likely to become more important over time. SPACs de-risk IPOs, mitigate adverse selection, and offer more certainty for the target to go public with a consistent valuation process, as we said. However, SPACs' standards have gone from profitable private companies, to earnings before interest, taxes, depreciation and amortization-positive companies, and to pre-revenue companies. Think of a hypothetical target company that promises to be the 'next Tesla' in the electric vehicle market. Following the business combination with the SPAC at a very high corporate valuation based on forward-looking statements, the newly listed entity might incur consistent leakage of shares' value. This is because of its possible inability to develop the electric vehicles that were supposed initially to justify such high corporate valuation at the acquisition phase. This inevitably has a negative effect on public investors. Indeed, the acquisition of high-growth companies by SPACs can generate a concern as zero-revenue companies are not an operating company, the SPAC is taking on a company that is making a promise. Hence, registration statements are key as well as an accurate due diligence of the target company. Appropriate disclosures are important in SPACs, and in target companies as the SEC endorsed between 2021 and 2022. Indeed, by the end of 2020, much had changed from a regulatory perspective in the US under the Biden administration. Since April 2021, SPACs listings have decreased following warnings from the US Securities and Exchange Commission. In September 2021, the new approach of the SEC intensified. The most important instance of this new approach is Professor Gary Gensler's statement as the new SEC Chair under the Biden administration. He associated SPACs with Bitcoin when he spoke of the need for better investor protections setting an agenda to implement further enforcement measures.[11] This approach is confirmed by the high-profile enforcement actions initiated in 2021 concerning, among others, Momentus Inc. and Nikola Corporation.[12] As a result, SPACs had already started to cancel their planned IPOs at the beginning of January 2022.[13]

Additionally, shareholder lawsuits are on the rise,[14] especially when SPAC sponsors do not fulfil their promises and breach fiduciary duties.[15] This aspect is, for example, addressed by the new directive by the SEC with regard to SPAC reform initiated in March 2022.[16] The directive proposes specialized disclosure and financial statement requirements of SPAC sponsors to report any potential conflicts of interest and dilution in connection with the SPAC's IPO and de-SPAC transaction.

For the sake of clarity, we shall highlight that this edited collection will not comment on the new SEC SPAC reform proposal due to two main remarks: at the time of writing, the SEC SPAC reform has not yet been approved; and more specifically, our work is mainly focused on the European Union and the U.K. with a specific address to the Italian legal system.

Undeniably, the SEC's activism has also affected investor sentiment dramatically increasing redemptions since the start of 2022. This trend has been noticed by SPAC sponsors too. In the second quarter of 2022, only 17 SPACs listed in the US raised $2.2 billion.[17] In July 2022, for the first time in five years, no new SPAC raised money in the United States.[18] Important de-SPAC deals were abandoned, such as Forbes.[19] Furthermore, well-known investment banks refrained from underwriting new SPAC offerings, and acting as advisors in de-SPAC transactions. This is creating a destructive disruption of the SPAC market, especially in terms of completion of de-SPAC deals. We argue that the SEC's activism has played a significant role. The descaling interest in SPACs does not necessarily have to be construed as an extreme increase in de-SPAC deals and consequent difficulty in finding targets. Regulatory uncertainty has disrupted both SPAC offerings and de-SPAC deals, affecting public investor sentiments by encouraging waves of new liquidations. Since 2021, the SEC under the Biden administration has implemented hostile regulation by enforcement. It necessarily follows that any financial entity would be irremediably confused, requiring clarifications or at least taking a 'wait-and-see' approach. Additionally, the current high inflation, in both the US and Europe, is not helpful. SPAC investors seeking liquidity prefer to redeem their shares and keep their warrants in the hope of exercising them at the de-SPAC phase, by taking advantage of the SPAC 3.0 model (see Chapter 1).

The decreasing interest in SPAC offerings does not affect the SPAC listing requirements that have already been codified. Indeed, before the 'SPAC boom' in 2020, US exchanges had already adopted listing requirements for SPACs as we said before. Since then, such financial regulatory frameworks and the constant evolution of SPACs' market practices have become an international standard or model to be 'copied' or imitated in terms of international financial regulation (see Chapter 1). Based on those models, several countries in Asia already have implemented financial regulations for SPACs, notably, Hong Kong, Malaysia, Singapore, and South Korea. Other exchanges have recently implemented or are considering the implementation of a new international financial and legal framework to accommodate IPO financed by SPACs, such as in the case of India and Indonesia.

These various reforms generate regulatory competitions among countries, in order to be able to attract capital and claim their-selves as accommodating an SPAC-friendly legal environment. Indeed, SPACs contain per se a political connotation and challenge for the future of financial markets. On the one hand, countries that have adopted or are considering adopting an SPAC-friendly legal environment can further attract capital into their economies, namely an inflow of capital in terms of SPACs' IPOs through the participation of national and foreign public investors. On the other hand, the total absence of an SPAC regulatory framework and the impossibility of attracting public investors and SPAC sponsors in a country can also signify and translate into an outflow of capital, and sometimes national private companies can become targets of foreign SPACs. Indeed, if you are not the sponsor, then you may become the target. Consider the Singaporean multinational mobile App leader for deliveries, mobility, and financial services in Southeast Asia: Grab Holdings Inc. (Grab). The company announced on 13 April 2021, the business combination with a US SPAC to list on NASDAQ in what has become the largest-ever US equity offering by a Southeast Asian company. India is registering the same trend. For example, consider the Indian company Flipkart that since 10 March 2021 has been exploring the possibility of being merged with an SPAC in New York. The same is also true in Europe, where two important U.K. companies are today listed in New York, after having merged with US SPACs, respectively, Cazoo Ltd. and Arrival Ltd. London-based Cazoo Ltd., the car dealership company that leaped head-first into online car sales, agreed in March 2021 to list in New York after selling itself to hedge-fund founder Dan Och's SPAC, in a deal valued at $7 billion. Arrival Ltd., a maker of electric vans and buses, backed by investors including

BlackRock Inc., completed the business combination in March 2021, with the SPAC GIIG Merger Corp., with an enterprise value of the combined listed entity set at $10.6 billion. Another significant example is the Italian fashion house Ermenegildo Zegna that, in summer 2021, listed via a $3.2 billion deal with Investindustrial Acquisition Corp., an SPAC whose chairman was Sergio Ermotti, former chief executive officer of UBS Group AG.

Those are just a few examples of how SPACs can represent a suitable exit strategy for companies to get listed on foreign markets, mainly N.Y. exchanges. In light of this, SPAC represents a new stage of evolution in capitalism by virtue of providing companies with liquidity. SPACs are flexible vehicles, enabling the valuation of the acquisition target to be settled through private negotiations. Indeed, the de-SPAC or business combination is a merger and acquisition (M&A) activity where the inclusion of forward-looking statements is justified as in any other acquisition, merger, or takeover.

Under US standards, SPACs are cash-shell companies with no operations set up with a particular purpose: to conduct a business combination or reverse merger with a target. The capital is raised via an IPO of shares and warrants, or unit securities composed of both. Then, the SPAC uses the proceeds to fund one or more mergers that form the basis of the ongoing public entity.

This model is not uniformly applied to Europe, where SPACs do not necessarily offer units framed following the US standards but instead might usually offer preference shares in a reserved offer to the SPAC sponsors. This especially applies to Italy and the U.K., sometimes even to public investors, such as in the case of 2MX Organic S.A. listed on Euronext Paris by the end of 2020. 2MX Organic, the SPAC founded by Xavier Niel, Matthieu Pigasse, and Moez-Alexandre Zouari, was listed through the admission to trading and direct listing of 30,000,000 preference shares and 30,000,000 stock warrants for a total amount raised of €300 million. By contrast, as we highlighted, a typical SPAC modelled on the US standards should issue units composed of common shares and warrants to be offered to public investors. Furthermore, in the United States, sponsors receive founder shares, the so-called promote, and founder warrants rather than preference shares.

As it is clearly visible, the SPAC concept is constantly evolving and developing. Such flexibility is not a negative feature per se; it also reflects the diversified uses of SPAC at the business combination moment. For example, the SPAC often involves acquiring pre-revenue or zero-revenue companies, namely high-growth companies, such as in the case of Arrival in the U.K. or Grab in Singapore. However, it can also be used to target operating companies and positive earnings before interest, taxes, depreciation, and amortization (EBITDA) companies. Furthermore, as evidenced in Chapters 1, 7, and 8 of this edited collection, SPACs can also pursue financing purposes that can make them similar to shadow banks or otherwise to white knights or financiers of distressed entities. Specifically, here the business combination is focused on the purchase of business units or assets or on the possibility of restructuring the finances of the distressed target entity, acquiring its control. Those instances highlight the importance of the multi-level definition of SPAC based on the functions that the business combination will serve from time to time.

Regarding the micro-regulatory aspects of SPACs in Europe, a significant point of concern, which does not conform to US standards can be traced to the redemption rights of public investors. The European Union is a complex international organization composed of many Member States. Although such Member States share a common legal culture in civil law traditions or families, they still have diversified corporation law frameworks that are not fully integrated and harmonized – at least – in the case of SPACs. This is not a minor detail because some of those corporate law frameworks, as this edited collection correctly points out, might limit redemption rights at the de-SPAC phase (see Part I and Part II of this book). Indeed, in several European countries, redemption rights might be subordinated or limited to specific circumstances provided by the law, such as in Belgium, France, Germany, and Italy. As a result, common law jurisdictions tend to be more SPAC-friendly about redemption rights of SPAC's shareholders. Nonetheless, a redemption right modelled on US standards might still be implemented in Europe, via a modification of bylaws unless mandatory corporate law provisions limit such opportunity (see Parts I and Part II).

From a macro-regulatory perspective, in the absence of secondary European legislation, either regulation or directive, dedicated explicitly to SPACs, the jurists shall refer to existing models of European regulations. In light of this, European SPACs might be perceived under the Alternative Investment Fund Managers Directive 2011/61/E.U. designed for private equity firms and hedge funds or the Undertakings for the Collective Investment in Transferable Securities (UCITS) Directive 2009/65/E.C. as subsequently amended, broadly designed for closed and open-ended funds. In both cases, the European Securities and Markets Authority (ESMA) has not taken a position. Indeed, SPACs in Europe are currently facing a lack of specific legal discipline, although the last public statement on SPACs by the ESMA (dated July 15, 2021)[20] has clearly outlined a model of regulation by objectives. According to this view, either exchanges or national financial regulators and lawmakers must take necessary steps in order to provide at least SPAC retail investors with appropriate protections and corporate safeguards especially in order to avoid the possible dilutional issues at the de-SPAC phase. However, the extent and degree of such protection are left to the discretion of each Member State and each national exchange. This paves the way for diversified legal frameworks about SPACs where each Member State might design more or less flexible SPAC listing requirements to attract further capital into their economies. The latter view is further explored in this edited collection with innovative remarks. Indeed, we qualify and summarize this particular feature of European SPACs' financial regulations as 'regulations by competition'.

Further remarks on the recent ESMA public statement are contained in Part I. A detailed analysis of the possible definition of SPACs, either AIF or UCITS, is luminously put forward by Professor Annunziata et al. in Chapter 2. Indeed, the central intake is that the SPAC, as any cash-shell company or a company vessel, tends to avoid definitions. Indeed, the current lack of a definition of the SPAC at the European level regarding hedge funds or investment companies also applied to the United States.

Are SPACs investment companies? This question was raised in the United States in the summer of 2021 when the SPAC, sponsored by hedge fund manager Bill Ackman, was at the centre of an interesting debate. Specifically, in August 2021, the former SEC commissioner, Robert Jackson, and Yale Law School Professor, John Morley, filed a lawsuit on behalf of Pershing Square Tontine Holdings shareholders, alleging that Ackman's SPAC should be registered as an investment company under the Investment Company Act of 1940 as amended (ICA). The doubt is generated because there is no legal or compulsory definition of SPACs in the World. Hence, a significant amount of speculation is focused on whether SPACs can be defined as investment companies under Section 3 (a) (1) (A) of the ICA in the United States. Similar debates – as mentioned earlier – exist in Europe with regard to whether SPACs can be classifiable as AIF or UCITS. The ICA establishes that an investment company is a company that invests primarily in securities or proposes to engage primarily in the business of investing, reinvesting or trading in securities. This type of company is often referred to as an 'orthodox investment company', a company holding itself as being engaged in an investment company business. In other words, investing in securities is all the company has ever done or proposed to do with the great majority of its assets. Those who claim such qualifications would like to make the IPO of SPACs more complex in terms of securities registration formalities. The correct answer to critiques as also confirmed by many top-tier American law firms[21] is that SPACs are not investment companies either under the US because:

I. SPACs are cash-shell companies with no operations;
II. as opposed to operating companies, SPACs seek a business combination with a predetermined time frame;
III. SPACs do not hold investment securities that would require their registration under the ICA, being the IPO proceeds held on trust invested in government securities (hence, exempted under Section 3 (a) (2) ICA);
IV. SPACs make private companies public via reserve takeovers. Hence, their primary purpose is not classifiable as a security investment. As a result, the SPAC vehicle is dissolved due to the reverse takeover with the target.

Nonetheless, as mentioned before, the SPAC can propose an unconventional transaction that includes features that deviate from the standard SPAC structure (namely, the reverse takeover). Indeed, an overlooked area of SPACs is the de-SPAC phase, which has been seen in recent years as a remarkable development. Moreover, reverse takeovers are not the only function of SPACs. Indeed, as we have briefly anticipated before, SPACs can:

I. Target distressed entities and conduct possible restructuring procedures. This function can assimilate SPACs to private equity deals in terms of buy-out or high-growth transactions;

II. Cash-out deals. Consider Accor Acquisition Company on Euronext Paris, sponsored by the Group Accor, a World leading hospitality company. The target company will benefit from Accor's network, scale, and global presence. This shows that a cash-out deal is still an SPAC, although it differs from a reverse takeover. In other words, an SPAC can be a company vessel to facilitate a group's expansion;

III. Be qualified as an emerging growth company (EGC) such as Alpine Acquisition Corp. in the United States. Following the business combination, the newly listed entity can continue to qualify as an EGC benefitting from being an EGC if it fulfils the rules under Section 2 (a) (19) of the Securities Act of 1933;

IV. Acquire individual units or assets such as vessels of shipping companies. This function can be assimilated into a banking function and, therefore, might give rise to possible issues of 'shadow banking'. The same consideration can be applied to the targeting of distressed entities as a form of new financing in a distressed company (see Part III of this edited collection);

V. Merge with zero-revenue companies. Look at Arrival and Cazoo in the U.K. or Grab in Singapore. This function can assimilate SPACs to venture capital late-stage rounds of financing.

This short excursus can provide evidence that the law or financial regulators cannot anticipate the different levels of complexity of the de-SPAC transaction. Disclosures of such complexities at the pre-IPO phase can be possible in prospectuses. However, such disclosures are necessarily illustrative rather than definitive subject to the detailed content of the de-SPAC transaction. For those reasons, SPACs cannot be defined a priori, as investment companies, but they might be at post-business combination. However, the SPAC entity vanishes at that stage, and a newly merged listed entity is required to fulfil new legal obligations.

Finally, opinions on SPACs generally tend to be extreme. On the pro-side: SPACs are speedier and provide more certainty when the target is identified because the public investment has already been made. On the other hand, those who invest in the SPAC initially have less confidence about the nature of the ultimate target. Additionally, the sponsor and associates are commonly allocated shares and warrants in the SPAC for a nominal consideration, in recognition of their efforts at identifying suitable targets, but this may significantly dilute other shareholders of the SPAC (see Chapter 1), although this issue in the US has surely been over-dramatized.

Book Overview

The edited collection is divided into three main parts. Part I examines the international financial regulation of SPACs and has a specific overview of the Italian financial regulation. Chapter 1 shows the variegated corporate law frameworks of several jurisdictions of the European Union: Germany, the Netherlands, Belgium, Spain, and Italy. The U.K. is also considered a third country that still belongs – at least geographically – to Europe. Indeed, the U.K. has become – especially after Brexit – the only European country to provide sponsors and public investors with a specific and harmonized legal discipline of SPACs. Both the consultation paper[22] and the policy statement[23] of the Financial Conduct Authority (FCA) outline not only specific listing requirements for the sponsors but also protective measures for investors both at the IPO phase and the de-SPAC moment. A comprehensive analysis of the U.K. SPAC reform about the future of SPACs in Europe is provided in Chapter 1 and Chapter 8. Chapter 2 is another building block of this edited collection, providing a complete overview of the Italian current financial regulation of SPACs and the future of Italian SPACs. Since 2017, Italy has been one of the European jurisdictions with the highest number of SPAC IPOs. The last IPOs between 2020 and 2021, with the particular case of Revo S.p.A., confirm the trend. It is also paving the way for a new concept in SPAC studies: the 'instant SPAC', namely an SPAC that has already identified a target company at the pre-IPO and IPO phase so that once listed on the market, the SPAC can immediately announce the business combination. Obviously, this practice is not without risks, especially if the SPAC's shareholders meeting does not approve the deal (see Chapter 3 of Raimondo Premonte and Donato Romano on this issue). Nonetheless, the 'instant SPACs' case is a very limited instance that has only recently occurred in Italy. This is because, in any other part of the world, an SPAC is not allowed to enter into any negotiation with the target company before the IPO (see Chapter 1).

Part II of this edited collection is specifically dedicated to the examination of SPACs within the Italian legal system, its corporate law framework, and the tax benefits or issues under the Italian legal framework. Specifically, in Chapter 3, Raimondo Premonte and Donato Romano, who are experienced lawyers of *Gianni Origoni & Partners*, share their expertise on the Italian SPAC markets. In particular, the authors highlight how Italian SPACs face legal issues regarding exercising redemption right, especially if listed in the Market for Investment Vehicles (MIV) segment. For these reasons, SPACs still prefer to list on the Alternative Investment Market (AIM) market, which is also beneficial, in terms of costs and timing of listing. Indeed, on the AIM, SPACs' listing is faster due to filing an admission document that is eventually approved by the Italian Exchange (*Borsa Italiana* S.p.A.), whereas on the MIV segment, a formal and more rigid prospectus is required. Moreover, it shall be filed with the Italian financial regulator, namely the *Consob*, to receive its approval before seeking the final opinion of *Borsa Italiana* S.p.A.

Furthermore, another peculiarity of the Italian legal system is the possibility of having an SPAC listed on the market with only a minimum capitalization of €10 million (euros) on the AIM. This is in line with the U.K.'s AIM, whose current minimum capital threshold of capital to be raised is £6 million (GBP). Furthermore, on the AQSE in the U.K., the capitalization is even lower, with only £2 million (GBP) (see Chapters 1 and 8).

This is an interesting trend for foreign SPAC initial investors, who currently face a higher limit of minimum capitalization on both US exchanges, the NYSE and NASDAQ. However, what can be defined as a 'micro-SPAC' is only a step away from becoming a possible future trend in other jurisdictions. Indeed, SPACs are analysed in terms of alternative acquisition models. In that case, a lower level of capitalization is not surprising in seeing SPAC as a corporate vessel that is deputed to finance restructuring plans of distressed businesses, or to acquire going concerns of companies that wish either to spin off specific business sectors or to restructure their corporate group. Furthermore, the 'micro-SPAC' could serve financing purposes that are more inherent to the Old Continent, and thus can better serve the needs of the European small- and medium-size companies as well as micro-enterprises rationales.

The SPAC corporate structure under the Italian law framework is further examined by Giuseppe Cavallaro in Chapter 4. The chapter focuses on the importance of shareholders' agreements in the corporate context more generally, and with a specific reference to SPAC's dynamics. Indeed, the author outlines the benefits and drawbacks of shareholders' agreements in SPACs and whether they can be implemented beyond the business combination.

Luisa Scarcella tackles tax issues of SPACs under the Italian legal framework in Chapter 5. Giovanni Romano illustrates the corporate governance issues of SPACs at both international and domestic levels, with a specific focus on the Italian legal framework in Chapter 6. He claims that SPACs are operating companies 'in the making'. This statement can give rise to legal issues, especially under Italian corporate law provisions that are mainly designed for operating companies. Furthermore, the author is critically analysing the function of the escrow account and whether the segregation of public funds in a bank account managed by a third party, that is, the escrow agent, can challenge the traditional fiduciary duties of directors. However, the conclusions are not so dramatic. Although the Italian system is a complex system of law in civil law traditions, the management and supervision of the escrow account are still in the hands of the escrow agent. This is confirmed by the fact that the release of funds is subject to public investors' positive approval of the business combination. The chapter is particularly interesting because it provides readers with a deeper understanding of the SPAC's transactional dynamics, outlining how some other civil law jurisdictions, including Germany and France, might find this investment model, or alternative acquisition model, as a potential challenge to pre-established legal principles, such as the private autonomy of private contractual parties.

Finally, Part III of this edited collection is devoted to the examination of 'experiments' in SPACs and to their role that is conceptualized as risk-free investments until the completion of the business combination. This critical connotation is prominently explained by Professor Shachmurove, who is conducting in Chapter 7 an economic analysis of the main potential issues of SPACs as shadow banks, examining the financing practices of non-banks. The edited collection is completed by Chapter 8, written by Giorgio Tosetti Dardanelli, who highlights a new perspective on SPACs that can be conceptualized as bridge companies, or venture companies, either to finance smaller private companies by reverse takeovers, or to provide direct forms of financing to distressed businesses.

Notes

1 Steven Kurutz, 'OK, What's a SPAC? A Once Obscure Financial Scheme Becomes a Celebrity Flex' (*The New York Times*, 27 February 2021).
2 Mary L. Shapiro, 'Seeking New Sanctions: Comments on Developments in the Commission's Enforcement Program' (1990) <http://www.sec.gov/news/speech/1990/030990schapiro.pdf> accessed 10 January 2023.
3 The North American Securities Administrators Association, *Resolution of the North American Securities Administrators Association, Inc., Declaring Blank Check Blind Pool Offerings to Be Fraudulent Practices* (Cm 7032, 1989). Nonetheless, it should be noted that the statement made by NASAA in 1989 that described the blank check companies as a fraudulent instrument per se can be misleading. Indeed, a company can never become a fraudulent instrument per se unless unscrupulous managers direct it. Therefore, this severe judgement on blank check companies is connected to a strict policy adoption and political justification, which aimed to avoid frauds and solve an urgent risk of market collapse in the Penny Stock Market.
4 Title 17, ch. II, C.F.R. § 240.3A51–1.
5 Securities Act of 1933, 27 May 1933, ch. 38, title I, 48 Stat. 74 (15 U.S.C. 77a *et seq.*).
6 57 F.R. 18043, 28 April 1992; see Title 17, ch. II, C.F.R. § 230.419.
7 'The SPAC IPOs Ride the Recovery' (White & Case Annual Review, 2020) <https://www.whitecase.com/insight-our-thinking/spac-ipos-ride-recovery> accessed 10 January 2023.
8 Daniele D'Alvia et al., 'The UK SPAC Reform: Preliminary Remarks' (*Oxford Business Law Blog*, 6 September 2021) <https://blogs.law.ox.ac.uk/business-law-blog/blog/2021/09/uk-spac-reform-preliminary-remarks> accessed 10 January 2023.
9 Jacob Adelman, 'The SEC Has Signalled More Oversight of SPACs. Big Banks Are Getting the Message' (*Barron's*, 20 April 2022) <https://www.barrons.com/articles/the-sec-has-signaled-more-oversight-of-spacs-big-banks-are-getting-the-message-51650477914> accessed 10 January 2023.
10 Andy Laszlo, 'Equity Capital Markets – Tech, Media & Telecom: Q1 2022 Review' (*Mizuho Group*, 8 April 2022) <https://www.mizuhogroup.com/americas/insights/2022/04/equity-capital-markets–tech-media–telecom-q1-2022-review.html> accessed 13 January 2023.

11 Gary Gensler, 'Testimony Before the Subcommittee on Financial Services and General Government of the US House Appropriations Committee' (14 September 2021) <https://www.sec.gov/news/testimony/gensler-2021-09-14> accessed 10 January 2023.

12 Andrew Hammond et al., 'How to Manage the Risks of SPAC Securities Fraud Actions in 2022' (3 March 2022) <https://www.whitecase.com/insight-alert/how-manage-risks-spac-securities-fraud-actions-2022> accessed 10 January 2023.

13 Nicholas Megaw and Nikou Asgari, 'Rising Number of Blank-Cheque Companies Call it Quits Before Listing: SPACs Cancel IPO Registrations in Fresh Sign of Fading Investor Enthusiasm' (*Financial Times*, 21 January 2022).

14 'SPACs: After the Boom Come the Lawsuits' (*Financial Times*, 31 March 2022) – Opinion Lex.

15 Sujeet Indap, 'A Court Battle That Has Raised Concerns About SPACs: Lawyers and Regulators Now Have Lopsided Financial Products in Their Sights' (*Financial Times*, 18 April 2022).

16 SEC, 'Special Purpose Acquisition Companies, Shell Companies, and Projections' (30 March 2022) <https://www.sec.gov/rules/proposed/2022/33-11048.pdf> accessed 10 January 2023.

17 PWC, 'Q2 2022 Overview' <https://www.pwc.com/gx/en/services/audit-assurance/ipo-centre/global-ipo-watch.html> accessed 10 January 2023.

18 Aziz Sunderji and Amrith Ramkumar, 'SPAC Activity in July Reached the Lowest Level in five Years' (*Wall Street Journal*, 17 August 2022).

19 Ortenca Aliaj et al., 'Forbes Abandons Plans to List Via SPAC' (*Financial Times*, 1 June 2022).

20 European Securities and Markets Authority ESMA, 'Public Statement' (*ESMA*, 15 July 2021) 32-384-5209.

21 Harvard Law School Forum on Corporate Governance, 'Special Purpose Acquisition Companies and the Investment Company Act of 1940' <https://corpgov.law.harvard.edu/2021/09/03/special-purpose-acquisition-companies-and-the-investment-company-act-of-1940/> accessed 15 October 2021.

22 Financial Conduct Authority, 'Investor Protection Measures for Special Purpose Acquisition Companies: Propose Changes to the Listing Rules' (April 2021) CP21/10.

23 Financial Conduct Authority, 'Investor Protections Measures for Special Purpose Acquisition Companies: Changes to the Listing Rules' (July 2021) PS21/10.

Part I
Analysing SPACs in Europe

1 The Financial Regulation of Special Purpose Acquisition Companies in the European Union and the UK

Daniele D'Alvia and Ettore Maria Lombardi

1.1 Introduction

The financial world has changed. The Special Purpose Acquisition Company (SPAC) has emerged as a viable alternative to traditional initial public offering (IPO), with lower costs and less formal requirements. By the end of 2020, more than 240 SPACs listed in the United States (on the National Association of Securities Dealers Automated Quotations [NASDAQ] or New York Stock Exchange [NYSE]) raised a record $83 billion, according to SPAC Research. SPACs have already surged past the 2020 year's record in the first quarter of 2021, raising $98.1 billion. However, the boom that made 2020 the 'Year of the SPAC'[1] started to cool in April 2021 following a warning from the US SEC.

The SPAC is an American innovation, and New York exchanges have adopted the financial regulation of SPACs regarding listing requirements. However, market practices have become an international standard or model to be 'copied' or imitated in international financial regulation. For instance, since 2020, many jurisdictions in the world have implemented or have started to discuss adopting specific SPAC listing requirements with some US features as well as distinguishing elements reflecting the interests of the different investment communities of each country. New reforms have been implemented in Asia with new listing requirements adopted by Hong Kong and Singapore; the Malaysian guidelines on SPACs issued in 2009 were updated in 2021; and new SPAC reforms have been implemented in the United Arab Emirates and Egypt between 2021 and 2022. India and Indonesia still discuss having an SPAC legal framework in their legal systems. The same is occurring in Europe, with Belgium and Spain taking the first regulatory steps, mainly the UK, which has developed a unique harmonized SPAC framework in Europe.

This chapter offers a comprehensive overview of the current international financial regulation of SPACs in the European Union (section 1.4) and in the UK (section 1.5) against the main legal system where the SPAC originates: the United States (section 1.2). Specifically, we will examine the European Union as a case study for SPACs due to its vast diversification of financial and corporate law frameworks at the Member State's level. In section 1.4, three

DOI: 10.4324/9781003169079-3

main European Union capital markets belonging to the Euronext Group are examined: the Amsterdam, Milan, and Brussels stock exchanges; the analysis will also involve two capital markets outside the Euronext Group, namely the Frankfurt and Madrid stock exchanges. The selection of those markets is based on two main considerations: the number of SPAC listings and the fact that some of those exchanges have specific listing standards for SPACs, or are progressing towards implementation of listing requirements. Consolidating remarks are provided in section 1.6.

1.2 The SPAC Definition

SPACs are cash-shell companies set up, as their name indicates, for a special purpose: to conduct an acquisition. The capital is raised via an IPO of unit securities composed of common shares and warrants. The gross proceeds, net of any upfront underwriting fees, operating expenses, and working capital, are put into an independent trust or escrow account until the acquisition occurs. The acquisition phase, where the capital is drawn down, is defined in the specific SPAC jargon as 'de-SPAC' or 'de-SPACing,' which will end with the liquidation of the vehicle.[2]

The acquisition and the subsequent release of funds for the acquisition generally take place between 24 and 36 months from the listing of the SPAC. However, this period can vary depending on the exchange practices and the jurisdiction in which the SPAC is listed. In case of failure of the acquisition, the SPAC will be wound up, and the funds will be returned to investors.

1.3 Key Features of US SPACs

Firstly, the SPAC's capital is raised via an IPO of unit securities composed of common shares and warrants. In the United States, sponsors buy founder shares and founder warrants. Founder warrants finance an upfront under-writing discount and post-IPO working capital, ensuring that 100% of the IPO proceeds would be kept in trust.[3] The sponsor will lose this amount if the SPAC does not complete a business combination within the settled time-frame. Founder warrants are the 'skin in the game' of the sponsor.

Secondly, the SPAC sponsors typically grant equity in the SPAC (founder shares) equal either to 25% of the capital raised at a symbolic nominal value (usually $25,000 in the United States) or to 20% of the fully diluted SPAC shares (i.e., shareholders of the target company paying the sponsor's fee in shares, which is known as the promote). Summing up, SPAC sponsors receive a promotion usually defined as the sponsor or compensation, or sometimes in a critical way as the SPAC bonanza.[4] For instance, Michael Klein had over $60 million from a $25,000 investment in his founder's shares in June 2020 (the merger between Churchill Capital Corp. IV and Clarivate Analytics PLC). This means that the initial investment of $25,000 converts into a slice of the equity of the newly merged entity when the SPAC finalizes a business combination.

The primary justification for the promotion has been its construction as compensation for the management's efforts in finding the target company and executing the merger, as well as providing the target company with 'extra financial value.'[5] On the other hand, the dilutive impact of these shares has contributed to the historical view that de-SPAC transactions can be more expensive from the seller's perspective than a traditional IPO.[6] Economic views on SPACs tend to be extreme. However, they have a competitive edge in that private investment in public equity (PIPE) offers SPACs (as well as other forms of debt financing) more equity leverage.[7] Furthermore, sponsors often invest more cash in the SPAC at the de-SPAC phase. For example, Mr Palihapitiya invested $100 million in Virgin Galactic at $10 per share when it went public (i.e., this is an additional form of 'skin in the game').[8] Other times, sponsors have been creative in proposing alternative promotion structures to align incentives and distinguish themselves.[9]

The SPAC sponsor promotion has received increasing attention from the SEC Division of Corporation Finance and is still under review when writing this chapter. Especially, in December 2020, the SEC issued its first guidelines relating to disclosures in SPAC IPOs and de-SPAC transactions concerning conflicts of interest and the nature of the sponsor team's economic interests in the SPAC.[10] The guideline makes it clear that, at the IPO stage, the SPAC should disclose the circumstances in which the financial incentives of a sponsor, director, officer, or affiliate may not align with those of the public investors. The same approach can be found in guidelines, opinions, or market rules issued by financial regulators in Europe. Finally, it is important to highlight that the promotion is mainly a US capital structure of SPACs that cannot be found in equivalent terms in Europe and the UK.

Thirdly, an SPAC cannot identify a target during the IPO under SEC rules. As an inducement to IPO investors to deposit their money in the escrow account while the SPAC searches for a target, investors are granted the right to redeem their initial investment. Until 2015, redemption rights in SPACs were limited to a portion of the initial investment (around 85%) upon liquidation or a vote by the applicable investor against a proposed merger: the de-SPAC transaction.

From 2015, these features were broadened in the typical SPAC to give investors the right to redeem 100% of their initial investment,[11] with interest, upon liquidation or a business combination, regardless of whether the investors vote for or against a transaction. In addition, SPACs usually permit IPO investors to retain their public warrants even if they have otherwise redeemed their public shares (the so-called SPAC 3.0 model),[12] namely while a public investor can redeem shares, the public warrants can be retained in the hope of buying later, at a discount, the shares of the newly merged entity, post-business combination.

However, this is possible if the new shares hit the warrant's strike price, which is conventionally set at $11.50. Otherwise, public investors are 'out-of-the-money,' and the warrants are worthless. From a sponsor perspective, the latter could, in theory, be able to win the acquisition vote but have insufficient capital to complete the deal. This deal feature is an important reason for SPAC sponsors to actively engage with their investors once a target has been identified. A sponsor must motivate its public investors beyond the need to obtain sufficient positive acquisition votes.

Finally, the risk of many redemptions is mitigated by the PIPE investment that finances part of the consideration price at the moment of the business combination. After that, the SPAC announces both the acquisition agreement and committed financing. This evolution partly lies behind SPACs' success, although it is also fair to say that PIPE investment currently lacks investors in the United States. For this reason, new transactional structures have appeared, such as convertible bonds issued by the target company,[13] facility agreements, or a combination of PIPE and one of those.[14]

1.4 SPACs in the European Union

In Europe, SPACs are a recent phenomenon. Unlike the United States, the Old Continent has experienced a far lower number of listings and IPO proceeds. In 2021, 38 SPACs were listed, raising almost €7 billion.[15] Among those offerings, the Netherlands has led the way with 16 SPAC listings in 2021, raising approximately €3.7 billion.[16] This means that in 2021 almost 40% of SPACs listed on European stock exchanges were listed on Euronext Amsterdam, according to the Netherlands Authority for the Financial Markets. Although Europe is behind the United States regarding IPO volume raised by SPACs, the number of deals in Europe has tripled, and the IPO volume raised has multiplied eight times in 2021 compared with 2020.[17]

In Europe, there is a harmonized regime of secondary legislation for SPACs, such as a regulation or directive establishing a specific legal discipline. The ESMA once issued its guidelines concerning Directive 2011/61/EU on Alternative Investment Fund Managers[18] without mentioning SPACs, nor did it clarify whether the Alternative Investment Fund Managers Directive (AIFMD) can apply to them. Since 2017[19], SPACs might also be characterized as a form of undertaking for collective investment in transferable securities, primarily if they focus on one business combination. Under the ESMA guidelines, an Undertaking for the Collective Investment in Transferable Securities (UCITS):

I.   does not have a general commercial or industrial purpose;
II. pools together capital raised from its investors for investment to generate a pooled return for those investors; and
III. and its unit holders – as a collective group – have no day-to-day discretion or control.

SPACs can be categorized as UCITS because they are cash-shell companies. Hence they do not follow industrial aims but aim to raise money in an IPO process. Moreover, they are directed by managers instead of unit holders, so the latter do not have direct control or discretion over the firm. Nonetheless, this is only a possible interpretation under the current financial and legal framework of the European Union, which has not yet received a practical application. This interpretation also makes SPACs similar to private equity funds, at least because they are a specification. However, some features distinguish them from the latter, such as their reliance on equity rather than debt. This statement is still valid in Europe, but it is developing in the United States, whereas SPACs are further relying on other sources of finance at the de-SPAC phase with an essential focus on debt instruments.

In July 2021, the ESMA published its first public statement on SPACs.[20] The ESMA still does not take a definitive position on whether SPACs are to be qualified as UCITS but provides the discipline of SPACs in the European Union with technical neutrality. Indeed, the public statement seeks to promote uniform prospectus disclosure and to protect investors in SPACs with a specific focus on retail investors. In addition, it encourages regulatory consistency among European national regulators. Hence, this document clarifies this area and applies to SPACs securities admitted to trading on an EU-regulated market. Most ESMA's points are based on existing disclosure requirements under the Prospectus Regulation.[21] The Prospectus Regulation provides a harmonized legal framework across the European Union regarding disclosure requirements. This means that in Europe, at least four sections of the prospectus will be relevant for European Union financial regulators:

I. The risk factors: these will include that the SPAC has no operating history and no specific targets have yet been identified.
II. The business description: the issuer will explain the parameters the SPAC will consider when seeking a business combination.
III. The offering section: where the SPAC's capital structure is described.
IV. The description of the management: it must contain a detailed description of the sponsor, founders, promoters, etc. because the investment experience of the SPAC's governing bodies is an essential driver of valuation.

Since an SPAC is a cash-shell company, drafting and reviewing the financial sections will consume less time than a traditional IPO. ESMA wants the SPAC's sponsors to inform investors of future scenarios during the de-SPAC phase. Specifically, the ESMA expects the SPAC prospectus to include future remuneration of the sponsors and their role after the SPAC has acquired the target; information about possible changes to the SPAC's governance after it has acquired a target; information about the future shareholdings of the sponsors and other related parties; and details of possible scenarios that might arise if the sponsor fails to find a suitable target, such as SPAC de-listing and winding up.

However, it would be desirable for European regulators to be more pragmatic and accept that pre-IPO disclosures are possibly illustrative rather than definitive because most of those features are negotiated at the time of the de-SPAC process.

1.4.1 SPACs in the Netherlands

Euronext Amsterdam and the Netherlands Authority for the Financial Markets or *Autoriteit Financiële Markten* (AFM) do not provide specific listing requirements for SPACs. Instead, they are treated as regular IPOs and subject to the Prospectus Regulation.

Shareholders can vote on the business combination and are allowed the redemption option. In addition, the structures of the financing and units are flexible in the Euronext Amsterdam market, allowing for replicating the US SPACs.

Regarding founder remuneration, the SPAC features on Euronext confirm that sponsors are not assigned with founder warrants.[22] Usually, shares are issued in a separate class as special shares, which could be converted into ordinary shares after a successful business combination at par value.

Euronext Amsterdam also permits BV or *Société à responsabilité limitée* (SRL),[23] namely private limited liability companies, to list which have the following benefit:

I. Permits lower voting thresholds to approve the combination;
II. Makes the requirement of prospectus redundant when using a vast pool of existing treasury shares as consideration on combination;
III. Mandatory offer and financial assistance rules do not apply.[24]

1.4.2 SPACs in Italy

In Italy, there was a wave of SPACs between 2017 and 2018, with over 30 listings on the Alternative Investment Market (AIM) and the Market for Investment Vehicles (MIV) segments. The MIV and the AIM (renamed Euronext Growth Marketing October 2021) segment are under the *Mercato Telematico Azionario* (MTA) market umbrella. So far, the AIM in Italy has been the preferred market to list SPACs due to its simplified listing process being a multilateral trading facility that only requires drafting an admission document rather than a prospectus.

The application of company law to SPACs in Italy might be problematic, especially with respect to the MIV. In fact, according to Section 2437, paragraph 4, of the Italian Civil Code (ICC), public companies on the MTA, and therefore on the MIV market, cannot provide investors with a full redemption right. This feature can prevent SPAC investors from redeeming their shares unless listed on the AIM. Indeed, the AIM being a multilateral trading facility, companies are not subject to Section 2437 ICC.[25] Therefore, the AIM in Italy is preferred due to its flexibility in modelling the redemption right on a US-style right.

Finally, regarding the SPAC's capital structure, public investors can buy units composed of common shares and warrants in the proportion of one warrant per share. The sponsor does not hold founder warrants but preference shares that are subsequently converted into ordinary shares after a successful business combination at par value.

1.4.3 SPACs in Spain

There are no specific SPAC listing requirements in Spain; therefore, general corporate and finance law provisions, including the Prospectus Regulation, will still apply. So far, no SPAC listing has ever occurred in Spain.

Spain is examining 2021, a possible SPAC reform to adapt its legal system to this new investment vehicle. The National Securities Market Commission or *Comisión Nacional del Mercado de Valores* (CNMV) refers to the preliminary Draft Bill of the Securities Market and Investment Services Law, recently subject to public consultation in Spain. This preliminary draft includes an amendment to the Companies Act of 2010 that would like to introduce a new section in title XIV of the Act, which regulates public companies, to contemplate the regime's features that apply to SPACs.

According to such reform, the SPAC must include in its corporate name the indication *'sociedad cotizada con propósito para la adquisición'* or its abbreviation 'SPAC S.A.' until the business combination is completed. Furthermore, under Spanish regulations, the 'redemption right' itself is not contemplated in the legal framework of the securities market. However, since it is one of the most attractive features of SPACs, it has been defined in the Draft Bill of the Securities Market and Investment Services Law. This reform guarantees that the investor's capital is adequately protected by allowing the SPAC to use either a statutory right of withdrawal[26] or the issuance of redeemable shares[27] as the redemption mechanism. Finally, suppose the SPAC undertakes to reduce the share capital by acquiring its shares for subsequent redemption. In that case, an SPAC might be required to file a takeover bid due to capital reduction. On 27 June 2022, the Council of Ministers approved the Draft Bill of the Securities Market and Investment Services Law, the full text published on 12 September 2022, to be submitted to the Spanish Parliament for approval.

1.4.4 SPACs in Germany

With the launches of Lakestar SPAC I SE, 468 SPAC I SE, 468 SPAC II SE, OboTech Acquisition SE, and GFJ ESG Acquisition I Se, modern SPAC listings similar in structure to the most recent wave of US SPACs reappeared on the Frankfurt Stock Exchange (FSE) in spring 2021 with the last SPAC IPO to date in early 2022. The FSE has seen SPAC listings in 2008 and 2010 with the IPOs of Germany1 Acquisition Ltd, incorporated in Guernsey, and Helikos SE and CleanTech I SE, both set up under the European Company model in Luxembourg.[28] However, their structures differed from modern SPACs.

In Germany and on the FSE, there are no specific listing requirements for SPACs. Therefore, the SPAC is subject to the Prospectus Regulation and the FSE rules governing the listing of shares on the regulated market.

In terms of capital structure, the rules of the German Stock Corporation Act raise several legal issues for the implementation of a US-style SPAC:

I. Firstly, the proceeds raised in the IPO must be freely disposable to the management board of the SPAC. As a result, depositing the total amount of the proceeds in an escrow account has raised legal concerns.
II. Secondly, warrants, as required in US-style SPACs, may potentially be issued by German stock corporations. However, there is considerable legal uncertainty if their specific terms can be implemented under German corporate law. Consequently, the only legal way under German law to replicate the US model would be by issuing preference shares. However, as preference shares (*Vorzugsaktien*), under German law grant, a preference in profit in return for waiving the right to vote, this is not in line with a US SPAC model.
III. Thirdly, shareholders might face difficulties under German law concerning redemption right. Per the German Stock Corporation Act, own shares can be acquired based on an authorization adopted at the annual general meeting. Although such authorization resolution is valid for up to five years, and such time limitation is in line with the functioning of an SPAC, the legal limit is a maximum of 10% of the share capital existing at the time of authorization. This is another hurdle for implementing an SPAC model for a German stock corporation or German SE. In addition, other ways to repay redeeming shareholders face various obstacles, limiting the ability to implement a functioning redemption model similar to a US-style SPAC.

For these reasons, all five SPAC IPOs since the spring of 2021 in Germany have been launched under Luxemburg law and Dutch law, which have more flexibility in corporate law.

1.4.5 SPACs in Belgium

In Belgium, there is no financial law framework specifically regulating SPACs. Hence, the SPAC sponsors will follow the general principles of corporate and financial law. The SPAC will be subject to the Prospectus Regulation as a listed company.

SPACs are new in Belgium, and no listing has occurred so far. The Financial Services and Markets Authority (FSMA) has not yet developed a specific practice nor issued any binding guidelines for SPAC prospectuses. However, the FSMA launched a consultation in May 2021[29] and issued an opinion in June 2021.[30] Specifically, the FSMA highlights minimum standards for listing SPACs with a specific focus on information on dilution at the de-SPAC phase. In addition, it recommends that the prospectus provide a quantitative analysis based on the conditions of the offer.

For SPAC purposes, listing private limited liability companies or BV (*besloten vennootschap*) might be a competitive option in Belgium. This is because Belgian corporate law establishes some constraints concerning share buybacks. Shareholders can vote on the business combination under Belgian corporate law.[31] However, the management is in charge of decisions on all matters unless they are reserved by law or by articles of association to the shareholders' meeting. Hence, it is possible to provide in the articles of association of the SPAC that any business combination would need shareholders' approval to replicate the US model. Shareholders who vote against the business combination can redeem their shares with similar limits to those we examined for Italian SPACs on the MIV. However, shareholders can be granted a put option, allowing them to sell their shares at a predetermined price to the sponsor of the SPAC.

Furthermore, the new Belgian Code of Companies and Associations – adopted in 2019 – provides for an 'exit at the expense of the company's assets'[32] that is not available for public limited liability companies or NV (*naamloze vennootschap*). According to this new procedure, a dissenting shareholder can exit the company by redeeming shares to the company against the payment of an exit fee whose amount is freely determinable in the articles of association. These mechanisms can be – for example – implemented in the event of a business combination.

Finally, in terms of capital structure, Belgian company law does allow both the issuance of warrants[33] and shares or preference shares to structure a possible SPAC project. Hence, the US-style founder remuneration can be replicated in Belgium, although it is very likely that the FSMA will not approve a highly dilutive promotion (funder shares).

1.5 SPACs in the UK

Regarding the UK market, between 2016 and 2017, there was a significant increase in the formation of SPACs, with 15 SPACs listed on the London Stock Exchange (LSE) in 2017 alone, raising £1.7 billion.[34] Since 2017 over 50 SPACs have been listed in the UK, and over £2 billion has been raised by SPACs on the LSE.[35] A small number of large IPOs have dominated the UK market. The four largest SPAC IPOs in the UK (J2 Acquisition, Landscape Acquisition Holdings, Ocelot Partners, and Wilmcote Holdings) represented 99.1% of the total funds raised by U SPACs in 2017.[36]

Historically there were two main differences between SPACs in the UK and the United States. Firstly the redemption right for investors, who choose not to support the acquisition of an identified target, has never been imposed as a listing requirement on the Standard segment of the LSE. Secondly, once the SPAC announces a business combination, the trading of shares is suspended per the UK Takeover Code. Those features came to the attention of the UK Government, and in March 2021, the UK Listing Review, chaired by Lord Jonathan Hill, recommended a series of reforms to make the UK a more attractive venue for IPOs post-Brexit.[37] However, those primary objectives were rapidly overturned by the Financial Conduct Authority (FCA) with the adoption of a conditional acceptance as stated in the final Policy Statement on 27 July 2021 (PS21/10)[38] and based on crucial differences:

I.   The SPAC has to raise a minimum size threshold of £100 million, excluding any funds the sponsor has provided, either in cash or in shares;
II. The SPAC shall obtain the shareholders' approval of the acquisition, and the founder and associates are excluded from voting;
III. The recommendation of the Hill report allowing dual-class shares for SPACs has been dropped;
IV. The SPAC shall put in place a specific ring-fenced procedure of public investors' money to fund an acquisition or the IPO proceeds shall be returned to shareholders in case of the failure of the business combination.

The sponsor unable to meet such conditions, or those choosing not to, will continue to be subjected to a presumption of suspension. This has created a dual system of regulation in the UK on the Standard segment of the LSE. However, SPACs in the UK have specific listing requirements today, and the UK is the first harmonized regime for SPACs in Europe. As a result, the SPAC can list on different exchanges, each with its specific requirements for listing as the following Table 1.1 summarises:

As can be seen following the SPAC reform in 2021, the redemption right of shareholders is a compulsory feature in each of those markets. However, the exception from the suspension of shares is today possible only for Standard listed SPACs that follow the specific requirements imposed by the FCA.

Furthermore, the FCA has also highlighted the importance of disclosures of key terms and risk factors at the point of the SPAC IPO and following the business combination. This feature is similar to the ESMA public statement, although such disclosures – as we previously said above – can only be illustrative rather than definitive. In light of this, the UK seems consistent with the international trend of guaranteeing more public investors' protections in SPAC deals.

However, new rules in the UK on the Standard segment prevent sponsors and anchor investors who participate in an SPAC's at risk-capital from voting on the acquisition.[39] This is a significant difference from other listing venues and might impact London's ability to compete in the SPAC market.

Table 1.1 Classification and listing requirements of London market segments for SPACs

	Standard Segment on LSE	AIM Listing	Access Growth Market on AQSE
Listing Document	FCA approved prospectus	AIM Admission Document	AQSE Admission Document
Minimum Capital Raise for IPO	£100 Million	£6 Million	No less than £2 Million prior to or at admission
Internal term for acquisition	Capital must be deployed within two years of listing	Capital must be deployed within 18 months or extension by shareholders' approval	Must execute strategy within two years of admission or face possible suspension by AQSE
Shareholder approval of the acquisition	Yes, shareholder approval is now required to disapply the presumption of suspension introduced as a part of the recent changes for SPAC listings	Yes, on the basis that it will be a reverse takeover for AIM Rules purposes	Yes, on the basis that it will be a reverse takeover, it will be conditional upon shareholder approval
Corporate Governance	Requires an annual corporate governance statement, which must include confirmation of the corporate governance code applied and explanations of any potential non-compliance with its provision	AIM companies must confirm the corporate governance code they have chosen to apply and explain how they comply with that code, and the reason/s for any non-compliance must be explained	AQSE companies must have due regard for the principles laid down by a 'recognized corporate governance code.'
Free float	10% of the shares must be in hands-on public admission to listing and at all times after that	AIM has no minimum percentage of free float requirement but will need to be comfortable that there will be sufficient liquidity post-IPO	25% of the shares must be in hands-on public admission to listing for enterprise companies (for entities other than SPACs, this is 10%)
Shareholder approval is required for de-listing	No	Yes	Yes

This is not a requirement on other exchanges such as NYSE, NASDAQ, and Euronext. Additionally, to avoid suspension of shares trading on the Standard segment of the LSE, the SPAC has to raise at least £100 million from public investors alone without counting the sponsors' or strategic investors' contributions pre-IPO. Again, this is not in line with the United States or with any other venue for SPACs in Europe. However, this threshold imposes the formation of a sound share capital with the investment by institutional investors, whose monitoring would, in turn, operate as a mechanism for investor protection; on the other hand, it is not competitive and might discourage sponsors from being listed in London.

Such statements have been confirmed in reality: only four SPACs listings have so far been witnessed under the new UK SPAC reform: Hambro Perks Acquisition Company limited with an IPO of £140 million in November 2021; Hiro Metaverse Acquisition I SA (a Luxembourg-based SPAC) that raised over £115 million in February 2022; New Energy One Acquisition Corporation PLC backed by Italian oil and gas group Eni S.p.A. with £175 million in March 2022; and Financial Acquisition Corp. that offered units for the equivalent of £150 million.

Further differences between the UK and the US SPAC regimes concern the funds held on trust such that under both the NYSE and NSDAQ rules, 90% of the gross proceeds raised during the IPO must immediately be deposited and held in a trust account and are subject to strict investment criteria. Furthermore, the SPAC must complete a business combination with a fair market value equal to at least 80% of the trust account at the time of the business combination. The UK does not have such requirements. This can give UK directors more autonomy when identifying a target because founders have more flexibility in using the funds in the short term. However, they have a fiduciary duty to deploy the funds in the best interest of the company and in the manner disclosed in the IPO prospectus/AIM admission document.

In the UK, SPACs usually issue founder shares as preferred shares and warrants for additional founder preferred shares. This is a major difference between the US promotion (founder shares and founder warrants) and a common European trait. In the United States, there is also a deferred underwriting fee, with a portion of the fee paid at the closure of the IPO and the remainder deferred until the closure of the initial acquisition. This is not the case in the UK, where underwriter fees are structured like for any other IPO.

One further commonality that the UK shares with the European Union is that entities listed on the AIM in London or Standard segment may, either on completion of the acquisition or subsequently, seek admission to a different market if that is considered more appropriate for the acquired business. This could involve, for example, moving to a premium listing on the LSE or to a listing venue in another jurisdiction, such as the NASDAQ or the NYSE. The same practice, for instance, has been followed in Italy by several SPACs. Hence, sometimes an SPAC can be seen as a 'bridge company' to plan and secure more prestigious listing venues.

Finally, London also offers a few advantages because operating under English law may be preferable to the US culture of securities litigation. A non-US SPAC may also appeal as a way to sidestep some onerous obligations around US GAAP accounting standards and the new disclosure requirements that are likely to be implemented in the United States by the end of 2022.

1.6 Conclusion

SPACs are cash-shell companies. This means that investors cannot access previous balance sheets, and the management investment decisions become the only valuable asset.[40] In light of this, the SEC is right, for instance, in stressing the importance of disclosure in terms of management's conflict of interests.

It is undeniable that the SPAC is a unique financial innovation, and the United States has established itself as the main legal formant in respect of the SPAC's corporate governance practices and listing requirements. Indeed, since the SPAC boom in 2020 in the United States, European regulators, mainly those in the UK, have studied the implementation of relevant financial regulation to facilitate SPAC listings in their jurisdictions and lure investors away from New York.

When a European Union Member State does not have specific legislation or market rules on SPACs, general principles and provisions of corporate and financial law are legal constants. It applies the saying that 'SPACs are without law, but outside of the law.'[41] National corporate law will be applied whenever there is no specific financial regulation regarding listing requirements. Furthermore, financial regulation of SPACs in Europe, if ever implemented at the domestic level, must abide by a minimum level of protection regarding retail investors' and sponsors' disclosures, with the necessary clarifications as illustrated in section 1.4. This is a regulation by objectives.

After examining European Member States, it is clear that in terms of SPACs, the jurisdiction most resilient to US standards is Euronext Amsterdam. Although that exchange does not have a specific financial regulation for SPACs, the flexibility of Dutch company law (such as BV entities) allows sponsors to replicate US-style features in their entirety; this is also by virtue of uncodified market practices such as preference shares in terms of founders' remuneration. The Amsterdam case directly illustrates that market practices and self-regulation matter in SPACs. It is not fundamental to have lenient financial regulation for SPACs if sponsors can implement market practices under their national corporate legal framework.

Currently, Italy, Spain, Germany, and Belgium have diversified legal regimes concerning redemption rights under their national company laws. This is creating difficulties for public investors and has obliged sponsors to be creative in setting up SPACs in other jurisdictions (see the case of Italy and Germany) by using more flexible corporate laws such as Dutch or Luxembourg law, which are closer to the flexibility of US corporate law from a de-SPAC perspective. This kind of forum shopping in Europe might act against the harmonization aims of domestic corporate law frameworks, but the establishment of regulation by competition is not necessarily negative. This shows that only SPAC-friendly legal systems can attract more SPAC listings, especially if the corporate law frameworks of such jurisdictions are flexible and consent to implement US-style SPAC features (see section 1.2). For these reasons, this chapter has demonstrated that lenient financial and legal frameworks are not the essential response to SPAC concerns. At the same time, they are not the only possible solution to lure investors from NY exchanges. Therefore, dynamic and flexible corporate law frameworks at the domestic level have more importance in terms of SPACs.[42]

Notes

1 Brooke Masters, 'Year in a Word: SPAC' (*Financial Times*, 1 January 2021).
2 Daniele D'Alvia, 'The International Financial Regulation of SPACs between Legal Standardised Regulation and Standardisation of Market Practices' (2020) 21(2) *Journal of Banking Regulation* 107.
3 Daniele D'Alvia, *Mergers, Acquisitions, and International Financial Regulation: Analysing Special Purpose Acquisition Companies* (Routledge 2021).
4 Ortenca Aliaj et al., 'The SPAC Sponsor Bonanza' (*Financial Times*, 13 November 2020).
5 David H. Hsu, 'What Do Entrepreneurs Pay for Venture Capital Affiliation?' (2004) 59 *Journal of Finance* 1805.
6 Bobby Reddy, 'The SPACtacular rise of the Special Purpose Acquisition Company: A Retail Investor's Worst Nightmare' (2021) 32 *Legal Studies Research Paper Series – University of Cambridge* 6.
7 Matt Levine, 'Money Stuff: Bill Ackman Wants a Mature Unicorn' (*Newsletter Bloomberg*, 23 June 2020).
8 Miles Kruppa, 'The Ex-Facebook Star Back in the Spotlight With Virgin Galactic Deal' (*Financial Times*, 11 July 2019).
9 Paul D. Thomas and Miles Kruppa, 'British SPAC King Plans First European Blank Cheque Listing' (*Financial Times* 11 May 2021).
10 US Securities and Exchange Commission – Division of Corporate Finance, 'CF Disclosure Guidance: Topic No 11' (22 December 2020) <https://www.sec.gov/corpfin/disclosure-specialpurpose-acquisition-companies#_ednref2> accessed 10 January 2023.
11 Specifically 100% of the SPAC's share can be redeemed by shareholders in connection with the business combination as long as the SPAC at all times has minimum net tangible assets of at least $5 million.
12 Daniele D'Alvia, 'From Darkness to Light: A Comparative Study of Special Purpose Acquisition Companies in the European Union, the UK, and the US' (2022) 23 *Cambridge Yearbook of European Legal Studies* 10.
13 Ortenca Aliaj et al., 'SPACs Forced to Fund Deals With More Expensive Financing' (*Financial Times*, 19 July 2021).
14 Amrith Ramkumar, 'Westrock Coffee to Go Public in $1.2 billion SPAC Deal' (*The Wall Street Journal*, 4 April 2022).
15 AFM, 'The Dutch SPAC market: An Overview' (January 2022) 5 *AFM Market Watch* 1, 2.
16 Ibid., 2.
17 Tomas De Heredia et al., 'The SPAC Boom: Europe Picks Up the Pace' (*Deloitte Insights*, 14 July 2021) <https://www2.deloitte.com/xe/en/insights/industry/financial-services/spacs-in-europe.html> accessed 10 January 2023.

18 ESMA, 'Consultation Paper – Guidelines on key concepts of the AIFMD' (*ESMA*, 19 December 2012) n. 845.

19 Daniele D'Alvia, 'SPACs: Limiti e Prospettive tra Hard Law e Soft Law' (2017) 12(4) *Rivista del Diritto Societario* 1167, 1187.

20 ESMA, 'Public Statement – SPACs: Prospectus Disclosure and Investor Protection Considerations' (*ESMA*, 15 July 2021).

21 Regulation (EU) 2017/1129 of the European Parliament and the Council of 14 June 2017 on the Prospectus to be published when securities are offered to the public or admitted to trading on a regulated market, and repleading Directive 2003/71/EC.

22 The possibility of issuing founder warrants in a reserved offer to the SPAC sponsor is not theoretically prohibited under Dutch law, but it is not common in practice.

23 A BV is similar to a private limited liability company under Belgian law in terms of corporate flexibility. It is also the most common form of limited company in the Netherlands and Belgium.

24 Article 5:70 of the *Wet Financieel Toezicht* or Financial Supervisory Act, and Article 2:98 (C) of the *Burgerlijk Wetboek* or Dutch Civil Code that has excluded the application of financial assistance provisions to BVs since 2012.

25 For further remarks on the financial regulation of SPACs in Italy, please see Chapter 2 and Part II of this edited collection.

26 See Article 346 of the Spanish Companies Act 2010, which provides for legal causes of withdrawal.

27 See Articles 500 and 501 of the Spanish Companies Act 2010.

28 Jochen Eichhorn and Kay-Michael Schanz, 'Deutsche SPAC unter Gesellschaft – und aufsichtsrechtlichen Aspekten' (2021) 3 *Recht der Finanzinstrumente* 186.

29 FSMA, 'Public Consultation by the FSMA about a Proposal for Minimum Standards for the Structuring, Information Disclosure and Trading in SPACs on Euronext Brussels' (*FSMA*, 5 May 2021).

30 FSMA, 'Opinion on Minimum Standards Governing the Structure of SPACs, the Disclosure of Information About SPAC Shares and Trading in Those Shares on Euronext Brussels' (*FSMA*, 21 June 2021).

31 Arnaud Coibion, 'Is Belgium Ready for the Rise of the SPAC?' (*Linklaters Publications*, 3 December 2020).

32 Article 5:154 of the Belgium Code of Companies and Associations (2019).

33 Article 5:55 of the Belgium Code of Companies and Associations (2019).

34 Price Waterhouse Cooper, 'IPO Watch Europe 2017' <https://www.pwc.co.uk/audit-assurance/assets/pdf/ipo-watch-europe-2017-annual-review.pdf> accessed on 20 January 2023.

35 London Stock Exchange, 'Special Purpose Acquisition Companies' <https://www.londonstockexchange.com/raise-finance/equity/spacs> accessed on 20 January 2023.

36 D'Alvia (n 2).

37 UK Listing Review (3 March 2021).

38 FCA, 'Investor Protection Measures for Special Purpose Acquisition Companies: Change to the Listing Rules' (July 2021) <https://www.fca.org.uk/publication/policy/ps21-10.pdf> accessed 10 January 2023.

39 D'Alvia (n 3) 118.

40 Usha Rodrigues and Mike Stegemoller, 'What All-Cash Companies Tell Us About IPOs and Acquisition' (2014) 29 *Journal of Corporate Finance* 111.

41 D'Alvia (n 19).

42 The truthfulness of this statement is further confirmed in the illustration of the Italian legal framework in Part II of this edited collection.

2 The Financial Regulation of Italian Special Purpose Acquisition Companies

Filippo Annunziata, Anna Chiara Chisari and Maria Lucia Passador

2.1 Introduction

Special Purpose Acquisition Companies (SPACs) have enjoyed, at least for some time, a fair degree of success in the Italian market. However, as in other jurisdictions, the relationship between the SPAC structure and financial market legislation is rather intricate: some areas of financial regulation potentially apply to SPACs, while others are not. In some instances, SPACs simply fall outside the scope of certain areas of the financial and capital markets legislation; in other cases, they benefit from specific exemptions from certain provisions; and finally, they may be entirely subject to certain types of regulation. In particular, it is worth considering the following areas: (i) the relationship between SPACs and the regulation of undertakings for collective investment, which arises, in Italy, from the implementation of the Alternative Investment Fund Managers Directive (AIFMD); (ii) the relationship between SPACs and the prospectus regulation; (iii) the regulation of trading platforms and SPACs, with particular attention to the Alternative Investment Market (AIM) experience; (iv) the regulation of corporate governance of listed companies and SPACs; (v) the peculiarities of SPACs vis-a-vis other similar regulated vehicles (including private equity funds, club-deals and family offices).

For each of these topics, this chapter will discuss how, and to what extent, SPACs are ultimately subject to the related relevant provision or are excluded from it and how they have developed their 'regulatory' strategies in approaching the Italian market.

Subsequently, this study will perform a quantitative analysis of Italian SPACs from January 2010 to December 2020, drawing some considerations and comparing their key characteristics with those of US SPACs.

2.2 From the United States to the EU: General Remarks on the Peculiarity of the Italian Market[1]

'Notably, the advance of European SPACs first occurred in July 2007 with the listing of the Pan-European Hotel Acquisition Company (PEHAC) on the NYSE Euronext Amsterdam.'[2] The following year, two additional SPACs

DOI: 10.4324/9781003169079-4

were listed on the NYSE Euronext Amsterdam; then, the two-year turndown is ascribable:

> [to the] collapse of global equity markets, with investors fleeing into safer and less volatile investment harbors such as gold and real estate. However, . . . the first overall IPO on the Frankfurt Stock Exchange in 2010 was the listing of Helikos SE, which also marked the introduction of SPACs into German capital markets.[3]

The US experience has represented a considerable driving force elsewhere,[4] especially in the pre-Brexit UK scenario[5] and in Italy. However, far from being interrelated, these two geographic areas share a peculiarity, namely the presence of a more flexible market (the AIM), that could, to some extent, explain the more limited recourse to SPACs (if compared to the 'US boom').

As to the former, it is worth reminding that UK Main Market rules require a (burdensome) trading suspension until SPACs issue a prospectus. However, its AIM's flexibility undoubtedly helped its expansion.[6]

As to the latter, the first SPAC came in 2011, with Italy 1 Investment, a company incorporated under the laws of Luxembourg and listed on the Market for Investment Vehicles (MIV), followed by Made in Italy, the first SPAC incorporated under the laws of Italy to be listed on the AIM Italia market, and promoted by the serial-SPAC sponsor Luca Fabio Giacometti. After a half-hearted start, also thanks to Law n. 232 of 11 December 2016, the market for SPACs expanded considerably until reaching a notable result in Italy, which is one of the few scenarios (although remotely) comparable to that of the United States. However, the Italian entrepreneurial network is affected by two key concerns: undercapitalization and systemic reliance on bank credit. This has resulted in the increasing use of private equity and initial public offerings (IPOs), while at the same time finding an appealing substitute for SPACs, also thanks to the US experience.[7]

At a regulatory level, it should be borne in mind that the Italian SPACs are also subject to the provisions of the Market Regulations and the AIM Regulations, recently amended on the issue in 2021 when *Borsa Italiana* S.p.A. became part of Euronext Group, providing that the SPAC issuer, for its admission, must raise at least 10 million euros in cash through a placement that ends on the date of admission or in the vicinity of such admission and establishing some criteria that SPAC promoters are required to meet to be admitted to trading shares on the AIM.[8]

2.3 SPACs and the AIFMD

Today, SPACs are not legally defined by any national legislation, apart from a couple of exceptions, such as the Bursa Malaysia. Furthermore, at the international level, and especially at the European level, there is a complete lack of any uniform and harmonized legal discipline regarding them.

The Italian regulation does not represent an exception, as it does not provide for specific regulations targeting SPACs. A complete lack of a uniform and harmonized legal discipline regarding SPACs is also found at the European Union level. The absence of a positive definition fueled the debate about the legal qualification of SPACs. It made questionable how and to what extent SPACs are ultimately subject to financial and capital markets laws – or, instead, should be excluded from their scope.

The first question to be addressed is whether SPACs could be identified as collective investment undertakings. At the European Union level, the general definition of collective investment undertakings is now contained in Directive 2011/61/EU on Alternative Investment Fund Managers (AIFMD), regulating all collective undertakings except those which require authorization under the Undertakings for the Collective Investment in Transferable Securities (UCITS) Directive.[9,10] The AIFMD proceeds negatively, applying to all collective investment undertakings – identified with the term alternative investment funds (AIFs) – which do not fall within the scope of the UCITS Directive.

Compared to the UCITS Directive, the AIFMD is broader in scope as it is aimed at regulating entities managing AIFs regardless of whether the AIF is of an open-ended or a closed-ended type, whatever the legal form of the AIF and whether or not the AIF is listed.[11] The definition of AIFs appears intentionally broad, aiming to capture the variety of forms and organizational schemes assumed by collective investment undertakings in the European Union market.

According to the definition of AIF contained in Section 4 of the AIFMD, AIFs are collective investment undertakings, including investment compartments, that:

I. raise capital from several investors to invest it in accordance with a defined investment policy for the benefit of those investors; and
II. do not require authorization pursuant to Section 5 of the UCITS Directive.

The European Securities and Markets Authority (ESMA), in its 'Guidelines on key concepts of the AIFMD'[12] (hereinafter, the ESMA's Guidelines), supplements this definition and establishes that a collective investment undertaking shall meet at least the following requirements to be classified as an AIF:

I. The undertaking does not have a general commercial or industrial purpose.
II. The undertaking should pool together capital raised from its investors for investment to generate a pooled return for those investors.
III. The unit holders or shareholders of the undertaking – as a collective group – have no day-to-day discretion or control.

Such broad drafting, however, creates severe problems of interpretation, making it difficult to reliably determine whether the AIFMD is capable of catching in its perimeter fund structures that appear as like AIFs, like SPACs, but that are not expressly included.

Within this framework, on 19 December 2012, ESMA published a Consultation paper[13] where the Authority raised the issue of applying the AIFMD to SPACs. However, after collecting market operators' responses, ESMA did not provide any clarification, and the question remained unsolved.

At this point, the attention can now be directed to better define the AIFMD perimeter, also by virtue of the exemption rules provided by the Directive. As already mentioned, the width of the definition of AIF gives rise to interpretative difficulties. Exemption rules are, therefore, crucial to delimit and circumscribe the reserve of activity in the field of asset management, which is required by the AIFMD and protected in almost all Member States.[14]

With specific reference to the Italian legal system, according to Section 32-*quater*, sub-Section 1, of Legislative Decree n. 58 of 24 February 1998 (the Consolidated Law on Finance or TUF), the professional practice of collective asset management (meaning the management of collective investment undertakings and the relative risks thereof) is reserved to the asset management companies, the SICAVs, the SICAFs, the EU management companies which manage Italian UCITS, the EU and non-EU alternative investment managers which manage an Italian AIF.

For the present discussion, among the exemption rules, the one that pertains to the holding companies seems to be relevant, set forth by Section 2, Sub-section 3 (a) of the AIFMD and implemented into national law with Section 32-*quater*, Sub-section 2 (d), TUF.

Section 32-*quater*, Sub-section 2 (d), TUF expressly excludes holding companies from the reserve of activity of Section 32-*quater*, TUF and defines holding companies as follows:

> companies which hold interests in one or more companies, to execute entrepreneurial strategies to contribute to the increase of value in the long term, through the exercise of control, considerable influence and the rights deriving from their holdings and which: 1) operate on their behalf and whose shares are traded on a regulated European Union market; or 2) are not established with the main purpose of generating profit for their investors by the disposal of their holdings in the companies they control or over which they have considerable influence or in which they hold interests, as proven by their financial statements and other company documents.

It should be noted that the Bank of Italy used the exemption under analysis to draw a distinction between certain entities, including SPACs, and AIFs. According to the Bank of Italy:

> SPACs are excluded from the reserve of Article 32-*quater*, TUF to the extent that they fall under Article 32-*quater*, para. 2(d), TUF about holding companies.[15]

In other words, SPACs could be covered by the definition of holding companies and could therefore fall under the related exemption if they meet the requirements set forth by Section 32-*quater*, Sub-section 2 (d), TUF, including the pursuit of 'entrepreneurial strategies. However, according to the Bank of Italy – referring to the definition of AIFs provided in ESMA's Guidelines – an entity pursuing an entrepreneurial strategy, meaning a commercial or industrial purpose, cannot be classified as an AIF. The latter, instead, is intended to deliver an investment return or profit for its investors, as it follows a financial purpose.

ESMA's Guidelines clarified the meaning of 'general commercial or industrial purpose' as follows:

> The purpose of pursuing a business strategy which includes characteristics such as running predominantly i) a commercial activity, involving the purchase, sale, and/or exchange of goods or commodities and/or the supply of non-financial services, or ii) an industrial activity, involving the production of goods or construction of properties, or iii) a combination thereof.

It seems reasonable to conclude that the 'special purpose' of SPACs, being the completion of the business combination,[16] appears closer to an entrepreneurial strategy than a financial purpose – as *Borsa Italiana* confirmed on several occasions.[17]

As recently pointed out in the literature,[18] the holding companies' exemption may not be a decisive argument. After the AIFMD implementation in Italy – regarding provisions concerning statutory collective undertakings (*Società di investimento a capitale fisso (SICAF)*)– the distinction between holding companies and collective investment undertakings became less immediate.[19]

Without prejudice to the above, it should be noted that the same outcome could be reached by relying exclusively on the definition of AIFs provided by the AIFMD, according to which any entity, including an SPAC, can be considered an AIF only if it meets all various elements provided by the AIFMD. Although SPACs share some characteristics that may recall the critical features of AIFs, one or more of the relevant criteria seem not to be met, including pursuing a financial purpose, as already mentioned.

Firstly, according to ESMA's Guidelines and the Bank of Italy,[20] AIF's investment policy is, by its nature, diversified, and the management activity implies both a choice of capital allocation and risk management. Instead, SPAC's business activity is incompatible with the logic of risk management and diversification: after the business combination is completed, SPACs investors will be only exposed to the business risk of the target company, as would any shareholder of a listed company. Secondly, it should be noted that the business combination is subject to the shareholder's meeting approval. This implies that while AIFs' investors have no day-to-day discretion or control over the entity, SPAC's investors partake in the investment decision process in their role as shareholders.

In conclusion, the absence of a positive definition and the structural and financial similarities between SPACs and AIFs do not seem sufficient *per se* to qualify SPACs as a possible form of AIFs. Moreover, the AIF definition provides a list of cumulative and specific requirements; SPAC does not seem to meet them.[21]

2.4 SPACs and Prospectus Regulation

As already mentioned, one of the first steps in SPACs' lifecycle is to raise capital through an IPO. The leading Italian legislative and regulatory instruments governing IPOs in Italy are the Consolidated Law on Finance and CONSOB Regulation n. 11971 of 14 May 1999, as subsequently amended and supplemented (CONSOB Issuers' Regulation) and the Rules of the Markets and related Instructions issued by *Borsa Italiana*.

The legal framework applicable to securities offerings in the European Union has constantly been evolving in recent years. Following a consultation process and as part of its Capital Markets Union action plan, the European Commission adopted a new prospectus regulation in June 2017. Regulation (EU) n. 1129 of 14 June 2017 (the Prospectus Regulation), with its relevant delegated and implementing acts,[22] repealed Directive 2003/71/EC (the Prospectus Directive), aiming at improving the prospectus regime previously designed by the Prospectus Directive.

With Legislative Decree n. 17 of 2 February 2021, the Italian Government aligned the national legislation with the provisions of the Prospectus Regulation. The Legislative Decree introduced significant amendments to the Consolidated Law on Finance. At the same time, CONSOB Issuers' Regulation had already been adapted to the Prospectus Regulation by CONSOB Resolution n 21016 of 24 July 2019.

In particular, pursuant to the Consolidated Law on Finance, when securities are offered to the public or admitted to trading on a regulated market in Italy, a prospectus (the Prospectus)– drawn up according to the Prospectus Regulation requirements – must be approved by CONSOB (or by the competent authority of another European Union Member State) and published. The Consolidated Law on Finance sets out the general provisions governing the offering of financial instruments to the public as well as the general principles and rules concerning, inter alia, the preparation, and contents of the Prospectus, the Prospectus liability regime, and the validity of the Prospectus.

Listing can take place in one of Borsa Italiana stock markets:

I. MTA – *Mercato Telematico Azionario*, a regulated market for medium-sized and large companies.
II. AIM Italia, a multilateral trading facility (MTF) dedicated primarily to small and medium companies and companies having a high growth potential; and
III. Market for Investment Vehicles (MIVs), a regulated market dedicated to listing vehicles that invest in the real economy.

SPACs can be listed on AIM Italia or MIV. Since MIVs is a regulated market, admission to listing is subject to the publication of a Prospectus. By contrast, being AIM Italia an MTF, the admission to listing on AIM Italia does not require a Prospectus. Consequently, the listing process is almost entirely governed by the rules issued by Borsa Italiana (AIM Italia Rules for Companies). On AIM Italia, the main transaction document is the admission document, subject to the requirements set out under the AIM Italia Rules for Companies. Those requirements do not include the preliminary approval by either Borsa Italiana or CONSOB. AIM Italia applicants are, in principle, free to prepare a Prospectus; in that case, the admission document is no longer required.

It is worth pointing out that the AIM Italia Rules for Companies require that the admission document discloses a set of information equivalent to the one provided by Annexes 1, 11, and 20 of Commission Delegated Regulation (EU) 2019/980 of 14 March 2019 (supplementing the Prospectus Regulation). To better understand the rationale behind this choice, reference should be made to the considerations detailed in the next section.

2.4.1 SPACs and Trading Platforms Regulation: The Case of AIM Italia

The problem of the regulatory gap between the legal framework applicable to issuers listed on regulated markets and those traded on MTFs is inherent to the legal design of European and national regulations.[23] As already pointed out in the Prospectus Regulation, some European Union regulations governing capital markets only apply to issuers listed on regulated markets: for instance, Directive 2004/25/EC of the 21 of April 2004 concerning takeover bids, Directive 2007/36/EC of 11 July 2007 relating to the exercise of certain rights of shareholders of listed companies and Regulation 596/2014 of 16 April 2014 on the discipline of market abuse (Market Abuse Regulation).[24]

MTFs are subject to the market rules set out by the entity governing the MTF, which is, in principle, relatively free to exercise its policy-making authority – including the extent to which the MTF rules should be aligned to regulated markets. However, with specific reference to AIM Italia, it should be noted that, given the qualification of AIM Italia as an SME growth market,[25] it benefits from relatively few regulatory alleviations compared to other MTFs.[26]

AIM Italia Rules for Companies are therefore structured and organized to find a balance between two needs:

I. the need for simplification inherent to alternative trading systems (compared to regulated markets) and their attractiveness toward issuers; and
II. the need to protect the market and the investors. According to the *Borsa Italiana* website, 'AIM Italia is the market dedicated to dynamic and competitive SMEs, which are looking for capital to finance their growth, thanks to a balanced regulatory approach, suitable for ambitious companies' needs.'

In this respect, AIM Italia Rules for Companies require applicants to include in their bylaws some requirements established under financial law and rules regarding mandatory takeover bids. The legal scheme of mandatory takeover bids, deriving from the consolidated law on finance and applying only to issuers listed on regulated markets, is therefore 'internalized' by the company bylaws.

Moreover, according to Section 6-*bis* of AIM Italia Rules for Companies, applicants shall adopt and maintain appropriate corporate governance provisions. These include, inter alia, the appointment of at least one independent director among candidates previously identified or positively evaluated by a Nominated Advisor (Nomad), the identification of a professionally qualified person (investor relations manager) who has the specific (but not necessarily exclusive) task of managing relations with an investor. The directors appointed by the applicant shall meet the requirements of integrity pursuant to Section 147-*quinquies*, TUF, and the statutory auditors shall meet the requirements of experience and integrity pursuant to Section 148, Subsection 4, TUF.

With specific reference to Nomads, AIM Italia applicants shall appoint a Nomad to be eligible for listing. Nomads are approved by Borsa Italiana and included on the AIM Italia Register. A Nomad can be a bank, an intermediary, or a company belonging to the network of a statutory auditing firm. They must assess the company's appropriateness to the admission to the market and assist and support the company on its responsibilities under the rules deriving from being listed on AIM Italia. The rules relating to the eligibility, responsibilities, role and activities of Nomads are set out in the separate AIM Italia rulebook (Rules for Nominated Advisers).

Admission standards applicable to the AIM Italia are more flexible, and listing admissions can be achieved in a shorter timeframe than MIVs. While MIVs are reserved for professional investors, AIM Italia has a Professional Segment but is also open to retail investors. According to AIM Italia Rules for Companies, the admission to trading on the AIM Italia is limited to 'AIFs and to companies established to purchase a specific business,' namely SPACs.

To be admitted to AIM Italia, SPACS shall raise at least EUR 10 million in cash via equity fundraising on or near the admission date. This minimum fundraising requirement does not apply to SPACs from demergers of other SPACs.

As a confirmation of the balanced regulatory approach pursued by AIM Italia, AIM Italia Rules for Companies identify some criteria to be satisfied by SPACs' promoters:

Only as concerns special purpose acquisition companies, promoters must be persons with proven experience and/or who held management positions in the area of (i) transactions on the primary capital market; (ii) private equity transactions; (iii) management of mid-sized companies; (iv) investment banking sector.

Moreover, according to AIM Listing Rules, an investing company[27] shall follow an investing policy and, in case of a material change, shall obtain the prior consent of its shareholders in a general meeting. Where an investing company has not substantially implemented its investing policy within 24 months of admission, it should obtain the consent of its shareholders for its investing policy at its next annual general meeting and on an annual basis thereafter until its investing policy has been substantially implemented.

AIM Listing Rules include two specific provisions for SPACs. First, SPACs are subject to a favorable regime regarding reverse takeover: listing suspension, according to Section 14 of AIM Italia Rules for Companies, shall not apply in the case of financial instruments issued by SPACs admitted to the Professional Segment. Also, Section 35 of AIM Italia Rules for Companies about the appointment of a specialist and research requirements do not apply to SPAC.

2.5 SPACs and Corporate Governance Rules for Listed Companies

As anticipated earlier, no special legislation regarding SPACs is set at both European Union and national levels. Recent studies nevertheless pointed out that SPACs can be defined as companies 'without law' but not 'outside law.'[28] This is because, in the European Union context, SPACs are subject to the provisions of the corporate law framework of each Member State.

Under Italian corporate law, SPACs are incorporated as joint-stock companies. When listed, those are regulated by the consolidated law on finance, the CONSOB Issuers' Regulation, and the relevant stock exchange's market rules. On the latter point, it should be noted that – contrary to what is required for AIM Italia – companies listed on MIVs must comply with the principles and recommendations set out under the Italian corporate governance.[29] Furthermore, in addition to listing requirements analyzed in the previous section, it is worth pointing out that SPACs admitted to MIVs and AIM Italia are also subject to Consob Regulation No. 17221 of 12 March 2010 regarding related party transactions, while SPACs listed on MIVs are required to establish in writing, maintain and apply an effective policy for the handling of conflicts of interest.

The most relevant corporate governance rules applicable to SPACs may be analyzed by looking at two steps composing SPACs' lifecycle:

I. identification of the target company; and
II. execution of the business combination.

After the target company has been identified, the SPAC shareholders meeting is required to vote on the decision regarding the execution of the business combination (Sections 2363 and following of the ICC).

The SPAC shareholders meeting usually resolves reserved matters according to the majorities required by the law. For example, suppose the SPAC has shares listed on a regulated market or widely distributed among the public.

In that case, it is classified as a company that 'serves the risk capital market' (Section 2325-*bis* of the ICC).[30] In this case, a positive vote of at least two-thirds of the share capital represented in the shareholder's meeting is required (Section 2368 of the ICC).

SPAC shareholders can vote for or against the completion of the business combination. Shareholders who do not participate in the vote (meaning those absent, dissented or abstained from voting) hold a right of withdrawal, pursuant to Sections 2437 and following of the ICC. In particular, the execution of the business combination implies a substantial modification of the corporate purpose and an extension of the company's duration, which are two of the circumstances set out by Section 2437 of the ICC, whereby a shareholder may exercise its right of withdrawal. Finally, it should be recalled that the possibility to introduce statutorily – and therefore additional – rights of withdrawal is exclusively reserved for companies that do not 'serve the risk capital market,' according to Section 2437, Sub-section 4, of the ICC.

The share liquidation value is calculated in compliance with Section 2437-*ter* of the ICC, setting out different criteria depending on whether the company is not listed or is listed on a regulated market. For example, suppose an SPAC is listed on an MTF, such as AIM Italia. In that case, the liquidation value is determined by exclusive reference to the company's assets and prospective profits and (if available) its shares market value. The bylaws can also provide for different evaluation methods, according to Section 2437-*ter*, Sub-section 4, of the ICC.

Regarding SPACs' management bodies, the board of directors is mainly composed of promoters, which usually own preferred shares. To avoid potential conflicts of interest and ensure investors' protection, the transfer of preferred shares is restricted until the business combination is achieved, ensuring that promotors cannot be replaced. Moreover, SPAC promoters are not entitled to receive a predetermined remuneration. Still, they are remunerated only at the time of the business combination through the conversion of preferred shares into ordinary shares at a reward conversion ratio. Promoters are usually appointed as a member of SPAC's supervisory board, according to Section 2397 and following of the ICC.

Securities and proceeds raised during the IPO are deposited in an escrow account or held in trust. The interests or dividends earned on the deposited funds cannot be distributed until an acquisition is completed. As mentioned earlier, SPACs must meet the business combination within an 18- to 24-month timeframe. The SPAC is liquidated at the end of the deadline for implementing the business combination.

Under Italian law, there are two legal instruments allowing SPAC's automatic liquidation:

I. to set in the bylaws a company's duration limited to 18–24 months (according to Section 2328, sub-section 2, n. 13 of ICC; or

II. to introduce in the bylaws a specific ground for winding-up (according to Section 2484, sub-section 1, n. 7 of the ICC.[31]

2.6 Descriptive Analysis of the Italian Market

The size of the Italian SPAC business is significantly smaller than the US one. Nevertheless, the market has been steadily growing since 2011, with a solid upward trend, given that in 2018, only seven listings will be framed in a general scenario of growing interest for Italian IPOs.

As reported by other authors, in 2006 and 2007, there was a great deal of fervor, with 37 transactions in 2006 and 66 in 2007. Then, the market collapsed significantly in 2008 (and in 2019, there was just one SPAC), and it gradually regained strength (7 SPACs in 2020). Finally, after a vigorous upturn in 2015, with the listing of 20 SPACs, and about four billion dollars raised, the trend was broadly upward, with the sole exception of 2016, when the volume of IPO transactions was reduced, as the capital was raised.[32]

The present analysis of the Italian scenario aims at complementing a recent Organisation for Economic Co-operation and Development (OECD) study focusing on the very same geographical context[33] and mirroring the results of a companion empirical study performed regarding a completely different geographical context, namely the US one.[34] Structurally, it is mainly divided into two areas, concerning which two quantitative analyses have been performed.

First, we considered how the firm's performance changed over time; then, we replicated the analysis concerning the percentage of shares owned by the different shareholders to verify whether any shareholder variation could be correlated with company results.

Following this initial analysis, we delved into the ownership structure of the SPACs analyzed, verifying both the composition of the clusters of the main investors and the possible long-term strategies within each firm of these investors.

The following analyses are based on the combination of data from both the Wharton Research Data Services (WRDS) and ORBIS databases. From the first one, all transactions classifiable as SPACs, with Italian-based companies as acquirers, from January 2010 to December 2020, have been selected. The list of resulting SPACs consists of 126 companies whose performance and shareholding characteristics were reviewed. The latter goal was possible thanks to the data available through ORBIS, based on a sample of 56 companies.

Changes in Operating Income

The data provided shows that, during the period under analysis, there was a predominant positive variation in operating income, amounting on average to 42.13% of total variations, corresponding to a minor negative variation of 33.45%.

Table 2.1 Classification of absolute changes in operating income (2011–2019)

	2011	2012	2013	2014	2015	2016	2017	2018	2019
Increased	2	4	4	6	6	7	12	14	0
Decreased	4	2	3	2	5	4	4	9	1
Unchanged	1	1	2	3	2	5	6	5	1
Total	7	7	9	11	13	16	22	28	2

Source: ORBIS.[35]

Table 2.2 Classification of relative changes in operating income (2011–2019)

	2011	2012	2013	2014	2015	2016	2017	2018	2019
Increased	28.57%	57.14%	44.44%	54.55%	46.15%	43.75%	54.55%	50.00%	0.00%
Decreased	57.14%	28.57%	33.33%	18.18%	38.46%	25.00%	18.18%	32.14%	50.00%
Unchanged	14.29%	14.29%	22.22%	27.27%	15.38%	31.25%	27.27%	17.86%	50.00%
Total	100%	100%	100%	100%	100%	100%	100%	100%	100%

Source: ORBIS.[36]

Changes in the Shareholding Structure

Considering the study of the changes in shareholdings, which are used in this analysis as a predictive tool concerning potential investment strategies, that is, those geared toward either the long or short term, we can observe that the short-term approach prevails over the long-term one in eight of the nine years reported.

This trend, essentially oriented toward the short term, leads to a reduction in the Delta analyzed and is reflected in the average values of the relative changes in equity investments for all types of investors.

Interestingly, suppose we divide the variations between institutional and non-institutional investors, considering the four most representative clusters (namely companies, individuals/families, banks, and financial institutions). In that case, we come up with two completely different results. First, while institutional investors tend to increase their investments (in 33.94% of cases), which indicates their preference for a medium-long-term strategy, non-institutional investors are not likely to alter the time horizons of their investments to any great extent.

Table 2.3 Classification of absolute changes in the shareholding structure (2011–2020)

	2011	2012	2013	2014	2015	2016	2017	2018	2019	2020
Increased	2	0	0	0	9	3	3	23	12	23
Decreased	3	1	1	0	8	10	8	52	52	25
Unchanged	6	8	31	30	37	49	53	48	78	142
Total	11	9	32	30	54	62	64	123	142	190

Source: ORBIS.

Table 2.4 Classification of relative changes in the shareholding structure (2011–2020)

	2011	2012	2013	2014	2015	2016	2017	2018	2019	2020
Increased	18.18%	0.00%	0.00%	0.00%	16.67%	4.84%	4.69%	18.70%	8.45%	12.11%
Decreased	27.27%	11.11%	3.13%	0.00%	14.81%	16.13%	12.50%	42.28%	36.62%	13.16%
Unchanged	54.55%	88.89%	96.88%	100.00%	68.52%	79.03%	82.81%	39.02%	54.93%	74.74%
Total	100%	100%	100%	100%	100%	100%	100%	100%	100%	100%

Source: ORBIS.

Table 2.5 Relative changes in the shareholding structure (2011–2020), considering all investor categories, on average

Changes	Average
Increased	8.36%
Decrease	17.70%
Unchanged	73.94%
Total	100.00%

Source: ORBIS.

Table 2.6 Relative changes in shareholdings (2011–2020) for institutional investors (banks and financial institutions), on average

Changes	Average
Increased	33.94%
Decreased	26.91%
Unchanged	39.16%
Total	100.00%

Source: ORBIS.

Table 2.7 Relative changes in shareholdings (2011–2020) for non-institutional investors (firms and individuals), on average

Changes	Average
Increased	8.92%
Decreased	8.84%
Unchanged	82.25%
Total	100.00%

Source: ORBIS.

Table 2.8 Absolute values and percentages of the presence of certain investors in the shareholder base of SPACs

Shareholders (clusters)	No.	Percent
One or more named individuals or families	179	40.68%
Corporate	112	25.45%
Bank	44	10.00%
Financial Company	34	7.73%
Mutual and pension fund, nominee, trust, trustee	21	4.77%
Insurance company	12	2.73%
Public authority, state, government	9	2.05%
Foundation, Research Institute	9	2.05%
No data fulfil your filter criteria	8	1.82%
Other unnamed shareholders aggregated	5	1.14%
Private equity firm	3	0.68%
Public	2	0.45%
Self-ownership	2	0.45%
Total	440	

Source: ORBIS.

Shareholding Composition

Shareholders are single individuals or family businesses in 40.68% of the cases (out of 440 shareholders analyzed), while they are other companies in 25.45% of cases. Therefore, more than 66% of the shareholders in this market are represented by non-institutional investors. This finding reflects the different economic and business background that characterizes our country, which is different from the United States, where the use of SPACs has recently reached unprecedented peak levels in terms of concluded transactions and capital employed.[37] Also, in our country, the banking system stands out as the leading institutional investor, with 10% of the total SPACs shareholding, a position that in the United States is held by financial institutions, insurance companies, and funds.[38]

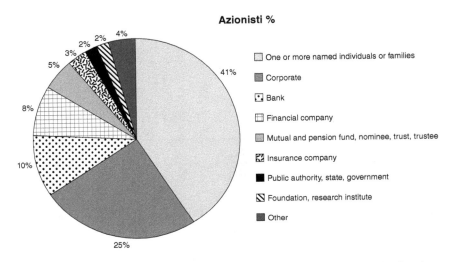

Figure 2.1 Percentage values of the participation of specific investors in the share-holder base of SPACs.

Source: ORBIS.

Banks

Table 2.9 Classification of relative and average changes in bank shareholdings (2011–2020)

	2011	2012	2013	2014	2015	2016	2017	2018	2019	2020
Increased	0.00%	0.00%	0.00%	0.00%	66.67%	20.00%	100.00%	37.50%	66.67%	54.55%
Decreased	50.00%	0.00%	0.00%	0.00%	33.33%	40.00%	0.00%	37.50%	16.67%	27.27%
Unchanged	50.00%	100.00%	100.00%	100.00%	0.00%	40.00%	0.00%	25.00%	16.67%	18.18%
Total	100.00%	100.00%	100.00%	100.00%	100.00%	100.00%	100.00%	100.00%	100.00%	100.00%

Trend	Average
Increased	34.54%
Decreased	20.48%
Unchanged	44.98%
Total	100.00%

Source: ORBIS.

Other Companies

Table 2.10 Classification of relative change and average change in other firms' shareholdings (2011–2020)

	2011	2012	2013	2014	2015	2016	2017	2018	2019	2020
Increased	33.33%	0.00%	0.00%	0.00%	0.00%	0.00%	0.00%	25.93%	8.11%	16.67%
Decreased	0.00%	0.00%	0.00%	0.00%	13.33%	10.53%	21.74%	18.52%	8.11%	16.67%
Unchanged	66.67%	100.00%	100.00%	100.00%	86.67%	89.47%	78.26%	55.56%	83.78%	66.67%
Total	100.00%	100.00%	100.00%	100.00%	100.00%	100.00%	100.00%	100.00%	100.00%	100.00%

Trend	Average
Increased	8.40%
Decreased	8.89%
Unchanged	82.71%
Total	100.00%

Source: ORBIS.

Financial Companies

Table 2.11 Classification of relative change and average change in financial companies' shareholdings (2011–2020)

	2011	2012	2013	2014	2015	2016	2017	2018	2019	2020
Increased	33.33%	33.33%	33.33%	33.33%	33.33%	33.33%	33.33%	33.33%	33.33%	33.33%
Decreased	33.33%	33.33%	33.33%	33.33%	33.33%	33.33%	33.33%	33.33%	33.33%	33.33%
Unchanged	33.33%	33.33%	33.33%	33.33%	33.33%	33.33%	33.33%	33.33%	33.33%	33.33%
Total	100.00%	100.00%	100.00%	100.00%	100.00%	100.00%	100.00%	100.00%	100.00%	100.00%

Trend	Average
Increased	33.33%
Decreased	33.33%
Unchanged	33.33%
Total	100.00%

Source: ORBIS.

One or More Individuals/Families

Table 2.12 Classification of relative change and average change in individuals/families' shareholdings (2011–2020)

	2011	2012	2013	2014	2015	2016	2017	2018	2019	2020
Increased	33.33%	0.00%	0.00%	0.00%	14.29%	0.00%	0.00%	21.88%	11.90%	12.90%
Decreased	0.00%	0.00%	0.00%	0.00%	7.14%	21.43%	3.70%	21.88%	9.52%	24.19%
Unchanged	66.67%	100.00%	100.00%	100.00%	78.57%	78.57%	96.30%	56.25%	78.57%	62.90%
Total	100.00%	100.00%	100.00%	100.00%	100.00%	100.00%	100.00%	100.00%	100.00%	100.00%

Trend	Average
Increased	9.43%
Decreased	8.79%
Unchanged	81.78%
Total	100.00%

Source: ORBIS.

Therefore, we can draw some remarks by analyzing the data of the holdings of the four main clusters, which represent 83.86% of the total shareholding.

In the case of non-institutional investors, one or more individuals/families and other companies tend to maintain their position unchanged in 81.78% and 82.71% of cases, respectively. Instead, comparing the different inclinations concerning the investment duration expressed through the increase or decrease in shareholdings, we can observe how a tendency to enlarge one's shareholding slightly prevails among companies (in 8.89% of cases). In comparison, individuals/families tend to decrease it (in 8.79% of cases).

In the case of institutional investors, such as banks and financial institutions, we find great variability in terms of an increase or a decrease in share quotas. In the case of banks, 20.48% of changes result in a decrease, and 34.54% of variations result in an increase. Thus, the prevalence of increasing variations fully reflects the major role played by credit institutions in Italy, compared, for example, to their US counterparts. Finally, as far as financial companies are concerned, substantial stability confirms the high degree of variability characterizing this cluster of investors.

2.6.1 *The Hallmarks of the Italian Landscape*

In recent literature, a comparison was made between all SPACs listed in Italy and all SPACs listed in the US in terms of structure and peculiarities: while US SPACs are sometimes liquidated before the completion of the relevant transaction, in Italy, this phenomenon is far less relevant (the first one was Ideami SpA, promoted by Banca Imi and Dea Capital, which was listed on Aim Italia in December 2017 after raising €250 million, €200 million of which from third-party investors and €50 million invested directly by promoters). This might occur due to two factors: in Italy, first, no investments are made in companies undergoing restructuring, and no business combinations are used to purchase business units or assets.[39] On the contrary, the latter is the case in the United States (e.g., see Navios Maritime Holding Corp., which acquired merchant or oil vessels and then merged them into the vehicle), where we have 'SPACs for restructuring,' as opposed to 'SPACs for growth.'

A preliminary comparison between the two contexts reveals that the timeframe is now more flexible in both countries, with the aforementioned 'extension amendment' provision in the United States, and a smoother transition to 24 + 6 months even in Italy, once a letter of intent with the chosen target group is signed. However, the difference in terms of remuneration of promoters is equally significant, as in the United States, an average conversion of 20% of the target capital ('the Magic 20')[40] post-business combination is possible if certain target share prices are exceeded. At the same time, in Italy, it is linked to the presence of special convertible shares, the achievement and exceeding of target share prices through a given conversion coefficient into ordinary shares.

In both countries, the number of warrants assigned to investors at the time of listing decreased, and the number of warrants allocated after the business combination to those who decided not to exit proportionally increased as a bonus. This strategy discouraged and almost ceased the practices of some institutional investors, who voluntarily hindered business combinations by purchasing units only to enjoy the more profitable return that warrants guaranteed.

As far as the price for the exercise of warrants assigned free of charge to investors is concerned, the same trend observed in the United States is being observed in Italy, too: we are moving from issuances in the money to those out of the money, but the trend observed is not as straightforward as overseas, where calibrating the issuance of units with warrants having an exercise price higher than the issuance price of ordinary shares on average by 1 or 1.5 dollars is standard. In Italy, on average, the exercise price of warrants does not exceed 10 euros, thereby being 15% lower than the average price in the US market. Moreover, while in the United States, the conversion of warrants into common shares is also carried out cashless, in Italy, the strike price is different from the exercise price, considering the former as the price at which the warrants are converted into common shares and the latter as the actual price to be paid for the conversion.[41]

Lastly, the US transactions are characterized by a remarkable internationalization, as overseas, they comprise cross-border acquisitions of business branches and restructuring transactions.

2.6.2 *The Importance of Benchmark Indices*

The first example of an index in Italy is the SPAC Index introduced by First Capital in March 2018, which includes all Italian SPACs, calculated using a price-weighted technique. First Capital's Studies Office draws up the SPAC Index© and, in addition to the monthly and historical performances, it covers the world of Italian small caps through the re-elaboration of market data, historical and prospective economic-financial data of companies and provides details on sectors and geography, statistics and valuations. However, there is a lack of distinction between those SPACs that have not achieved the business combination yet, and those who have already done so; concerning whom, at the time of the merger, it is negligible to estimate the capital raised as a weighting index, whereas it is advisable to estimate the company's capitalization to cover those cases where the price has not been determined exclusively by the book drawn up during the IPO phase.

Nevertheless, it seemed appropriate to develop a new index based on the value-weighted method, ideally resembling the one devised by Mediobanca in 1996–1997 – using floating capital as a benchmark (as Mediobanca felt that all holdings above 3% should be stripped of their value, except for those held by trustees or asset management companies), thus being comparable with the methodology used in the FTSE index series.

It would then be worthwhile to elaborate a new index containing all the SPACs until the approval of the business combination, to track SPAC performance as investment vehicles for short-term liquidity purposes. As a proxy for floating capital, the number of ordinary shares multiplied by the closing price on the chosen date should be used, excluding shares belonging to the opponents of the relevant transaction from the date of the announcement of the option offer results until the exclusion of the SPAC from the index. In fact, at the bylaws level, it is envisaged that the units will be reimbursed, and the actual award of the shares will be after the effectiveness of the business combination. Consequently, the withdrawn stocks will not contribute to forming the price until the merger becomes effective.

All those SPACs that announced the business combination should be considered the second index, as the value of the shares will depend on the promoters' ability and management to increase the company's value from the very moment of the merger. To attribute to the index a significance in terms of sample size, even for the results, the time period goes from 1 January 2017 up to three years from the business combination. Compared to the first index, a return is forecast to grow linearly over the entire period under review. In light of the literature examined and the data considered for this study, companies are expected to have lower performances in the post-business combination phase than those of corporations listed in the STAR market segment.

However, it would not consider any additional returns achieved through SPACs. To examine the individual extra returns, it is necessary to look at warrant regulations for each SPAC, as each vehicle can decide on the most suitable design to attain its goals.

Notes

1 Although this chapter is the result of the authors' joint work, section 2.2 is attributable to Filippo Annunziata, sections 2.3, 2.5 and 2.6 are attributable to Anna Chiara Chisari, while sections 2.1, 2.6 and 2.7 are attributable to Maria Lucia Passador.
2 Axel Moeller, *Alternative Initial Public Offering Models the Law and Economics Pertaining of Shell Company Listings on German Capital Markets* (Mohr Siebeck 2016), 3 and fn 4; 10 and fn. 33–4.
3 Ibid., 10 and fn 35.
4 It is surely remarkable to recall a study about EU SPACs from 2005 to 2013 (only 19), which shows that, despite their listing on EU stock exchanges, most SPACs do not have a EU-wide focus, either in terms of investors or in the choice of target companies, and are very heterogeneous, particularly in the selection of target companies (Elena Ignatyeva, Christian Rauch and Mark Wahrenburg, 'Analyzing European SPACs' (2013) 17 *Journal of Private Equity* 64.
5 Paul Amiss, 'SPAC to the Future: The Recent Resurgence of UK SPACS and Latest Trends' (2018) <https://www.winston.com/images/content/1/4/v3/142888/SPAC-to-the-Future-the-Recent-Resurgence-of-UK-SPACs-and-Latest.pdf> accessed 15 September 2021.
6 Still, the Main Market was preferred because of its prestige and procedural rules (see Daniele D'Alvia, 'The International Financial Regulation of SPACs between Legal Standardized Regulation and Standardization of Market Practices' (2020) 21(2) *Journal of Banking Regulation* 107, 119–20. See also Chapter 1 of this edited collection where the suspension of trade of SPACs' shares is specifically analyzed considering the Hill Report in the UK (March 2021).
7 Marco Fumagalli, *Lo Sviluppo della SPAC (Special Purpose Acquisition Company) in Italia. Un nuovo modo fi fare private equity e di quotare le imprese in borsa* (EGEA 2014) 133. For an immediate comparison with the American situation, see the graph, created using the same graphical methods already adopted in the report *PE Jumps into the SPAC Markets* (2017), 2 <https://privateequityreport.debevoise.com/~/media/per/spac.pdf> accessed 10 October 2021. For an updated examination of the spread or, more correctly, as defined here, of the acceleration that the phenomenon has undergone in the last years, Roberto Schiesari, 'Le SPAC tra crescita dei mercati finanziari e lo sviluppo delle imprese' (2018) 35 *Strumenti Finanziari e Fiscalità* 85. This report shows how the increase in the number of SPACs can be a positive element to boost investment opportunities and reduce the risk of a speculative bubble, both because its greater competitiveness can lead to beneficial effects for the reduction of the implicit costs arising from the remuneration mechanism, allowing the target to effectively negotiate its valuation in exchange rates. It also offers an interesting outlook on how the SPACs have been able to benefit from the large amount of liquidity generated by the success of individual savings plans, a liquidity that is likely to further grow in the coming years, given the tax exemption mechanism established for such plans with annual and total investment limits.
8 In 2018, the minimum capital requirement for an SPAC was 30 million euros rather than the new 10 million requirement. See Andrea Sacco Ginevri, Giovanni Filippo Pezzulo, 'Appunti sulle "Special Purpose Acquisition Companies" ("SPAC") (Diritto Bancario' <https://www.dirittobancario.it/sites/default/files/allegati/sacco_ginevrei_a._e_pezzullo_g.f._appunti_sulle_special_purpose_acquisition_companies_spac_2018.pdf, par. 4, fn 26 and 27> accessed 10 October 2021.
9 Directive 2009/65/EC, as subsequently amended.
10 Filippo Annunziata, *Gli organismi di investimento collettivo del risparmio (OICR): fattispecie e forme* (EGEA 2017), 29.

11 Recital 6 of the AIFMD.
12 ESMA, *Guidelines on key concepts of the AIFMD*, 13 August 2013, n. 611.
13 ESMA, *Consultation Paper – Guidelines on key concepts of the AIFMD*, 19 December 2012, n. 845, 33.
14 Filippo Annunziata, 'Collective Investment Undertakings in the EU: How to Frame a Definition After the AIFMD' (21 April 2017), RTDF N° 1–2017, Bocconi Legal Studies Research Paper No. 2956246.
15 *Borsa Italiana S.p.A., Regolamento sulla gestione collettiva del risparmio – Resoconto della consultazione*, 2014, 6.
16 In particular, SPACs do not carry out any business operations at the time of their incorporation and until the target company is identified and the business combination arranged. This circumstance gave rise to a debate – currently outdated – among scholars concerning the compatibility of the SPACs' company purpose with Article 2248 of the Italian Civil Code (Arianna Paoletti, 'Le Special Purpose Acquisition Companies (SPAC)' (2017) 4 *Rivista di Diritto Societario* 1151).
17 *Borsa Italiana S.p.A., Avviso n.3584, La riconducibilità dell'attività sociale allo schema della gestione collettiva del risparmio* (12 March 2015); *Borsa Italiana S.p.A., Disciplina in materia di gestione collettiva del risparmio. Recepimento della direttiva 2011/61/UE (AIFMD) e ulteriori interventi di modifica* <https://www.bancaditalia.it/compiti/vigilanza/normativa/consultazioni/2014/gestione-collettiva-risparmio/commenti-ricevuti/Borsa_italiana.pdf> accessed 15 September 2021; *Borsa Italiana S.p.A., I mercati degli Investment Vehicles gestiti da Borsa Italiana e la nuova AIFMD* <https://docplayer.it/2123709-I-mercati-degli-investment-vehicles-gestiti-da-borsa-italiana-e-la-nuova-aifmd.html> accessed 15 September 2021.
18 Filippo Annunziata, *La disciplina del mercato mobiliare* (Giappichelli 2020) 220.
19 For a detailed analysis about the relationship between AIFs and holding companies, see Luigi Ardizzone, *L'esercizio dell'attività di impresa nel private equity* (EGEA 2018); Eugenio Barcellona, *La "gestione collettiva del risparmio" a seguito della direttiva GEFIA. Investment companies, family offices, club deals, spac, holding companies* (Giuffre 2018).
20 Banca d'Italia, *Regolamento sulla gestione collettiva del risparmio* (Banca d'Italia 19 January 2015) as subsequently amended and supplemented.
21 Pierluigi De Biasi, 'La SPAC, uno speciale veicolo di investimento e quotazione' (2018) (2/3) *Rivista delle società* 713 ff.; Giulio Sandrelli, 'Raccolta di capitali e attività di investimento. Note sulla nozione di organismo di investimento collettivo del risparmio a seguito dell'attuazione della direttiva sui fondi alternativi' (2015) 60 (2/3) *Rivista delle Società* 445 hh.
22 Commission Delegated Regulation (EU) 2021/528 of 16 December 2020, Commission Delegated Regulation (EU) 2019/980 of 14 March 2019, Commission Delegated Regulation (EU) 2019/980 of 14 March 2019 and Commission Delegated Regulation (EU) 2019/979 of 14 March 2019.
23 Filippo Annunziata, 'AIM Italia e disciplina degli emittenti, 10 anni dopo' (2020) 1 *Rivista delle società* 242.
24 It should be noted that the Italian Legislative Decree No. 101 of 17 July 2009 has already extended the provisions on market abuse to MTFs, before the Market Abuse Regulation has entered into force. Therefore, AIM Italia companies must comply with the provisions of the Market Abuse Regulation, including the disclosure to the market of privileged information. In particular, the Nomad assists and supports the AIM Italia company in complying with disclosure requirements set out in Market Abuse Regulation.
25 In accordance with the requirements set out by Section 33 MiFID II, implemented in Italy with of Section 69, Subsection 2 (a), TUF. These minimum requirements brought the discipline of SME growth markets close to that of regulated markets

and have acted as a disincentive for MTFs to seek registration as an SME growth market.

26 Regulation (EU) 2019/2115 of 27 November 2019 introduced additional proportionate alleviations to adequately foster the use of SME growth markets.

27 According to AIM Listing Rules, the investing company is an AIM Italia company admitted to trading before the effective date of the provisions on AIFs (31 August 2015) and which did not apply for the relevant authorization, or a company established with the purpose of purchasing a specific business.

28 D'Alvia (n 5).

29 According to section 123-*bis*, TUF: 'The management report of issuers with securities admitted to trading on regulated markets shall contain a specific section entitled: "Report on corporate governance and ownership structures", providing detailed information on: . . . 2. In the same section of the report referred to in paragraph 1, information shall be provided regarding: a) adoption of a corporate governance code of conduct issued by regulated stock exchange companies or trade associations, giving reasons for any decision not to adopt one or more provisions, together with the corporate governance practices actually applied by the company over and above any legal or regulatory obligations. The company shall also indicate where the adopted corporate governance code of conduct may be accessed by the public'.

30 According to section 2-*bis* of CONSOB Issuers' Regulation, Issuers of shares widely distributed among the public shall also mean Italian issuers that contemporaneously: (a) have different shareholders to the majority shareholders accounting for more than 500, overall holding an at least 5% share in the share capital and (b) exceeds two of the three limits of Section 2435-*bis* of the ICC about financial statement in abbreviated form. SPACs typically meet the requirements set out by Section 2435-*bis* of the ICC with the consequence that, in that specific case, SPACs listed on AIM Italia, should not be considered issuers of shares widely distributed among the public.

31 Further elements about SPACs and corporate governance rules can be found in Vincenzo Donativi and Piero Corigliano, 'Le SPAC (Special Purpose Acquisition Companies): il modello internazionale e la sua compatibilità col diritto italiano' (2010) 29(1) *Società* 17; Gimede Gigante and Andrea Conso, *Le SPAC in Italia. Stato di un fenomeno in evoluzione* (EGEA 2019).

32 EY, *Global Trends* (2016) 4Q <https://www.ey.com/Publication/vwLUAssets/ey-4q-2016-global-ipo-trends-report/$FILE/ey-4q-2016-global-ipo-trends-report.pdf>, at 2 and 14>.

33 *OECD Capital Market Review of Italy 2020. Creating Growth Opportunities for Italian Companies and Savers*, 2020 <https://www.oecd.org/corporate/ca/OECD-Capital-Market-Review-Italy.pdf>.

34 Maria Luisa Passador, *In Vogue Again: The Re-Rise of SPACs in the IPO Market* (Bocconi 4 April 2021). Bocconi Legal Studies Research Paper No. 3820957; University of Luxembourg Law Working Paper No. 2021–005 <https://ssrn.com/abstract=3820957>.

35 The choice of this time frame is related to the fact that compared to the year 2020, ORBIS was not providing significant financial statement data to complete the analysis.

36 Ibid.

37 See Jessica Bai, Angela Ma and Miles Zheng, *Reaching for Yield in the Going-Public Market: Evidence from SPACs* (1 January 2021) <https://ssrn.com/abstract=3746490 [https://perma.cc/SCR4-BL8Z]>; Minmo Gahng, Jay R. Ritter and Donghang Zhang, *Investor Returns on the Life Cycle of SPACs* (29 January 2021) <https://docplayer.net/202917488-Investor-returns-on-the-life-cycle-of-spacs.html [https://perma.cc/7JZ7-CKBS]>; Minmo Gahng, Jay R. Ritter and

Donghang Zhang, *SPACs* (29 January 2021) <https://ssrn.com/abstract=3775847 [https://perma.cc/9QM7–6B4E]>; Michael D. Klausner, Michael Ohlrogge and Emily Ruan, *A Sober Look at SPACs* (28 October 2020). Stanford Law and Economics Olin Working Paper No. 559, NYU Law and Economics Research Paper No. 20–48, YALE J. REG. (2021, forthcoming) <https://ssrn.com/abstract=3720919 [https://perma.cc/7DT8-D3NQ]>; Passador (n 33).
38 Passador (n 33).
39 Valter Conca and Linda Longhi, 'C'è Spac e Spac. I casi italia e USA' (2018) *Economia & Management* <http://www.palladiocf.it/static/upload/art/articolo-rivista-bocconi.pdf> accessed 15 October 2021.
40 Usha Rodrigues and Michael A. Stegemoller, 'Exit, Choice, and Reputation: The Evolution of SPACs' (2013) 37 *Delaware Journal of Corporate Law* 849, 870–9, 891–95, 920–2.
41 Fumagalli (n 6) 88.

Part II
SPACs and the Italian Legal Framework

3 The Special Purpose Acquisition Company in the Italian Corporate Experience

Raimondo Premonte and Donato Romano

3.1 Introduction

The Special Purpose Acquisition Company (SPAC)[1] is an investment model introduced relatively recently in the Italian legal system based on the US experience.

Such SPACs originated from the American "blank check companies," that is, companies that began to operate in the United States starting from the 1980s and that were defined by the Securities and Exchange Commission as "a development stage company that has no specific business plan, or purpose, or has indicated in its business plan that is engaged in a merger or acquisition with an unidentified company, other entity, or person,"[2] were *ad hoc* newly incorporated companies through an initial public offering (IPO) and pursued the same aim as current SPACs.

As opposed to SPACs, American blank check companies were not subject to public authorities' supervision, given that they were listed on the market created ad hoc for smaller companies (the so-called Penny Stock Market or PSM), where significant exceptions to strict rules for the drafting of prospectuses and other documentation required in connection with the listing of companies' shares on the main markets applied, pursuant to the Securities Act of 1933.[3] As a result, these companies were operating de facto in the absence of a clear regulatory framework and strict rules to protect investors; therefore, subscribing to these issuers' shares was equivalent to signing a blank check (hence, the name "blank check") in favor of these companies.[4]

Following certain abuses and frauds perpetrated against investors, the Securities and Exchange Commission issued the Securities Enforcement Remedies and Penny Stock Reform Act of 1990, as implemented by Rule 419,[5] which introduced strict regulation of the placement of these penny stock companies' securities, providing a system of controls and protection instruments for investors, as well as a set of operating requirements for SPAC's sponsors.

DOI: 10.4324/9781003169079-6

3.2 The Italian SPAC Structure

In a nutshell, the SPAC is a corporate vehicle incorporated as an Italian joint stock company (the so-called *Società per Azioni*) and incorporated by a group of promoters or sponsors, who raises a certain amount of capital, then proceeds with the listing on the stock exchange (the IPO) on a regulated market or a multilateral trading facility (namely, the Euronext Growth Milan market, formerly known as AIM, in Italy) and uses the capital raised to invest, acquiring stakes in another operating company (the target company).

Once this acquisition of the target company has been completed, the SPAC will merge[6] with the target company (the business combination), carrying out a reverse merger, namely a merger where the incorporating SPAC is smaller than the incorporated target,[7] or the so-called inverted merger (or *fusione inversa* in the Italian language), where the target company will incorporate the SPAC parent company, becoming a listed company as a result.[8]

As an alternative to acquisition followed by a merger structure, it could also proceed directly with a merger by incorporating the corporate vehicle into the target company, determining the exchange ratio between the shares of the two companies.[9]

As we said, the SPAC shall be incorporated as a joint stock company by one or more promoters, who provide the initial capital required to finance the SPAC's operational management and current expenses up to its listing.[10] Essentially, the SPAC involves four main stages:

I. Incorporation of the SPAC by the promoters and sponsors, making a capital increase.
II. IPO with the assignment of shares and warrants. Under the IPO, subscribers receive one or two shares and one warrant, which can be traded separately.
III. Identify a company to be acquired, known as the target company.
IV. The business combination or the winding up of the SPAC if no business combination is completed within a predetermined time frame, which is typically short.[11]

Such promoters are generally individuals, well-known in financial markets, with a solid network of contacts and consolidated merger and acquisition (M&A) or private equity track records, also having entrepreneurial and management skills as well as scouting ability relating to specific sectors selected by the SPAC.[12] The SPAC's board of directors comprises promoters or sponsors and independent directors.[13] SPAC's promoters:

> do not receive a predetermined fee for their office, nor – unlike the managers of a private equity fund – a fixed amount of commission calculated on the amount of the capital managed (so-called management fee).[14]

However, at the time of the business combination, they will receive a warrant to subscribe for ordinary shares on favorable terms or special/preferred shares with a favorable exchange ratio.[15]

Following the incorporation of the SPAC, the promoters will approve a capital increase beneficial to the company's listing to provide the SPAC with any resources necessary to carry out the business combination.[16] The capital amount raised by the investing shareholders besides the promoters remains deposited in a separate escrow account, which can be used only for the transaction. As correctly highlighted,[17] such separation does not create separate assets,[18] but it derives only from the agreement of the shareholders, which is not enforceable against third parties.

The business combination must be approved by the shareholders' meeting of the SPAC within a set period, namely between 18 and 24 months from the listing; if the transaction is not completed, the SPAC will be wound up, and it will pay back any capital amount – which was, deposited, as already mentioned, in the escrow account – to each public investor.[19] In addition, the SPAC's directors are tasked with researching and identifying a company (the target) operating in a specific industry; such research and acquisition represent the SPAC's unique purpose.

The economic sector is generally identified in the informative prospectus or the admission document, which indicates, inter alia, the industrial sector, the target company's features, and the geographical areas to achieve the business combination. Once the promoters have identified the target company, the shareholders' meeting will be called to approve the transaction. At such meetings, the shareholders will be provided with any details relating to the target company, including information on its activities and sectors of operations.[20]

Public investors are provided exhaustive information about the promoters' track record and the target company's corporate overview. This considerably reduces one of the principal risks of investing in the SPAC: "the impossibility for a potential investor to rely on the past performance of the company."[21] At the shareholders' meeting, the SPAC's public investors may vote for or against the business combination at the shareholders' meeting. It is essential to highlight that any SPAC shareholder who does not contribute to the approval of the business combination will have a withdrawal right pursuant to Section 2437 of the Italian Civil Code.

Concerning the *quorum* requirements, the shareholders' meeting of the SPAC will validly resolve the transaction with the majorities established by the law. In this respect, the *quorum* requirements will change depending on whether or not the SPAC qualifies as a "company operating on a regulated capital market" under Section 2325-*bis* of the Italian Civil Code. In light of this, Section 2325-*bis* applies to SPACs listed on the regulated Market for Investment Vehicles (MIV) segment of *Borsa Italiana* S.p.A. On the other hand, the same legal provision does not apply to SPACs listed on a multilateral trading facility such as the Euronext Growth Milan market of *Borsa*

Italiana S.p.A. This means that in the Euronext Growth Milan market, the redemption right can be framed in the relevant bylaws more liberally. As a result, the bylaws of Italian SPACs tend to condition the effectiveness of a shareholders' meeting resolution deliberating on the business combination subject to failure of exercising withdrawals and redemption rights, to an extent exceeding a predetermined threshold.[22]

The investment in the target company can be made in various ways. However, the method widely preferred in Italian practice involves merging the target company into the SPAC. Following this approach, the acquired company will automatically become a listed company.

However, it cannot be excluded that the merger takes place through a direct merger, namely merging the SPAC into the target company. In this case, the shareholders of the SPAC will receive shares in the target company in exchange. Meanwhile, the target company will have started and completed the listing process to allow SPAC's shareholders to receive shares in a listed company in exchange for shares they hold in the SPAC.

The SPAC could acquire a stake in a target company without proceeding to further corporate integration. In this scenario, the SPAC would operate as a holding company.

As mentioned earlier, if the business combination has yet to be completed on the expiry of the SPAC, the SPAC will be wound up.[23] Some bylaws of the Italian SPACs indicate details of the liquidator to be appointed at the early stage of incorporation in case a business combination is not achieved. This is made to avoid the need to call a shareholders' meeting to appoint a liquidator should the SPAC not complete a business combination within the duration set out in the bylaws.[24]

The SPAC is an alternative route to the traditional listing process, together with other innovative instruments connected to the SPAC, such as the so-called pre-booking company scheme, where investors subscribe to convertible bonds in shares of the target company. Such a scheme has the advantage that the corporate vehicle – which issues financial instruments subscribed by investors – does not have to be listed, thus providing a benefit in terms of time and cost savings.[25]

3.3 The Italian Legal Framework

SPACs operating in Italy can choose between two markets for listing, both managed by *Borsa Italiana* S.p.A., which today is also part of Euronext Group: the MIV segment and the Euronext Growth Milan market.[26]

The Italian practice shows a clear preference for listings on the Euronext Growth Milan, due to more accessible access to the market, in terms of both costs and time, compared to the listing on the MIV, which is usually preferred by larger SPACs.[27] The MIV is a regulated market, exclusively addressed to investment vehicles, accessible only to professional investors, as defined according to Annex II, parts 1 and 2, of Directive n. 2014/65/EU.

Pursuant to the Market Rules organized and managed by *Borsa Italiana* S.p.A.,[28] SPACs are defined as:

> *società costituite con lo scopo di acquisizione di un business il cui oggetto sociale esclusivo prevede l'investimento in via prevalente in una società o attività nonché le relative attività strumentali, le società derivanti da operazioni di acquisizioni perfezionate da queste ultime società.*

Essentially, the Market Rules are introducing the SPAC as an investment company that can be listed on the MIV segment and trade and negotiate its shares in such a market. Furthermore, the SPAC is an investment company whose business purpose is to acquire another company. Finally, the definition also reminds us that once the SPAC takes over the target company, this latter can also be listed in the MIV segment. This is a direct recognition of one of the SPAC's main objectives: to act as a "back-door-listing" in addition to the other functions outlined in section 3.2.

The listing on MIV requires the drafting of an informative prospectus, which much be approved by the Italian National Commission for Companies and the Stock Exchange (*Consob*), and the appointment by the issuer of a sponsor, as well as further requirements; in this regard, it is worth noting that, pursuant to the Market Rules, the SPAC's bylaws must provide for

> a duration of the company not exceeding 36 months to carry out one or more significant investments[29] with the possibility of extension only where evidence can be shown that there are actual negotiations underway to reach a significant level of investment.[30]

Additionally, there are other conditions to be met in order to be admitted to trading on the market, namely the shares must have the following requirements:

I. Foreseeable market capitalization of at least €40 million. However, *Borsa Italiana* S.p.A. may admit shares with a lower capitalization if it deems they will have a good market.[31]
II. Sufficient circulation is presumed to be achieved when shares are distributed to professional or institutional investors and retail investors for at least 25% of the share capital represented by the category to which they belong.

However, the SPAC may decide to proceed with the listing on the Euronext Growth Milan market, which is – as we said – a multilateral trading facility[32] that provides a simplified procedure for listing in terms of costs and time. To list on such a venue, it is sufficient to file an admission document, which will not be subject to *Consob*'s investigative activity. For admission to the

Euronext Growth Milan, SPACs are defined as "companies incorporated to acquire a specific business," which, in order to be listed, must raise a minimum of €10 million[33] in cash through placement, which should end on the admission date or close to the admission itself. This minimum capitalization does not apply to SPACs resulting from the demerger (in the Italian language, *scissione*) of other SPACs.

Moreover, Part I – Section 8 of the Issuers' Regulations of the Euronext Growth Milan set forth that, for admission to trading of SPACs and investing companies:

> promoters must be either individuals or legal entities with proven experience and/or have held senior positions in (i) transactions on the primary capital market; (ii) private equity transactions; (iii) management of medium-sized companies; (iv) the investment banking sector.

It should be noted that most companies are listed on the Euronext Growth Milan following an IPO reserved for professional or institutional investors. In contrast, with listings related to SPACs and related business combinations (which account for about 10% of listings), IPOs were not reserved for professional or institutional investors.[34]

Euronext Growth Milan's regulatory provisions contain specific rules concerning the investment policy, which must be defined and pursued by the investment company. In addition, this latter must obtain the prior approval of the shareholders convened at the shareholders' meeting for any material change to its investment policy. Finally, the investment company has 24 months to implement its investment policy effectively; if this does not occur within 24 months following the admission, the company must obtain the shareholders' approval at the first meeting available and every year after that until such a policy has been implemented.[35]

Finally, according to the AIM Rules, a reverse takeover is defined as one or more acquisitions within 12 months for an AIM issuer:

I.   exceeds 100% in any relevance index; or
II. results in a material change in the issuer's business, board of directors, or change of control; or
III. in the case of an investment company, differs significantly from the investment policy (as described in the admission document or approved by shareholders in accordance with Euronext Growth Milan Rules).

Any agreement that may lead to a reverse takeover must be:

I.   subject to the shareholders' approval convened at the shareholders' meeting;
II. communicated without delay, providing the information specified in Schedule 4 of the Euronext Growth Milan Rules, and where it is entered

into with related parties, any additional information required pursuant to Section 10 of *Consob* Rules adopted by resolution no. 17221 of 12 March 2010; and

III. supported by the publication of an information document relating to the enlarged entity resulting from the transaction and by a notice of call for the shareholders' meeting to be published at least fifteen days before the date of the shareholders' meeting.[36]

As we said, Italian SPACs prefer the Euronext Growth Milan market option for listing due to faster procedures and lower costs. Specifically, the most relevant difference concerns the documentation that SPACs are required to produce: while on the Euronext Growth Milan, it is sufficient to produce an admission document, on the MIV, it is necessary to prepare an informative prospectus which must comply with the provisions of the so-called prospectus regulation (i.e., Regulation (EU) no. 2017/1129 of the European Parliament and of the Council of 14 June 2017) and the implementing provisions, as well as Sections 93-bis et seq. of Legislative Decree no. 58/1998 (Consolidated Law on Finance).

When listing, a package of financial instruments, including shares and warrants, is structured innovatively for traditional Italian practice.[37] Traditionally, Italian-listed companies issue warrants, which grant the option right to subscribe to capital increase by a set deadline; the investor undertakes to pay a certain amount and, in return, receives the right to subscribe to newly issued shares.

It is undisputed that options have three economically relevant quantities: (a) the premium (i.e., the issue price of the warrant), (b) the strike price (the subscription price of the compendium shares); and (c) the exercise ratio (the number, even fractional, of compendium shares that can be subscribed through the exercise of a warrant).[38] Generally speaking, the strike price is higher than the market price of the underlying share at the time the warrant is issued. This means that the option right granted in the warrant is "out of the money." However, the warrant is valuable. The price of an option is de facto composed of two elements: (a) the intrinsic value (the difference between the strike price and the market price of the underlying share); and (b) the time value (the value of time during which the market price could rise to make positive any difference with the strike price). It is clear. Therefore, those warrants create a dilution risk for the old shareholders, which depends on several factors, namely the number of warrants in circulation, the exercise ratio, the number of options exercised, and, finally and respectively, the strike price.[39]

SPACs' warrants often have one or more peculiar characteristics. Firstly, they have a long duration, equal to five years from the completion date of the business combination; however, the issuance regulations may provide for an early expiry date in case the underlying share reaches specific prices, thus placing a limit on its appreciation. Furthermore, the strike price is immediately "in the money," that is, lower than the subscription price of the underlying share; it is fixed and different from the subscription price, which can be variable.[40] More in detail, one of the original features of the Italian SPACs' warrants is that they are very often cashless, that is, they have a nihil subscription price, thus not requiring a predetermined payment by the investor for the subscription of a fixed number of shares, but providing for the charge-free transfer of several shares (with no par value), which varies according to the price of the shares themselves.[41] Finally, the option right granted by the warrants falls within the American type of options,[42] which means that it can be exercised anytime between the date of issuance and the expiry date.

3.4 Investors' Protection

The Italian legal framework grants some protection instruments for SPACs investors. The directors will have to submit the business combination transaction to the shareholders' meeting, allowing investors to vote on the transaction. Moreover, the business combination will change the SPAC's corporate purpose, and any shareholders voting against the relevant transaction may exercise the withdrawal right from the SPAC.[43]

Moreover, SPACs have a concise duration, and, in the absence of a merger, it would be necessary to resolve upon an extension. This would trigger the provisions of Section 2437, paragraph 2, letter (a) of the Italian Civil Code, pursuant to which shareholders not taking part in the resolution to extend the duration may exercise the withdrawal right.[44] As correctly noted, the withdrawal right is governed by general rules and is therefore fully enforceable; however, it would perhaps be appropriate to enact, by way of legislation, *ad hoc* rules governing withdrawal rights from SPACs, considering that investors opt to invest expecting that the SPAC will, at some point, change its corporate purpose, as a consequence of the completion of the business combination for which the SPAC itself was incorporated.[45]

Concerning the determination of the liquidation value pursuant to Section 2437-*ter* of the Italian Civil Code, the company's assets will be equal to the capital contributions made at the date of the resolution triggering the withdrawal right. At the same time, the foreseeable income criteria would not apply, given that the company does not make an economic result until the corporate integration.[46]

For the sake of completeness, it should be specified that it does not seem possible in Italian SPACs to determine an individual limit to the number of shares held by the specific investor concerning which the withdrawal right could be exercised by the same investor, as it is the case in international practice. In this case, the withdrawal right is based on the legal cause of withdrawal due to a change in the corporate purpose, pursuant to Section 2437, paragraph 1, letter a) of the Italian Civil Code. The reason for this negative response would be found in the provisions of Section 2437, last paragraph, of the Italian Civil Code, according to which "any agreement aimed at excluding or making more onerous the exercise of the withdrawal right in the cases provided for in the first paragraph of this Section is null and void."[47]

Any individual limit on the number of shares subject to withdrawal would therefore be null and void as it would exclude or render the shareholder's withdrawal right more onerous. However, as already mentioned, it is possible – and indeed likely – that the bylaws of the SPAC would provide, as a condition for the implementation of the business combination, a maximum threshold of withdrawals, so that if this threshold is exceeded, the business combination would not be implemented.

3.5 The Issue of SPACs With a Pre-identified Target Company

There are some concerns regarding the admissibility of SPACs with a pre-identified target company. In such cases, the SPAC would be admitted to listing after having already agreed with a specific target company, already identified, and which would complete a so-called accelerated business combination. Sometimes this practice can also identify SPACs as "instant-SPACs."

This type of scheme, which has been used in Italy in some instances in the past,[48] requires the SPAC and the target company to approve the accelerated business combination and merger before admission to the listing. Consequently, withdrawal rights would only be triggered in favor of the investors who would acquire the shares following the admission to the listing. Therefore, such a scheme could represent an obstacle since investors would not have one of the essential protections regarding SPACs, namely the redemption right.

In this respect, there could be an issue from a regulatory standpoint. SPACs are excluded from the scope of the alternative fund's regime due to the absence of diversification in the investment policy, which in SPACs is usually aimed at identifying a single operating company for investment and merger purposes. This operating method would not be compatible with the risk management rationale. Moreover, the SPAC would not have an industrial (or commercial) strategy itself; this industrial and/or commercial strategy would only become effective and definitive following the business combination. Finally, Nomads on the Euronext Growth Milan Market usually require the sector where the SPAC intends to operate and a list of target companies that could be communicated to the investors during the roadshows.

According to Borsa Italiana, the industrial transformation (and the corresponding change in the corporate purpose) would characterize the SPAC from its incorporation and represent an original and typical feature. Furthermore, the SPAC's shareholders participate and influence this strategy in an incisive way since the transaction is subject to the approval of the shareholders' meeting, with full disclosure of the characteristics of the target company: business description, financials, and technical details of the acquisition. Furthermore, at the shareholders' meeting, shareholders can vote for or against the acquisition; in the latter case, they have the redemption right regarding their investment.[49] In this context, investors would be deprived of the possibility to exercise their withdrawal right, thus removing one of the safeguards and preconditions for excluding SPACs from the rules on collective asset management.

Further issues concern that competent authorities' controls, once admitted to listing, would be limited to the SPAC, whereas the target company would be excluded from such controls. In this respect, in order to proceed with such a scheme, the investment is, in each case, decided by the investors, who may decide to invest or not in the SPAC.[50]

Nonetheless, public investors would still be protected since they would already know the target company at the time of the purchase of the shares on the market, so there would be no need to recognize a redemption right, as in the case of SPACs with "standard" business combinations. Therefore, in the admission document or prospectus, the SPAC should provide and disclose to the market detailed financial information, even on a pro-forma basis, relating not only to the SPAC itself but also to the target company. This, however, would entail a high risk for the target company, which would be compelled to disclose highly sensitive financial data before being admitted to listing when there is still a significant risk that the transaction is open. Summing up, we believe that, de jure, the case could be made for allowing an SPAC with a pre-identified target to be listed; however, de facto, this could imply high risk, especially for the target company: it is definitely interesting to assess the evolution of the SPAC market in Italy in this respect.

3.6 Conclusion

The evolution of the SPACs in the Italian market is decidedly characterized by an intense initial period of great euphoria followed, in recent times, by a relative decline.

Introducing specific laws or regulations governing SPACs could provide a solution to specific issues hindering the emergence of SPACs in Italy.

In particular, the general framework concerning the exercise of withdrawal right does not seem to be entirely appropriate in the context of the SPACs, considering that investors that decide to invest in the SPAC already know, at the moment of the investment, that the SPAC will, at some point, change its corporate purpose, as a consequence of the completion of the business combination; a business combination that represents the real purpose underlying the decision to set up an SPAC. In such a respect, specific rules for SPACs could be welcome. For example, the SPACs could be exempted from the general application of the rules set forth under Section 2437 of the Italian Civil Code on withdrawal rights (and specifically, concerning withdrawal rights as a consequence of a change in the corporate scope of the SPAC) or at least it could be introduced a separation between shares and warrants, so that the withdrawal from the SPACs would not necessarily imply a withdrawal from both the shares and the warrants, thus allowing the withdrawing shareholder to keep the warrants. Similarly, it could be appropriate for the regulatory and financial authorities to clarify the admissibility of the "instant-SPACs" in Italy.

Notes

1 The term "SPAC" was filed as a trademark by D. Nussbaum in 1992; however, in 2000, it expired for lack of use (Daniel S. Riemer, 'Special Purpose Acquisition Companies: SPAC and SPAN, or Blank Check Redux?' (2007–2008) 85(4) *Washington University Law Review* 931).
2 Cristina Chiomenti and Leonardo Graffi, 'La Special Purpose Acquisition Company' (2010) 37(3) *Giurisprudenza Commerciale* 445; Yochanan Shachmurove and Milos Vulanovic, 'SPACs IPOs' in Douglas Cumming and Sofia Johan (eds), *Oxford Handbook of IPOs* (OUP 2017); James Murray, 'Innovation, Imitation and Regulation in Finance: The Evolution of Special Purpose Acquisition Corporations' (2017) 6(2) *Review of Integrative Business and Economics Research* 1; Andrea Sacco Ginevri and Giovanni Filippo Pezzulo, 'Appunti sulle "Special Purpose Acquisition Companies" (SPAC)' (2018) *Rivista di Diritto Bancario* <http://www.dirittobancario.it/approfondimenti/capital-markets/appunti-sulle-special-purpose-acquisition-companies-spac> accessed 23 September 2021.
3 Chiomenti and Graffi (n 2) 445.
4 Pierluigi De Biasi, 'Le SPAC, uno speciale veicolo di investimento e quotazione' (2018) 2(3) *Rivista delle Società* 713.
5 The Securities Enforcement Remedies and Penny Stock Reform Act was implemented from the following rules: Rule 419 of Securities Act of 1933, Offerings by Blank Check Companies, 17 C.F.R. § 230.419 (1992); Rule 15g-8 of Securities Exchange Act of 1934, Sales and Escrowed Securities of Blank Check Companies, 17 C.F.R. §240.15g-8 (1992); and from an amendment to Rule 174 of Securities Act, Delivery of Prospectus by Dealers, Exemptions Under Section 4(3) of the Act, 17 C.F.R. §230.174(g) (1992). See Chiomenti and Graffi (n 2) 445.
6 De Biasi (n 4) 713.
7 Marco Fumagalli, *Lo Sviluppo della SPAC (Special Purpose Acquisition Company) in Italia. Un nuovo modo fi fare private equity e di quotare le imprese in borsa* (EGEA 2014)
8 De Biasi (n 4) 713.
9 Ibid., 714.
10 Sacco Ginevri and Pezzulo (n 2).
11 See Borsa Italiana S.p.A., 'La SPAC di Borsa Italiana' <https://www.aim-italia.it/component/content/article/56-spac/93-spac-in-borsa.html> accessed 10 September 2021.
12 Eugenio Barcellona, *La "gestione collettiva del risparmio" a seguito della Direttiva GEFIA* (Giuffre 2018).
13 De Biasi (n 4) 714.
14 Chiomenti and Graffi (n 2) 456.
15 Sacco Ginevri and Pezzulo (n 2), the authors outline how: "The special shares owned by the promoters of the transaction may have the following characteristics: (i) they lack voting rights in the ordinary and extraordinary shareholders' meetings; (ii) they are not admitted to trading and are non-transferable until the effective date of the business combination and, in any case, for the entire period of the company's duration and, in any case, for a maximum period of 5 years; (iii) they are convertible into ordinary shares, under the terms and conditions provided for by the company's bylaws; (iv) they are excluded from the right to receive profits which the company resolves to distribute until the thirty-sixth

month following the date on which the relevant transaction becomes effective, while they grant their holders the right to the distribution of available reserves; (v) in case of dissolution of the company, they grant their holders the right to have their share of the liquidation shareholders' equity liquidated with priority over the holders of ordinary shares."

16 Sacco Ginevri and Pezzulo (n 2).
17 De Biasi (n 4) 714.
18 Francesco Pacileo, 'Secondo la Cassazione i fondi comuni d'investimento non hanno soggettività giuridica mentre la società di gestione e risparmio ha la titolarità del patrimonio del fondo' (2010) *Dircomm.it* <http://www.dircomm. it/2010/n.1/05.html> accessed 15 September 2021.
19 De Biasi (n 4) 714.
20 Sacco Ginevri and Pezzulo (n 2).
21 Chiomenti and Graffi (n 2) 456.
22 Sacco Ginevri and Pezzulo (n 2).
23 Ibid.
24 Marco Fumagalli, 'Brevi considerazioni sugli statuti delle SPAC e sui regolamenti dei warrants (di Space S.p.A. e di Capital for Progress 1 S.p.A., in particolare)' (2018) 2(3) *Rivista delle Società* 743.
25 De Biasi (n 4) 718.
26 For any further remarks in terms of financial regulation of those market segments please refer to the comprehensive Chapter 2 in this work written by Annunziata and Passador.
27 See Sacco Ginevri and Pezzulo (n 2).
28 *Borsa Italiana* S.p.a., 'Regolamento dei Mercati Organizzati e Gestiti da Borsa Italiana S.p.A.' (26 April 2021) <https://www.borsaitaliana.it/borsaitaliana/ regolamenti/regolamenti/regolamentodeimercati-26042021_pdf.htm> accessed 15 September 2021.
29 Market Rules of *Borsa Italiana* S.p.A., Title 2.2, section 2.2.36. Significant investments are those "investments . . . considered significant if they collectively represent more than 50% of the company's assets."
30 Market Rules of *Borsa Italiana* S.p.A. Title 2.2, section 2.2.36.
31 Market Rules of *Borsa Italiana* S.p.A., Title 2.2, section 2.2.1, paragraph 2: "In the case of companies already admitted to trading on another regulated market or multilateral trading facility, the Euro 40 million requirement is calculated on the basis of the average market capitalization of the last three months preceding the decision to admit them to trading. For this purpose, the average market capitalization is calculated on the basis of the average of the official prices of the reference period."
32 The Euronext Growth Milan is a multilateral trading facility pursuant to Section 1, Paragraph 5-octies, letter a) of Legislative Decree no. 58/1998 and not a regulated market pursuant to Section 1, Paragraph 1, letter w-ter) of Legislative Decree no. 58/1998, that is, it is a multilateral facility managed by an investment firm or a market operator that allows the meeting, within it and according to non-discretionary rules, of multiple purchase and sale interests of third parties with regard to financial instruments.
33 This is a new requirement that has been recently approved on the Euronext Growth Milan market after *Borsa Italiana* S.p.A. has entered the Euronext Group. See *Avviso* n. 24575 of *Borsa Italiana* S.p.A. issued on 19 July 2021 and <https://www.borsaitaliana.it/borsaitaliana/regolamenti/avvisi/avviso24575-aimitalia_pdf.htm> accessed 15 September 2021.
34 F. ANNUNZIATA, *AIM Italia e disciplina degli emittenti, 10 anni dopo, Riv. Soc.*, 1, February 2020, 242 et seq.

35 Section 8 of the Issuer's Regulations of the Euronext Growth Milan Market of *Borsa Italiana* S.p.A.
36 Section 14 of the Issuers' Regulations of Euronext Growth Milan also specifies that "no later than the date of publication of the information document, the Euronext Growth Milan issuer and the Nominated Adviser must issue to *Borsa Italiana* S.p.A., at least, the statements required, respectively, by Schedule 7, part I, of the Issuers' Regulations and Schedule 4, part I, of the Nominated Advisers' Regulations. In any case, close to the effective date of the acquisition, the Euronext Growth Milan issuer and the Nominated Adviser must issue to *Borsa Italiana* S.p.A. the statements required, respectively, by Schedule 7, part II, of the Issuers' Regulations and by Schedule 4, part II, of the Nominated Advisers' Regulations, even when already provided. This last provision also applies in the event that the Euronext Growth Milan issuer is a company set up for the purpose of acquiring a specific business and incorporates the target company achieving the same effects of a reverse take-over."
37 Fumagalli (n 24) 745.
38 De Biasi (n 4) 728.
39 Ibid., 728.
40 Ibid.,.
41 Fumagalli (n 24) 729.
42 De Biasi (4) 729.
43 Vincenzo Donativi and Piero Corigliano, 'Le SPAC (Special Purpose Acquisition Companies): il modello internazionale e la sua compatibilità col diritto italiano' (2010) 29(1) *Società* 17; De Biasi (n 4) 727.
44 Donativi and Corigliano (n 43) 22.
45 On this point, De Biasi (n 4) 727; Chiomenti and Graffi (n 2) 457.
46 De Biasi (n 4) where it is specified that "the competing criteria, applicable to listed companies, of the arithmetic average of the official prices in the previous six months will normally give a lower value than the first one, because the hypothetical sale-purchase transaction on the market will result as the attribution of a value to a non-interest bearing cash, tied up for a period, which translates into a discount on the value of this cash, which will be a function of the theoretical residual duration of the company (net of the relevant transaction) and of the interest rates paid by the market at that time."
47 Donativi and Corigliano (n 43) 24.
48 For instance, see SPAC GEAR 1 S.p.A.'s admission document. In such a context, we report SPAC REVO S.p.A.'s admission document and although no business combinations were included in it, the company announced almost immediately the business combination with Elba Assicurazioni S.p.A.
49 *Borsa Italiana*'s communication to Consob and Bank of Italy, concerning "*Disciplina in materia di gestione collettiva del risparmio. Recepimento della direttiva 2011/61/UE (AIFMD) e ulteriori interventi di modifica*" <https://www.bancaditalia.it/compiti/vigilanza/normativa/consultazioni/2014/gestione-collettiva-risparmio/commenti-ricevuti/Borsa italiana.pdf> accessed 18 September 2021.
50 On this point, see also Barcellona (n 12) 77.

4 Special Purpose Acquisition Companies

Shareholder's Agreements under Italian Law

Giuseppe Cavallaro

4.1 Introduction

Special Purpose Acquisition Companies (SPACs) are investment vehicles set up by one or more promoters with the purpose of listing (initial public offering, IPO) on a regulated market (the Market for Investment Vehicles [MIV] in Italy) or on a multilateral trading system (Alternative Investment Market [AIM] Italy, renamed Euronext Growth market since October 2021). Their special purpose is to conduct a business combination (generally through acquiring holdings or a merger) with one or more existing operating companies (target companies). In Italy, it is not possible to find specific SPAC listing requirements as developed under international standards based on the US SPAC-style features. As stated in Part I of this edited collection, market practices and Italian company law are the main legal formants. Special purpose vehicles set up in Italy have taken the legal form of joint-stock companies and have therefore been subject to the related regulations.[1] This circumstance has led to several legal issues, primarily focused on the difference between the functioning of SPACs, which are incorporated as cash shell companies, and joint stock companies, which are generally operating entities.

One legal profile that has proved critical to implementing special purpose vehicles in Italy is that inherent in shareholders' agreements. It is the aspect that I will focus on after having illustrated the typical features of the SPAC model under the Italian company law framework.

4.2 Introduction to the Origins of SPACs

SPACs have their origin in blank check companies. These companies began to operate on the US market at the beginning of the 1980s and were defined by the Securities and Exchange Commission as:

> A development stage company with no specific business plan, purpose, or has indicated its business plan is to engage in a merger or acquisition with an unidentified company, other entity, or person.[2]

DOI: 10.4324/9781003169079-7

Initially, the regulation of blank check companies was simplified concerning larger listed companies since the former issued penny stocks and operated on the penny stock market. However, after notorious financial scandals, mainly caused by the lack of regulation of the activities of blank check companies, the SEC adopted Rule 419, containing stringent discipline on the placement of securities by these entities.[3] It is from voluntary adherence to this discipline – which was dictated for blank check companies and not for SPACs – that modern purpose vehicles were born.[4]

4.3 The Peculiarities of the 'SPAC' Business Model

As mentioned, the term 'SPAC' refers to companies set up by very well-known business entrepreneurs (the promoter or sponsor) who provide the working capital necessary to finance the operational and current expenses of the SPAC until its listing.

Following the constitution of the SPAC, the sponsors take it to the listing, placing units (consisting of one or more shares and one or more or a fraction of warrants) on the market. At this stage, the vehicle provides for disclosure to the market. However, the disclosure is exceptionally streamlined, given that the balance sheets of SPACs revolve around liquidity items. Therefore, the public investors' evaluations are mainly focused on the reputation and ability of the promoters, and on this depends the resolution of a capital increase aimed at providing the vehicle with the funds and resources needed to complete a business combination with a target company within a period of 18 months, which can be extended up to 24 months.[5]

A typically Italian tendency in this regard is to identify a target company with significant growth prospects (so-called high-growth company). At the same time, in the United States, special-purpose vehicles are also used to restore companies on the verge of bankruptcy.[6]

The identification of the target company is left to the managers of the SPAC, who, in most cases, coincide with the promoters.[7] These are typically individuals with recognized entrepreneurial and management skills and scouting ability in the sector, able to boast an extensive network of contacts or professionals with a solid track record in merger and acquisition (M&A) and private equity.

The promoters of an SPAC do not receive a predetermined fee for their work or – unlike the managers of a private equity fund – a fixed amount of commission calculated on the amount of capital managed (so-called management fee). Instead, their remuneration takes the form of the allocation of special shares (so-called founder shares)[8] and, if the business combination is successful, warrants to subscribe to ordinary shares at particularly advantageous conditions or special shares, with rewarding conversion ratios. If the transaction is not completed within the deadline, the promoters do not receive compensation, and the paid-up capital is returned pro rata to the shareholders.[9]

Once the promoters have identified a target company (operating and unlisted) that has the characteristics indicated in the 'investment policy' adopted by the SPAC, they submit the transaction to the shareholders' meeting, with full disclosure of the characteristics of the target company, including information relating to the business of the latter and the specific sector in which it operates. This allows investors to control how the money invested is used by the managers of the SPAC, thus mitigating one of the main risks inherent in the investment, namely the impossibility of a potential investor relying on the company's past performance (so-called track record).[10]

At the meeting, the shareholders of the SPAC may vote for or against the completion of the business combination, with the specification that those who have not taken part in the adoption of the decision will have the right of withdrawal, which in the Italian legal system is contemplated mainly by Sections 2437 and following of the Italian Civil Code.[11]

Usually, the shareholders' meeting of an SPAC resolves the matters reserved to it with the majorities provided for by law, depending on whether or not it qualifies as a company that makes use of the risk capital market pursuant to Section 2325-*bis* of the Italian Civil Code, it being understood that it is typical for the by-laws to condition the effectiveness of the resolutions functional to the realization of the business combination to the failure to exercise the right of withdrawal and redemption to an extent exceeding a predetermined threshold.

The investment in the target company can be made in different ways, although market practices have shown that the target company is reversed merged into the SPAC, with the result that the acquired company – which was previously a 'closed' company – automatically obtains the status of a listed company; however, the target company may incorporate the SPAC, with the consequence that the shareholders of the vehicle will receive in exchange shares of the target company (which, in the meantime, will have started and completed the listing process so that, when the merger takes effect, the shareholders of the SPAC can receive listed shares of the target without interruption).[12]

It could also happen that the SPAC limits itself to acquiring a shareholding in the target company without proceeding to further company integration; as a result, the SPAC takes on the nature of a holding company. Finally, as mentioned before, it may occur that – at the end of the company's duration – the SPAC has not completed the business combination: in such a scenario, the SPAC is put into liquidation, and the shareholders have the right to reimbursement of the capital contributed to the vehicle.

4.4 The Italian Listing Requirements Under *Borsa Italiana* S.p.A.

The listing requirements (Market Rules) organized and managed by *Borsa Italiana* S.p.A. read SPACs

[are] companies set up to acquire a business whose exclusive corporate purpose is to invest primarily in a company or activity as well as the related instrumental activities or among those companies whose investment strategy has not yet been stated or completed and/or is characterized by particular complexity . . . whose shares are traded on the professional segment of the 'MIV' market (*Mercato Telematico Degli Investment Vehicles*) reserved to professional investors.

It should highlight that – with specific reference to the admission requirements for the shares of companies in the Professional Segment of the MIV market – the Market Regulation expressly provides that

(i) The Articles of Association provide . . . for a duration of the company of no more than 36 months to make one or more significant investments, with the possibility of extension only if it is demonstrated that there are concrete negotiations underway to reach a significant level of investment, and (ii) Investments are considered significant if they represent overall more than 50% of the company's assets.

SPAC listing of SPACs can occur not only on the MIV but also on AIM Italia (renamed Euronext Growth market in October 2021).[13] The decision to list an SPAC on the regulated MIV market rather than on the unregulated AIM Italia market depends essentially on the size and the different peculiarities of the vehicle, without prejudice to the fact that listing on AIM Italia (renamed Euronext Growth market since October 2021) has so far been the solution chosen by most operators, given the greater ease of access in terms of cost and time.[14]

One of the main differences between the MIV and AIM segments is focused on the documentation the issuer must make available to investors during the IPO. For example, SPACs listed on the MIV must draft a prospectus – pursuant to Section 94 TUF and submitted to Consob (the Italian financial regulator) for approval. By contrast, an SPAC that is listed on the AIM just has to submit an admission document whose content, although similar to that of the prospectus (given the reference made by the AIM Regulation to the Prospectus Regulation to draft the Admission Document), is not subject to Consob's preliminary investigation. Instead, it must only be sent to the Italian Exchange (*Borsa Italiana S.p.A.*) for final approval.[15]

4.5 Shareholders' Agreements and SPACs – New Applicative Prospects in the Italian System

Precisely for the regulation of the specific position of SPACs, it is discussed whether it is possible to resort to the stipulation of so-called shareholders' agreements. These are agreements usually present within dynamic market contexts but, about these figures, assume certain contents and raise problems.

4.5.1 Shareholders' Agreements: Typical Clauses and Relationships Between Investors

The statute or memorandum of association represents the heart of the company. The Articles of Association outline the company's objective and all the internal rules and regulations to be observed to ensure it is achieved. Alongside the Articles of Association, the company may also provide for shareholders' agreements, that is, extra-corporate agreements, whereby some shareholders submit to restrictions on administrative rights or limits on the transferability of shares.

More specifically, pursuant to Section 2341-bis of the Italian Civil Code, it is possible to identify three main types, such as (i) shareholders' agreements concerning the exercise of voting rights; (ii) those aimed at limiting the right of the shareholder to the transfer of its equity investment or its shares; and (iii) agreements whose purpose or effect is the exercise of a dominant influence on the company.

The non-corporate nature of these agreements implies that they only imply obligations for the parties signing them. It follows that their violation will not affect the company and its resolutions but only contractual breaches by those who violate them. Some specific provisions of these agreements relate to restrictions on the transfer of shareholdings (e.g., drag-along or lock-up clauses) or the right of representation (whereby the investor will have its representatives appointed to administrative bodies).

Generally, in order to ensure greater compliance with shareholders' agreements, their provisions are also transferred (at a later date) to the Articles of Association. This is because, as mentioned earlier, shareholders' agreements are contractual, and their violation does not produce social effects. On the contrary, including their provisions in the Articles of Association will make them more binding since any violation would affect the validity of the shareholders' meeting resolutions.

Section 2341-*ter* of the Italian Civil Code limits the maximum duration of shareholders' agreements to five years. This happens because the rationale of these contracts lies in the need to guarantee to the company itself a real stabilization of the social balance in terms of ownership structure. Precisely because their effect is to produce a so-called piloted balance of corporate governance, it can only be allowed for limited periods and must be known to all investors.

Among the typical clauses of shareholders' agreements relating to the rights of the shareholder, there are provisions governing: (i) obligations relating to the expression – by some shareholders – of a uniform vote as regards the replacement of the management team when specific circumstances occur, such as the failure to achieve economic targets; (ii) obligations relating to the expression – by some shareholders – of a uniform vote as regards the appointment of at least some members of the board of directors (iii) obligations for certain shareholders to abstain from holding specific positions of control, in order to leave them to other subjects, during a predefined period of time; and (iv) agreements relating to intervention in the taking of decisions that are particularly important for the company.

Moreover, although the investor who draws up a shareholders' agreement is usually a minority shareholder, it can also happen that he/she holds majority stakes. It is precise with reference to the hypotheses in which there is a majority acquisition of the investor in management buy-outs that the agreements in question often find application.

Shareholders' agreements stipulated between non-majority shareholders typically include, inter alia, clauses aimed at (i) defining the powers that can be exercised autonomously and those that instead require the approval of a predetermined number of shareholders; (ii) regulating the economic rights of managers, should they cease their role; (iii) regulating any joint sale obligations; and (iv) establishing the type of investment that may be required of the manager in companies or increases in his existing shareholdings.

To summarize, shareholders' agreements qualify as a contractual mechanism of particular importance within investments in companies. Especially in the context of stock exchange listing, where there is a fragile corporate governance balance, they represent a fundamental tool for maintaining an internal balance, albeit limited in time. Moreover, where they are stipulated (also or exclusively) between professional investors, the function of shareholders' agreements appears even more critical. This is because these parties can assume both a minority position (as is usually the case) and a majority position.

In both cases, it is advisable to adopt agreements that regulate relations between the company, the so-called ordinary shareholders, and this particular group of ad hoc investors. This is especially so since these are medium-short-term investors and therefore concentrated in a high investment risk. There are various foreseeable regulations among which, in addition to those already highlighted, we find those relating to their disinvestment (such as way out or lock-up clauses). We are faced with a particularly complex discipline because there are various limits to be respected to stipulate an agreement of this type; in fact, they are governed not only by the Italian Civil Code but also by the TUF under Sections 122 and 123. Moreover, since they are contractual, they are not as binding as the provisions of the Articles of Association. In some cases, it might be appropriate to transpose the contents of the agreement into the Articles of Association.

In conclusion, although the application of shareholders' agreements within SPACs is debated, a reading of the regulatory data would lead to the conclusion that it is plausible to apply them also to these categories of investment entities, albeit for a limited period of time, in order to regulate relations between investors employing a non-corporate instrument.

4.5.2 Shareholders' Agreements in the SPAC Model

Shareholders' agreements are significant concerning the shareholdings in the SPAC. Assuming that these agreements are characterized, inter alia, by a duration of fewer than five years, their main purpose is to support the investment for a medium-short-term period. For this reason, shareholders' agreements help promote social balance for the period of intervention of the investor, who is granted special corporate governance rights.

However, the nature of special-purpose vehicles does not always lend itself to the shareholders' agreements outlined earlier. In the first place, the maximum duration of shareholders' agreements (five years) is calibrated to the physiological duration of the life of a joint-stock company, which is generally shorter than the maximum duration of SPACs (18/24 months). In the latter, the agreements in question cannot perform the same function of sustaining the investment in the medium-short term.

Indeed, the shareholders' agreements stipulated by the shareholders of an SPAC could be drafted in such a way as to be kept alive even after the business combination operation. However, by operating this way, the shareholders would act uncertainly. At an early stage, these do not have an overview of the structuring of the business combination, nor do they know the target company.

Looking at the question from another perspective, the stipulation of parasocial pacts between the partners of the SPAC could be an advantage for the managers: they would know in advance – compared to the meeting to approve the business combination – the will of the partners. This circumstance would considerably limit the risk surrounding the vote on the business combination and, as a result, the success of the same.[16]

Moreover, as regards shareholders' agreements as a means of fostering a balance between shareholders and corporate bodies, some clarifications are necessary. The logic of the SPAC model unhinges – albeit only partially – the relationships between shareholders and bodies in a joint-stock company. In fact, it is possible to identify two moments in the purpose vehicles. In the first phase, powers are intensely concentrated on the promoters-managers, promoters of the initiative, and called upon to make strategic choices, especially during negotiations with the target company. In the second phase, that is, from raising capital through the IPO, it is customary to say that control passes to the investors.

In this regard, the shareholders have absolute veto power regarding the business combination at the shareholders' meeting. In other words, if the shareholders disagree, the managers cannot implement the transaction. It follows that the stipulation of shareholders' agreements could further strengthen the shareholders' position (given the cohesion among them) to the detriment of the managers.

Finally, it should be remembered that the promoters of SPACs are used to providing – in the Articles of Association – clauses to the effect that, if a particular share of capital (usually 30%) were to exercise the right of withdrawal (which is due to dissenting shareholders regarding the business combination), it would not be possible to carry out the operation. This cannot be reconciled with the stipulation of shareholders' agreements. If the minority investors agree, by means of an agreement outside the company, to express an opinion contrary to the business combination, then exercising their right of withdrawal, they could cancel the entire operation without any possibility remaining for the directors.

This scenario is particularly critical in an SPAC, where the managers are (possibly) remunerated only after the company merger. In other words, there would be a risk of abuse – by the shareholders – of their position.

4.6 Conclusion

With reference to investors, the characteristics of the SPAC that have made this form of investment particularly popular are mainly the following: (i) the investment has a relatively low-risk profile, since, in the event of failure of the planned initiative, the investors obtain the repayment of the initial investment (with a minimum remuneration represented by the investments made from the escrow account with which the SPAC had deposited the capital raised during the IPO phase); (ii) each investor (as a shareholder of the SPAC) may withdraw from the SPAC following the shareholders' meeting called for the business combination (receiving back, also in this case, the capital invested with the accrued income); and (iii) the valuation and acquisition of the target company is usually carried out 'at a discount' with respect to market values, and therefore the SPAC investors – immediately after the business combination with the target company – may immediately benefit from a potential appreciation of the listed shares of the target company.

From the perspective of the entrepreneur owner of the target company, the SPAC has the advantages of (i) accelerating the listing process of the target company itself; and, at the same time, (ii) mitigating the risk that, at the time of setting the offer price for the IPO (of the target company), market conditions (in terms of valuation, volatility, etc.) do not allow for a sufficient appreciation of the stock brought to the listing. On the other hand, by resorting to the SPAC scheme, the valuation of the target company (in terms of exchange ratios, etc.) is established autonomously by the parties independently of market conditions (avoiding the book-building mechanism). These elements have made the SPAC one of the most appreciated forms of investment in current market conditions, competing with more traditional ones.

However, the implementation of special-purpose vehicles continues to give rise to reflection on the possibility of applying to them the regulations dictated for joint-stock companies without any modification. The institution of shareholders' agreements is an excellent example of this. In fact, from what has been said earlier, it might seem appropriate to provide for an ad hoc regulation for non-corporate agreements entered into by the shareholders of an SPAC. In this regard, one solution could be eliminating the duration limit for such agreements.

Acting in this way, the shareholders would be free to draft the terms of the agreement as they see fit. However, a limit would be imposed on them by the very nature of the special purpose vehicle: shareholders would not be able to make long-term forecasts, as they would not have a proper balance sheet. On the other hand, the directors could make forecasts regarding the evolution of the meeting called to express their opinion on the business combination, representing – as has been said – a moment of fundamental importance.

Notes

1 An exception in this regard is represented by the first SPAC implemented in our legal system (in 2011): Italy Investment S.A., a vehicle under Luxembourg law. See D. K. Heyman, 'From Blank Check to SPAC: The Regulator's Response to the Market, and the Market's Response to the Regulation' (2007) 2(1) *Entrepreneurial Business Law Journal* 531–552.
2 It should be noted that this definition, as will be discussed, was partially amended by the Penny Stock Reform Act, which included it within § 77g of the Securities Act of 1993.
3 The powers by virtue of which the SEC adopted Rule 419 were granted to the authority in question by the US Congress, pursuant to the Securities Enforcement Remedies and Penny Stock Reform Act. On this point, see Arianna Paoletti, 'Le Special Purpose Acquisition Companies (SPAC)' (2017) *Rivista del Diritto Societario* 1145; Daniele D'Alvia, 'SPACs of Everything: Challenging Financial Regulation in Times of Crisis' (27 July 2021) <www.thefinregblog.com> accessed 10 January 2023.
4 It should be noted that SPACs cannot be assimilated in toto to blank check companies since the latter, unlike the first ones, are considered as issuers of penny stocks. In fact, it was the voluntary adhesion of SPACs to the regulations dictated for blank check companies that marked the beginning of their history.
5 The capital raised at the time of the IPO is deposited in an escrow fund or in a trust and the directors cannot dispose of it until the business combination has been carried out, except for investments with a very low rating.
6 For further remarks, please see Chapter 8 of this edited collection.
7 On the typical characteristics of the promoters of a SPAC, see Michael Klausner et al., 'A Sober Look at SPACs' (2022) 39(1) *Yale Journal of Regulation* 230; Magnus Blomkvist, Giacomo Nocera and Milos Vulanovic, 'Who Are the SPAC CEOs?' (2021) <www.ssrn.com> accessed 10 January 2023.
8 The special shares in question are often characterized by the absence of the right to dispose of them, at least until the realization of the corporate aggregation operation. Marco Fumagalli, *Lo sviluppo della SPAC (Special Purpose Acquisition Company) in Italia. Un nuovo modo di fare private equity e di quotare le imprese in borsa* (EGEA 2014) 47; Filippo Garramone, 'An Overview on Special Purpose Acquisition Companies' (2020) *Banca Impresa Società* 138.
9 Vijay M Jog and Chengye Sun, 'Blank Check IPOs: A Home Run for Management' (2007) *SSRN* 1–31.
10 In fact, the SPAC, as a cash shell company, does not have a proper balance sheet. It follows that the shareholders of the vehicle have no way – prior to the aforesaid meeting – of assessing the validity of the initiative.
11 Vincenzo Donativi and Piero Corigliano, 'Le SPAC (Special Purpose Acquisition Companies): il modello internazionale e la sua compatibilità con il diritto italiano' (2010) 29(1) *Le Società* 17–25.
12 For the consequences of the choice of one rather than the other legal form through which to carry out the operation of company aggregation, see Carlo Santagata,

La fusione tra società (Morano 1964) 155; Antonio Serra and Ivan Demuro, *Tras-formazione, fusione, scissione* (Zanichelli 2014).
13 See Chapters 2 and 3 of this edited collection.
14 See Part I of this edited collection.
15 Daniele D'Alvia, 'SPAC: Limits and Perspectives between Hard Law and Soft Law' (2017) *Rivista diritto societario* 1168.
16 This category of covenants is – in general – structured differently depending on the cause of the termination of the office of the members of the board of directors (e.g. due to their own decision or the intervention of the professional investor).

5 The Tax Legal Framework of Special Purpose Acquisition Companies

An Italian Prospective

Luisa Scarcella

5.1 Introduction

Under the acronym SPAC, the financial world has been indicating so-called Special Purpose Acquisition Companies. The set-up of an SPAC and the completion of the business combination are part of the life cycle of an SPAC. This makes SPAC an alternative route to list companies with more certainty than the traditional initial public offering (IPO).

Between 2017 and 2018, over 30 SPACs were listed in Italy on the Alternative Investment Market (AIM) and Market for Investment Vehicles (MIV) segments. Scratching beneath the surface of the acronym, SPACs are companies set up for a special purpose to carry out a business combination. Historically, we have already seen in Part I of this edited collection how SPACs started in the US in the 1980s and were considered the direct descendants of blank check companies[1] or, better, a new phoenix rising from the ashes of blank check companies.[2]

Since SPACs have also been defined by many as the new drivers of a merger and acquisition (M&A) era, the types of tax concerns that might arise in SPACs are indeed the traditional and more specific tax issues that could arise from any merger and acquisition (M&A) transaction. Currently, the Italian legal system does not provide for any particular tax rule on SPACs. Thus, traditional rules on M&A – also from a tax perspective – will apply in SPACs. Nonetheless, specific tax questions might still arise with SPACs.

Some of these questions have already been addressed by the Italian Revenue Agency (IRA), namely the national tax authority in Italy. In fact, between 2018 and 2019,[3] the IRA has already been consulted three times by taxpayers. Specifically, those taxpayers have used the so-called *interpello* instrument (essentially, a specific formal request that taxpayers can file with the IRA to ask for its opinion on their possible future behavior that might be tax-relevant) to ask for the IRA's advice concerning the tax consequences deriving from a merger in the context of an SPAC. These questions concern the continuity of the tax consolidation, the effect on previous losses, and the possibility of tax and accounting backdating. While SPACs do not seem to open new questions, they still require an assessment of the possible application of

DOI: 10.4324/9781003169079-8

already-existing provisions and a direction about which provision shall apply to SPACs. On this matter, the responses given by the IRA provide a first overview of how these questions shall be solved.

Other tax questions do not concern the M&A side or could arise in a cross-border context of a de-SPAC transaction. At the same time, tax questions may arise with the managers acting as sponsors for the SPAC and SPAC public investors. However, in this area, there is no specific direction, and the IRA has never issued so far an *interpello* or any guidance. However, the chapter is also addressing those potential new issues.

At the same time, with tax benefits, SPACs might also be entitled to tax credits. Again, the reference is to a tax credit provided for listing SMEs on the exchange. In addition, there has been interest in promoting access to public capital markets for SMEs or high-growth companies at the national and European levels. In this field, SPACs could play an exciting role.

The following sections explore tax issues in the area of M&A, and the possible access to the tax credit for promoting SME listing will be analyzed. Finally, the last section provides the reader with consolidating remarks.

5.2 Continuity of the Tax Consolidation: First Remarks

The possibility of continuing a tax consolidation after the IRA has addressed the business combination in a specific *interpello* request presented by a taxpayer. By reading the *interpello*, it is possible to find out that the petitioner's name is unknown due to confidentiality issues. However, the conclusions of this *interpello* are fascinating. Indeed, the petition for a ruling was submitted in accordance with Section 124, Paragraph 5, of the Italian Consolidated Tax Act (and, therefore, to obtain confirmation of the continuation of a tax consolidation regime that had already been launched) by an Italian company operating as an SPAC and incorporated as a Special Investment Vehicle (SIV).

The SPAC, which at the time of applying was probably listed on the AIM managed by *Borsa Italiana* S.p.A., identified a target company (which was the holding of a group). As a result, the business combination was completed in 2017 in the form of a direct merger by which the target company was merged with the SPAC and automatically listed on *Borsa Italiana* S.p.A. Following the completion of the business combination, the SPAC held 53.15% of the former target's company share capital (namely, the majority and control of the target), and the SPAC changed its business name and corporate purpose transforming from an SIV into an operating company pursuing industrial aims.

After the de-SPAC transaction, the former SPAC filed a new prospectus with *Borsa Italiana* S.p.A. to list its ordinary shares and warrants on a new market segment different from the AIM probably related to the STAR segment or MIV under the leadership of *Borsa Italiana* S.p.A. The exchange consented to this new listing, and it did not backdate the effects of the merger for tax purposes. Consequently, the main question was whether the newly merged entity had achieved its consolidation objectives. This is because the SPAC was merging with a holding company. Indeed, under Italian tax law, companies belonging to the same group can elect for domestic tax consolidation. This regime allows the determination of a single IRES (corporate income tax imposed under Presidential Decree 917 of 22 December 1986) taxable base comprising each participating entity's taxable income and losses. The tax consolidation does not operate for IRAP (regional production tax) purposes.

In the case under examination, the SPAC and the target company are technically two and do not belong to the same group. Hence, the question on tax consolidation was fascinating.

5.3 Neutrality of the Incorporation of the Target Company

The IRA upheld that the best answer focused on continuing the consolidation with the target company. Essentially, under Section 2504-*bis* of the Italian Civil Code, the acquiring company shall succeed in every legal relationship, even including liabilities of the target company that necessarily comprise corporate income tax (IRES).

Thus, by the inheritance effect that characterizes merger operations, incorporating SPAC in our scenario takes over all the legal relationships of its predecessor (the target company), including its controlling relationships with the consolidated companies.

5.3.1 Tax Consolidation and Limits to the Use of Previous Year's Losses

Two tests must be considered when addressing the effects of continuing tax consolidation. The first one is the so-called equity test. This test is contained in Paragraph 7 of Section 172 of the Testo Unico delle Imposte sui Redditi (T.U.I.R.), which limits the acquiring company that wishes to take over tax losses, excess interest expense, and ACE (*Aiuto alla Crescita Economica*) surpluses[4] accrued by a target company. In particular, such regulatory provision provides that the company's tax losses (including the acquiring company) may be deducted from the company's corporate income tax resulting from the merger. Deductions can be made for the part of their amount that does not exceed the amount of their shareholders' equity as shown in the latest financial statements and, if lower, without taking into account the contributions and payments made in the last 24 months prior to the date to which the balance sheet refers.

The second test, in addition to the limit mentioned above on shareholders' equity (the so-called equity test), is the vitality test for loss-making companies. This test is based on the revenues earned and the expenses for employee services incurred during the last financial year. Specifically, the company's income statement, whose losses may be carried forward, must show revenues and proceeds from core business activities, staff expenses, and related contributions greater than 40% resulting from the average of the previous two financial years.

The equity and vitality tests described earlier also apply to non-deductible interest carried forward, and the excess ACE carried forward. At the same time, it is still possible to appeal to the tax authorities[5] to request the disapplication of the aforementioned provisions. Finally, companies involved in the merger, including the acquiring company, must determine their result for the period, relating to the time interval between the beginning of the tax period and the date before the merger becomes legally effective. Any loss from this calculation is subject to the described asset and economic viability limits.

5.4 MLBO, SPV, and the SPAC

The tax authorities' guidelines regarding merger leverage buy-out (MLBO) transactions (debt acquisition transactions)[6] must also be considered applicable to the case of a merger by incorporation or a direct merger with a target company. The expression "leveraged buy-outs" – which refers both to a single transaction and to a series of transactions, even of different forms – defines the acquisition of a company or of a controlling or wholly owned interest in a given target company through the creation of a Special Purpose Vehicle (SPV), which is financed partly, even minimally, by equity and partly by debt. The choice of sources for financing a given business acquisition (asset deal) or share deal (share deal) is fundamentally linked to the use of debt as "leverage," which entails the emergence of incremental benefits (and risks) as long as the cost of debt is lower (or higher) than the return on risk capital.

These transactions, therefore, are characterized by the existence of a single cause, which is the acquisition of a company or a shareholding that allows control of the target company. Transactions in which the SPV acquires a shareholding in the target company (share deal) are usually characterized by the subsequent merger of the target company into the SPV with the consequent approximation of the debt to the assets securing the loan and the generation of the cash flows necessary for the progressive extinction of the debt as well as for the discharge of the financial charges connected with it.

It is easy to observe how both MLBO operations and those carried out by the SPAC are characterized, in substance, by identifying a target company and its subsequent merger into the "vehicle" company. The fundamental difference that characterizes the two mentioned operations is represented by the modalities of financing of the investment in the target: in the first case, the sources of financing are mainly represented by debt, while, in the second case, they are represented by capital raised on the stock market at the time of the listing of the SPAC.

In both cases, however, the vitality test and the shareholders' equity limit, as governed by Paragraph 7 of Art. 172 of the T.U.I.R. are generally not respected.

It should be pointed out that, in such transactions:

I. with regard to the vitality test, in most cases, the special purpose vehicle, being newly established, does not have the financial statements for previous years on which to carry out this test;

II. in relation to the quantitative limit on shareholders' equity, if the shareholders' equity of the SPV or SPAC were to be reduced by the contributions/disbursements made in the last 24 months, these companies would have no shareholders' equity.

These circumstances, in themselves, would have the effect of blocking the carry-over of any tax losses, non-deducted interest expense – deriving from the indebtedness contracted by the SPV for the acquisition of the target company – and the ACE surplus formed, in the case of the SPAC, as a result of the IPO.

However, the taxpayer can request the disapplication of the anti-avoidance provision contained in Section 172, Paragraph 7, of the T.U.I.R., by demonstrating that, in the particular case, the anti-avoidance effects that the provision intends to counteract could not occur.

With particular reference to NewCo's (SPAC or SPV) set up as part of listing or MLBO operations, it should be remembered that, as regards the vitality test, the absence of previous financial statements with which to carry out the comparison required by the regulation does not exclude, ex se, the possibility of investigating the substantial vitality of the company involved in the extraordinary operation, since the company involved in the extraordinary operation, since it is possible to have recourse to other valuable factors to demonstrate the existence of this requirement. In this sense, the "vitality" of NewCo, in both cases, can be easily demonstrated by the performance of the functions instrumental to the search, identification, selection, and reorganization of the operating target company.

As far as the limit of the net equity is concerned, it must be considered that the initial contributions in favor of the "vehicle" company can be considered *"physiological"* in the context of the realization of an MLBO operation or the listing of the SPAC and, therefore, not aimed at allowing a full, as well as artificial, recovery of tax losses and ACE surpluses.

5.5 Tax Backdating and Accounting Backdating

The IRA has also addressed some concerns in relation to tax backdating in its answer to an *interpello* presented in 2019. With the answer no. 405/2019, the IRA examined the *interpello* request. The SPAC declared that it acquired the target company Alfa in July 2018. In the same month, it completed the merger, attributing backdated fiscal and accounting effects to the operation to 1 January 2018. After the merger, the incorporating company (namely, the SPAC that had taken on the purpose and operational business of the incorporated company Alfa) deliberates the transition to use IAS/IFRS international accounting standards.

The petitioner points out that backdating for accounting purposes is prohibited in applying IFRS 3 on business combinations. Hence, the merged company was asking whether or not, in the absence of accounting backdating. However, in the presence of a retroactivity clause for income tax purposes contained in the merger deed, a "final" tax return should be prepared for the merged company. The Italian Revenue Agency has clarified that in SPAC's business combinations, the IFRS 3 does not apply because the SPAC is a non-operating company.

The answer is no. 405/2019, therefore, confirms that the fiscal backdating envisaged by Section 172, paragraph 9 of the T.U.I.R. meets the needs of simplification, which are closely interconnected with those which are at the basis of accounting backdating and which consist in the possibility offered to the companies participating in a merger operation to determine in a unitary manner the statutory and fiscal result of the interim period between 1 January of the year of the merger and the effective date of the operation. This is why the IRA concluded that the fiscal backdating envisaged by Paragraph 9 of Section 172 of the T.U.I.R. could not operate if the accounting backdating is not also implemented since the standards adopted by the companies involved did not allow it.[7] As a result, the incorporated company (i.e., the target) must submit a corporate tax return (based on an independent profit and loss account) referring to the pre-merger closing tax period.[8]

5.6 Possible Tax Benefits on Italian Financial Markets

One last aspect that could be relevant for SPACs is a tax credit that was initially introduced by the Italian lawmaker with the 2018 Budget Law for advisory costs incurred by small- and medium-sized enterprises for the IPO; the tax credit is only due to the extent that the IPO procedure is successful.

The new Budge Law for 2023 (approved by the Italian Parliament on 29 December 2022), effective from 1 January 2023, provides several tax measures that may interest multinational enterprises with Italian operations. In particular, the tax credit available for advisory costs incurred by SMEs for IPOs is extended to 2023 with an increase of the maximum qualifying cost from €200,000 to €500,000. The tax credit is equal to 50% of such cost. In an Italian entrepreneurial scenario characterized by the widespread presence of SMEs, this measure is expected to impact the beneficiaries' growth prospects and the development of the AIM Italia market dedicated to them (now Euronext Growth).[9]

The measure is part of a series of tax incentives for listing companies with low capitalization, reducing, as mentioned, the costs associated with the procedure and contributing to the strengthening of the capital structure of SMEs and the reduction of the debt-to-equity ratio. Indeed, facilitating access to listing on regulated markets or in Italian and European multilateral trading systems will allow smaller companies to raise new capital by using an alternative instrument to bank debt, given the greater rigidity of providing bank loans. Recourse to the capital market could represent an opportunity for SMEs to significantly improve their net financial position and operating performance, in terms of increasing turnover, net profit, and EBITDA, as a prerequisite for developing growth strategies and evaluating new acquisitions thanks to the capital raised.[10]

According to the European Commission, SMEs represent 99% of all businesses in the European Union. The definition of an SME is, therefore, essential to finance these enterprises. The SMEs are defined in the EU recommendation 2003/361, and the main factors determining whether an enterprise is an SME are:

I.   annual turnover of no more than €50 million;
II. annual balance sheet total of no more than €43 million; and
III. AWUs ("Work Units – Year") of fewer than 250 units.

Therefore, SMEs fall into the so-called small-cap issuers (companies with a small market capitalization). Given the size requirements of the beneficiaries and the simplified path for admission to listing, it is foreseeable that the Tax Credit for SMEs will significantly impact the AIM Italia market. Thus, SPACs could represent an exciting instrument for listing SMEs also benefiting from a tax credit.

5.7 Conclusion

This chapter has outlined how tax consolidation is achieved in de-SPAC deals and has given rise to new perspectives on tax benefits that target companies can achieve by merging with SPACs. Specifically, because of the peculiarities of the listing process on the AIM, the range of advisory expenses in support of the IPO that can be hypothetically facilitated could include the following:

I.   Feasibility studies and evaluation of competitors, drafting of the equity story and business plan, assistance in the placement of the stock and investor relations before and after listing (typical activities of the financial advisor)
II. The verification of the adequacy of the financial and legal due diligence and the issue of the issuing company's statement of appropriateness (typical activities of the Nomad);
III. The promotion of the issuing company toward the financial community, the management of investor relations and the marketing phase, and the book-building activity (typical activities of the global coordinator)
IV. Legal, due diligence, the issue of the comfort letter, the drafting of the admission document with the Nomad, and support in contractual matters (typical activities of the law firm)

V. Tax due diligence (carried out by the tax firm)

VI. The financial statement opinion and the issue of the comfort letter by the auditing firm[11]

Finally, due consideration should also be given to the potential critical issues that the listing could entail concerning a redefinition of the company's ownership structure and, in particular, a dilution of the controlling interest of existing shareholders. In addition, the risk of losing control deriving from hostile "takeovers," although remote, must be considered during the IPO.

Notes

1 Daniel S. Riemer, 'Special Purpose Acquisition Companies: SPAC and SPAN, or Blank Check Redux?' (2007–2008) 85(4) *Washington University Law Review* 931, 934.

2 Daniele D'Alvia, 'The International Financial Regulation of SPACs between Legal Standardised Regulation and Standardisation of Market Practices' (2020) 21(2) *Journal of Banking Regulation* 112, 124.

3 Italian Revenue Agency, Risoluzione n.13/E/2018, 2 February 2018; Italian Revenue Agency, Risposte 405 and 406/2019.

4 The ACE (aid to economic growth) is a benefit-measure introduced in 2011 to encourage the strengthening of the capital structure of companies and the Italian production system. Section 1, Paragraph 1080, of Law no. 145 of 30 December 2018 repealed the ACE as of the tax period following the one in progress as of 31 December 2018. However, the same paragraph of Section 1 allows the use of past ACE surpluses by establishing that the provisions referred to in Paragraph 2 of Section 3 of the Ministerial Decree of 3 August 2017, in relation to the amount of the notional yield exceeding the total net income for the tax period in progress as of 31 December 2018.

5 Pursuant to Section 11, Paragraph 2 of Law no. 212 of 27 July 2000, containing the Statute of Taxpayers' Rights.

6 Ibid.

7 As also reported by L. Gaiani, 'Fusioni societarie: riporto perdite, consolidato fiscale e retrodatazione al vaglio dell'agenzia dell'entrate' (2019) 46 *il fisco* 4435.

8 Art. 172, comma 8, T.U.I.R. e art. 5-*bis*, comma 2, D.P.R. n. 322/1998.

9 As defined by Recommendation no. 2003/361/EC of the European Commission of 6 May 2003, implemented in Italy by the Decree of the Ministry for Productive Activities of 18 April 2005.

10 F. Molinari and F. De Bernardis, "Credito d'imposta per le pmi sui costi IPO per la quotazione in mercati regolamentati e non" (2018) 16 *Il Fisco* 1532.

11 This list of potential expenses draws upon the one by Molinari and De Bernardis (n 10) 1532.

6 The Special Purpose Acquisition Company

Special Purpose and Corporate Governance Structure

Giovanni Romano

6.1 Introduction

This chapter considers the adaptation of the internationally standardized Special Purpose Acquisition Company (SPAC) model under Italian company law. It aims to ascertain whether the national corporate framework is inclined to support the special nature of the SPAC as a shell vehicle formed to raise capital for a business to be acquired in the future under a peculiarly designed corporate governance structure.

SPACs have rapidly become one of the mainstream financial products of Wall Street. Their growing popularity has made them an important financial innovation, but at the same time, it has attracted the attention of financial regulators and governments. The SPAC seems a useful financial invention, but some adjustments must be implemented or studied in depth. To this end, section 6.2 of this chapter outlines the transactional structure of the SPAC as it is shaped by international market practices, pointing out the unique combination of heterogeneous mechanisms that such an investment vehicle is used to deploy in achieving its economic objective. Subsequently, the focus of section 6.3 is on how the main features of the SPAC structure interact with the Italian legal system, intending to assess how this spontaneous product of financial innovation should be domestically qualified and regulated. In contrast, section 6.4 discusses some company law issues pertaining to the special corporate purpose of the SPAC, the internal distribution of corporate powers, and the use of the trust/escrow account as an external investors' protection device. Finally, consolidating remarks are provided in section 6.5.

In a nutshell, I argue that a minimal set of tailored legislative provisions would help remove residual uncertainties about SPAC operation and that more specific regulatory measures can be expected to be implemented in the future.

6.2 The Transactional Structure of the SPAC

When approaching SPAC, the Italian business law scholar is particularly struck by the multifaceted combination of devices to protect public shareholders in such a 'one-shot' investment vehicle.[1]

DOI: 10.4324/9781003169079-9

The safeguards against the risks implied in the business combination to be carried on by the management team result from a peculiar interaction between heterogeneous elements derived from company, contract, and fiduciary law. Such interplay is not entirely new, as it has already been discussed in venture capital-backed firms about issues arising from trade sale techniques.[2]

However, while SPACs share certain characteristics with private equity and venture capital,[3] some key differences remain in how the former choose their targets and design their investment horizons and exit strategies.[4]

One of the most qualifying features lies in the contractual arrangements governing the relationship between managers and investors. While the commitment to an investment fund typically puts the investor in a passive position, the public shareholder in an SPAC is given the decisive right to vote for or against the only transaction to which she exposes her capital.[5]

Furthermore, an SPAC initial public offering (IPO) intends to provide broader access to investment opportunities that, in the field of private equity, would normally be available to sophisticated investors only. And since SPAC shares are publicly traded, another consequence is that the investment is liquid daily.[6]

Finally, the commitment in an SPAC is expected to become effective within a minimal horizon, as the management team has a short timespan to find a suitable target.

On the other hand, the IPO proceeds are placed in a trust/escrow account.[7] Once the target is announced, dissenting shareholders may exit the deal by receiving a pro-rata share of the trust/escrow fund.[8] On the contrary, if no business combination is finalized, the SPAC is dissolved and liquidated.[9]

In addition to a solid reputation of sponsors/managers compensating for the lack of any track record of the shell company, the involvement of all these 'voice' and 'exit' mechanisms are amongst the most prominent advantages of investing in an SPAC.[10] To achieve such goals, the international practice has designed a corporate vehicle that uses the heterogeneous legal devices mentioned earlier.[11]

Firstly, contractual freedom is involved to the extent that SPAC shells raise the need to adapt, through private arrangements, the by-laws in a manner functional to their corporate purpose, claiming formal recognition vis-a-vis the legal system for their alleged potential as efficient alternatives to traditional IPOs.[12] Secondly, fiduciary law seems to come into play on a twofold basis. The execution of the 'blank mandate' given to the directors—who basically set up a shell company and then take it public on the promise that they will strive to complete the acquisition of a target within a short timeframe—undoubtedly entails their duties of care and loyalty to mitigate possible conflicts of interest.[13]

However, this only happens after the shareholders' meeting has approved the proposed business combination, making it possible to release the IPO proceeds deposited in the trust/escrow account.[14] Thus, the trustee/escrow agent's fiduciary obligation somewhat seals that the management team's primary duty is to scout for a business. At the same time, the execution of the acquisition becomes a subordinate task.[15]

6.3 The SPAC and the Italian Law: Preliminary Remarks

Considering the multidimensionality of its transactional structure, the distinctiveness of the SPAC results from the strict terms and conditions under which its special purpose is to be achieved, as well as from the temporary and reversible nature of the IPO investors' commitment.[16] Such features are intended to comfort the investing public against the initial vagueness of the SPAC prospects.[17]

More precisely, by straddling the boundary between the private equity sector and capital markets, the SPAC combines the nature of an open company with some elements of the contractual relationship between managers and investors in a private equity fund.[18] In crafting this combination of 'contract' and 'company,' the SPAC appears to result from a financial experiment with a significant impact on corporate governance.[19]

This is quite self-explanatory in Italy, where, with the sole exception of the redemption right established by a legal provision in the Italian Civil Code,[20] almost every safeguard granted to investors has a contractual nature. Such contractual design leads to the result whereby, rather than being exposed to multiple investment/divestment choices made by others, in an SPAC, the public shareholders decide, as a class, whether to carry out just one relevant acquisition. Following this decision, divestment becomes an individual choice.[21]

Hence, while the position of the individual investor is characterized by great walk-out flexibility,[22] the internal governance structure of the SPAC is relatively rigid in regulating the inter-relationship among its main corporate constituencies.[23] Moreover, an external party is here involved, namely the fiduciary, who holds the account where the IPO proceeds are locked-up. Most of the company's assets are not at the directors' disposal until the shareholders' meeting approves the business combination.[24]

Surprisingly, however, such a dynamic corporate results from 'soft law' provisions. In fact, in Italy (as elsewhere),[25] the standardization of SPAC terms has not taken place through ad hoc legal provisions but rather via the stock exchange regulations adopted by the Exchange, in our case *Borsa Italiana* S.p.A., which represent private standards that issuers need to comply with if they wish to have their securities listed on the market.[26]

By analyzing such rules, legal scholars have noticed that an SPAC

I.   exhibits an internal organization like an ordinary joint-stock company;
II. has a capital structure resembling the typical asset organization of an Undertaking for Collective Investment (UCI);
III. operates toward the target like a parent holding company; and
IV. tends to invest like a vehicle pertaining to the private equity universe.[27]

However, although this empirical description correctly grasps the SPAC complex aptitude, it must be pointed out that, in legal terms, an SPAC does not qualify as an investment company (i.e., as an Alternative Investment Fund or AIF).[28]

This issue has been addressed by both the Bank of Italy and *Borsa Italiana* S.p.A. The first assumed that SPACs are exempted from the Alternative Investment Fund Managers Directive 2011/61/EU (AIFMD) as far as they meet the holding company definition therein. In contrast, Borsa *Italiana* S.p.A. noted that SPACs are distinguished by:

> (1) an initial phase . . . which includes the constitution of the vehicle, the raising of the cash, and the search for the target . . .; and (2) a final phase, consisting in the approval and implementation of the business combination. [During the first phase] the managers do not carry out any upstream management of the money raised, which remains deposited in the escrow account, [whereas in the final phase] the assets of the SPAC are not managed by the managers autonomously from the public investors: in fact, the management has only a function of proposing the business combination which, in any case, needs the approval of the shareholders' meeting.[29]

This second interpretation seems more accurate, as it directly emphasizes that the SPAC is not a UCI since it does not 'provide the service of the collective management of assets.[30]

An SPAC is not intended to be liquidated as a collective investment portfolio. By contrast, it shall merge so that the cash raised by public investors is not eventually liquidated. Furthermore, the sole and fundamental 'management' operation (i.e., the business combination) is here conditioned upon the direct decision of investors.[31]

However, there is no doubt that the objective of the SPAC is not to pursue a commercial activity but only to seek, by means of the management team's scouting skills, an investment opportunity in an operating profit-driven firm.[32] Yet, in Italy, the most reasonable option is to regulate it under general company law.[33]

This condition highlights the importance of accurately detailing its 'special purpose' and accordingly coordinating the allocation of corporate powers so that the modern SPAC's distinctive features can serve such a purpose.[34] It is precisely here that the need arises to identify potential obstacles stemming from mandatory company law provisions. Although being an operating company 'in the making' might be the key to tackling some conceptual issues, it remains to be evaluated whether some ad hoc enabling provisions would ultimately be preferable to eliminate residual applicative uncertainties.

6.4 Company Law SPAC-Specific Challenges

The first issue related to the 'hyper-specificity' of the SPAC corporate purpose[35] concerns the entity qualification vis-a-vis the typological boundary marked by Sections 2247–2248 ICC, which perform the systematic task of 'identifying the case of the company.'[36]

Since a company cannot be incorporated to enjoy or hold one or more assets, this leads to a potential systematic inconsistency. Indeed, before the acquisition and throughout the life of the SPAC, the impossibility of having an immediate or instantaneous business combination might indirectly lead to the assumption that the SPAC is just carrying out a static and conservative investment activity.[37]

However, it must be highlighted that, within the provisions mentioned earlier, 'enjoyment' postulates an activity instrumental to merely preserving the assets according to their normal economic use.[38] This is not the case with the SPAC.

The activity carried out by the SPAC is certainly not aimed at preserving an indirect form of enjoyment of the profits of the cash fund provisionally held on trust but rather at 'converting' that pool of money into a capital contribution to the target company, with a definitive involvement in its business purpose. But, of course, the SPAC organizational structure per se merely combines segregated financial resources on the one hand and the scouting skills of the promoters on the other. This means that the relationship between the capital raising and its allocation to the merger and acquisition (M&A) market, namely the functional connection of the 'company' to the 'firm,' which in abstract terms could fulfill the 'productivist' criterion implicit in the ICC provisions, only stays as a potential development within the life cycle of an SPAC.[39]

Nonetheless, the fact that an SPAC conducts a mere search for an investment opportunity, which does not qualify as an entrepreneurial activity in the technical sense,[40] should not preclude a legitimate use of the corporate form under general company law.[41]

Firstly, it has been recognized that the general notion of company provided by Section 2247 ICC is not only incomplete, leaving out corporate structures with specific purposes already known to the Italian legal tradition but also somewhat outdated. Significantly departing from the Civil Code's original approach, subsequent legislative developments have led to what scholars define as the 'neutrality' of the organizational form regarding the corporate purpose, the latter remaining freely moldable by private autonomy.[42]

Since an SPAC is not an investment company, but a cash-shell vehicle without an operating business that pursues a profit-making goal in a subjective sense only, it may operate under general Italian company law while simultaneously avoiding the obligation to be incorporated either as an SICAV or as an SICAF.[43]

Secondly, in today's economic environment's complexity, influential academic literature has highlighted the importance of considering the overall meaning of a given (although 'atypical') economic transaction when addressing the functional relevance of private autonomy choices through the legal hermeneutical process. Assumed as a conceptual category, the 'economic operation' is conceived as a tool to overcome the inability of purely formal schemes to catch the substantive and multiform attitude of the interests at stake.[44] In our case, this approach may contribute to adequately enhance the overall teleological relevance of the SPAC 'special purpose,' namely the SPAC IPO as a means on the way to the 'de-SPACing' transaction, which is, in turn, the process that eventually leads the raised investments to a 'to-be-scouted' operating business.

Recently, however, following such a functional approach, a widely echoed paper has raised some doubts in this respect. Finding that nearly all pre-merger shareholders exit at the time of the acquisition, this research claims that the extent of redemption rights and refinancing in connection with SPAC mergers by virtue – for instance – of PIPE investments would show that an SPAC IPO and a de-SPAC transaction are largely independent of one another as an empirical matter, thus leading to a critical review of the overall purpose underlying the SPAC transactional structure.[45]

Although crucial, this aspect mainly pertains to the regulatory merits of the SPAC in comparison to both private equity and more traditional IPO processes, opening up a debate that cannot be furthered here.[46]

6.4.1 Corporate Powers and Business Combination Approval

Other issues arise because of the mutual conditioning between the SPAC's special purpose and the activity to fulfill it. Indeed, the strict teleological nature of the shell vehicle requires the capital raised through public subscriptions to be exclusively deployed to carry out the business combination. Until then, such sums must remain unimpaired so that they are eventually used for this purpose or returned to investors. This implies a different regime between the sponsors' contributions – which will serve as the SPAC working capital – and the public shareholders' ones – which will be segregated in the trust/escrow account while waiting for the shareholder approval of the targeted business.[47]

In the case of an Italian SPAC, the question arises whether such a conventional regime of non-disposability of the corporate assets potentially conflicts with Section 2380-*bis* (1) ICC concerning the exclusive power of the directors to 'manage the firm.'[48] On closer examination, this issue involves two distinct, although functionally related, profiles within the SPAC standard design. The first relates to a restriction in the management of the firm. The second concerns the unavailability of the company's assets as a consequence of the powers conferred on a third party to guarantee such a 'limited' management activity on the part of the directors. Here I deal with the former question, while the latter will be discussed in section 6.4.2.

Given its internal relevance, the first problem must be addressed by considering the relationship between the prerogatives of the directors and those attributable to the shareholders' meeting. In this sense, an attempt could then be made in the light of the functional distinction between the 'management of the firm' and the 'organization of the company.'

In general, it can be said that the latter relates to the structure of the shareholders' interest as established in the by-law, which then becomes the yardstick for the negative delimitation of the former.[49] First, however, regarding the corporate stock form, the scope of the distinction must be verified in accordance with the systematic interpretation of Sections 2364 and 2380-*bis* ICC. These clarify that, except for the limited space allowed under Section 2364 (1) (5) ICC, the by-laws may not extend the competence of the shareholders' meeting to nullify the residual managing responsibility of the directors. However, the exact legal value (whether a veto power or a mere consultation) of a possible shareholders' meeting authorization is arguable.[50]

In this respect, it must first be observed that, by not qualifying as a UCI, the SPAC organizational structure is not conditioned by the problem of whether Section 2364 (1) (5) ICC provision would be admissible within the by-laws of an investment company since it could substantially hinder the stricter autonomy prerogative of the managing partners in providing the upstream collective investment management service.[51] Once again, the question must be addressed under general company law. And it could reasonably be argued that the reservation of consent on the business combination in favor of the shareholders' meeting is to be classified as an act of organization of the (shell) company rather than one of management of the firm. In the end, the main hallmark of the SPAC contract is that the traditional features of a 'fir' are temporarily absent. Indeed, the IPO-stage investors intend to make a 'light commitment' which does not yet include any operating business risk exposure. The only risk they are planning to bear is narrowed to the time factor, along with the inability/impossibility of the management team to find a suitable business to acquire. Otherwise stated: if there is no firm, directors have no exclusive power to manage it.

The SPAC is a case of a 'company without a business.' This then makes it possible to enhance the organizational significance of the purpose clause as an element for defining the specific risk conditions that the organized group of the *in pectore* investors intended to assume.[52]

The discussion thus leads to a full appreciation of the SPAC-shell special purpose as an ex-ante bargaining chip.[53] Moreover, the dialectic between corporate powers is here strictly stipulated so that the business combination essentially results in an amendment to the original purpose, thus also functioning as a leeway for individual divestment decisions by dissenters.[54]

This is particularly evident in the by-laws of Italian SPACs, which provide that the completion of the business combination in whatever technical form to be finalized (whether a merger, an equity interest, or an asset purchase), and in any case intended as a unitary transaction entails a prior amendment of the corporate purpose on the part of the shareholders' meeting.[55]

6.4.2 *Shares Subscription and Trust/Escrow Account*

In light of the above, the SPAC corporate governance structure is characterized by a distinctive sovereignty of the shareholders' meeting. By the explicit competencies established within the by-laws, shareholders can approve the business combination, which is the transaction intended to lead the SPAC shell to an operating business. In turn, the board of directors has the primary task of scouting a suitable target, while the execution of the acquisition becomes a subordinate duty.[56] Equally evident, such an internal balance of powers is coupled with a strong protective device provided by segregating the sums contributed by the public investors in the trust/escrow account.[57]

It could be argued that because of the fiduciary obligation of the trustee/escrow agent not to release such sums pending the shareholders' resolution, the 'absence of the firm' discussed earlier exhibits a sort of tangible evidence too. The capital held in trust/escrow is not at the free disposal of the directors, for it cannot be used to carry out any other corporate activity.[58] In light of this, some argue that the use of the escrow account by SPACs is intended to mimic the organizational solution typical of investment funds, resembling the intervention of an independent depositary between the fund manager and the investors.[59]

However, as noted earlier, the SPAC does not exhibit any delegated upstream management of investors' 'financial property' out of which a pooled return is to be extracted through multiple investment/disinvestment decisions. Instead, what stands out here is a participating corporate position, which, without any diaphragm and indeed in force of direct consent by the 'owners' themselves, aims to evolve into a stake in some business risk.

The fact that the SPAC is an operating company 'in the making' makes such a triangular structure more reminiscent of the situation typical of the incorporation phase when contributions in cash have to be deposited with a third party (i.e., a bank) while waiting for the company to be definitively set up.[60] This interpretation is preferable as it better emphasizes the provisional 'absence of the firm,' confirming that, from a functional perspective, the real IPO is the future (and hypothetical) business combination for public investors.

At the same time, the consequent unavailability of the sums on the part of the management board highlights the actual size of the problem anticipated in section 6.4.1. A preliminary question can be readily addressed by considering that the voice on the fundamental 'management' decision (namely, the business combination) is kept by the shareholders and that the trustee/escrow agent is bound to act according to a stringent mandate.[61] Hence, it can be inferred that no core corporate power is transferred outside the company's organizational structure.[62]

Nonetheless, challenges remain in other features.[63] For example, assuming that the participation in an SPAC by public investors can be implemented through a capital increase in exchange for money, several scholars have argued on the potential clash between those statutory rules that – by being rooted in a creditor protection system – establish that the amounts called on the new shares are to be made available to the SPAC's directors,[64] and the SPAC provision whereby such sums must instead be held in trust/escrow.[65]

Consequently, to the extent that the trust/escrow account purported to function as a genuine special asset partitioning mechanism, it would ultimately be at odds with the corporate entity itself as a phenomenon of asset allocation governed by its own typical rules.[66] The question, therefore, remains as to whether and in what technical form such agreements on the use of funds would be permittable vis-a-vis the relevant statutory corporate provisions.[67] According to some, being a mere contractual arrangement, such segregation does not hold against third parties since it would in no way create a 'separate patrimony.'[68]

However, it is remarked that the SPAC is a shell company with no operating business and that, typically, sponsors' contributions are calculated to cover the expected costs of setting up and running the vehicle for 24–36 months, its IPO process, scouting the target and merging with it. If the transaction is not realized in time, or if the shareholders reject it, the contributions of the IPO-stage investors will be reimbursed to them. At the same time, the sponsors' products will be used and presumably consumed in the company's liquidation. Hence, unless there is gross mismanagement by the directors, an SPAC should not incur any additional liability.[69] Yet, as a matter of law, this empirical consideration alone cannot solve the problem of identifying a contractual scheme that can be entirely consistent with the corporate framework. Although some doubts persist, it may be useful to consider the option toward which market practice has followed.

A glance at the listing documents and the by-laws shows that Italian SPACs used to sign a *mandato di amministrazione fiduciari* with a so-called stati trust company.

This deed, the Italian counterpart of the Anglo-Saxon escrow agreement, does not technically constitute a type of trust and does not produce any 'bilateral' asset segregation effect.[70] The 'entrusting' of the assets is here 'transparent' and merely formal, conferring on the agent the only power to administrate them while the full ownership remains with the principal. Hence, the assets, although indeed separated from the trust company's general patrimony (and therefore protected from the claims of its creditors), are still subject to possible suits on the part of the creditors of the principal. In addition, the agent must administer the assets in strict adherence to the instructions received from the principal, who therefore does not lose control over the property.[71]

This is evident from the listing documents, where it is stated that the risk of a reduction of the escrowed amounts due to third-party claims against the SPAC cannot be excluded.[72]

Indeed, the use of the escrow account seems intended to ensure a differentiated *ex ante* allocation of the risk of failure of the SPAC transaction with internal effects only. The distinguishing feature is the fiduciary duty that the escrow agent must fulfill toward the public shareholders by ensuring that the management team respects the dedicated investment function of their contributions. This is achieved by providing that the release of the escrow fund for any payment of goods (whether equity interests or assets) in connection with the business combination is only possible after the directors have filed with the fiduciary (namely, the escrow agent) the shareholders' resolution (or the public notary extract thereof) authorizing such transaction.[73]

This appears to make the overall agreement under consideration resembling a deposit in the interest of a third party, a well-known contractual scheme under Italian law by which the restitution of the *res deposita* to the principal-depositor cannot take place (namely, the deposit is not released) without the consent of the said third party.[74] And it shall be highlighted that the fact that the fiduciary mandate and the deposit of the IPO proceed thereto is (also) 'in the interest of' and not 'in favor of' a third party[75] might be the key ultimately leading to the conciliatory result being sought within the SPAC settings. Since the restitution will, in any event, be made in favor of the depositor (i.e., the SPAC) and not to a third party (namely, the individual investor), it should be then confirmed that there is no attributive transaction other than the one generated by the initial contribution in the context of the SPAC IPO, which will then remain governed by mandatory company law.

The prevalence of company law over private autonomy is evidenced by the listing documents themselves, which, by reproducing the essential clauses of the escrow agreements, maintain the principle of free disposability of funds on the part of the directors for the payment of the 'liquidation value' to redeeming shareholders as well as when the business combination is not finalized in time, and the company must be wound up. For their part, the by-laws reiterate that, in both scenarios, the escrowed capital must be liquidated in accordance with the general principles of company law (namely, such sums are not simply 'returne' to investors). Being third-party interests (i.e., corporate creditors) potentially involved here, no fiduciary protection can interfere with corporate financial structure rules.[76]

6.5 Conclusion

The SPAC represents a financial innovation that, in several respects, has hitherto lived as a sort of an 'in-the-between' entity. Indeed, it stands at the edge between private equity and IPOs, acting as a public shell company aiming to combine with an operating business. It is subject to a mix of 'soft law' permissions and potential 'hard law' limitations.

The SPAC transactional structure reveals its special nature mainly regarding the purpose clause and the internal balance of corporate powers, relying on a highly specific relationship between statutory and contractual provisions, with some important fiduciary implications arising from there. In a sense, the intersection point of all these components is represented by the trust/escrow account, with the resulting obligation of the fiduciary sealing the agreement between the SPAC shareholders and the sponsors/managers. The vibrant debate on SPACs recently initiated in the more developed

US market offers valuable insight into the regulatory merit of the phenomenon vis-a-vis more traditional IPO processes.[77]

A hypothetical regulator, faced with this evidence, should attempt to set out rules capable of curbing the possible negative externalities while at the same time enhancing the favorable aspects of the SPAC innovation in terms of collective well-being.[78]

To this end, a preliminary choice must be made at the formal legal level. Alike elsewhere, Italian SPACs have mainly operated under the provisions of general company law, with some contribution from stock exchange regulations. While in the adaptation phase, the promptness of a 'soft law' solution has perhaps represented a valuable resource, the consolidation of the SPAC experience – and the defense of its reputation – probably requires greater legal certainty about the complete application of its fundamental characteristics. As our analysis has shown, several doubts remain in this respect. A feasible option could be to address them with a narrow set of enabling legal provisions dedicated to better supporting the legitimacy of stock exchange rules.[79]

This seems unavoidable because general company law is not always inclined to support the special nature of the SPAC as a shell company, and – more specifically it's an operating public company 'in the making.' At the same time, some institutional changes within the SPAC structure have become increasingly evident in recent years. This evolutionary trend is markedly oriented toward reducing the investors' voice while further strengthening the exit options granted to them.[80] Such changes respond to concrete needs that emerged in market practice.

However, while this makes it all the more pressing to clarify the consistency of specific typical SPAC mechanisms with mandatory company law, the question arises to what extent such changes can be implemented without blurring the distinguishing features of SPACs from more traditional collective investment schemes.[81]

In any event, sooner or later, SPACs will be subject to more specific regulations.[82] Whether punitive or supportive remains to be seen, most likely depending on the outcomes of the huge wave of SPAC offerings experienced between 2020 and 2021.[83]

Indeed, regarding legal taxonomy, it is hard to imagine that the SPAC will be much longer permitted to live 'among those who are suspended.'

Notes

1 G.O. Nilsson, 'Incentive Structure of Special Purpose Acquisition Companies' (2018) 19 *European Business Organisation Law Review* 253.
2 Alberto Mazzoni, 'Patti di co-vendita e doveri fiduciari', in Antonio Crivellaro (ed), *Trasferimenti di partecipazioni azionarie* (Giuffrè 2017) 211. In relation to further remarks on SPACs and venture capital see Part III of this edited book.
3 Usha Rodrigues and Mike Stegemoller, 'Exit, Voice and Reputation: The Evolution of SPACs' (2013) 37 *Delaware Journal of Corporate Law* 849, 851.

4 Eugenio Barcellona, *La 'gestione collettiva del risparmio' a seguito della Direttiva GEFIA* (Giuffrè 2018) 50, 92.
5 Pierluigi De Biasi, 'La Spac, uno speciale veicolo di investimento e quotazione' (2018) 63 *Rivista delle Società* 713, 717.
6 OECD, *Capital Market Review of Italy* (2020) OECD Capital Market Series, 48.
7 Giovanni Cristofaro, 'Il trust nella quotazione delle Spac (Special purpose acquisition companies)' (2009) 10 *Trusts e attività fiduciarie* 272.
8 However, they can keep the 'in-the-money' warrants offered within the IPO 'units,' thus still possibly making a profit out of the post-merger share market price. See De Biasi (n 5) 728.
9 Nilsson (n 1) 254.
10 G.A. Tasca and L.F. Giacometti, *La SPAC tra Diritto, Finanza e Impresa* (Giuffrè Francis Lefebvre 2020) 1, 58.
11 Daniele D'Alvia, 'The International Financial Regulation of SPACs Between Legal Standardised Regulation and Standardisation of Market Practices' (2020) 21 *Journal of Banking Regulation* 107.
12 OECD (n 6) 49.
13 The management team is compensated trough special 'founder shares' and warrants that in most cases expire worthless in liquidation. Hence, founders/managers might face the pressure of finalising the business combination by the drop-dead date, closing their eyes to 'red flags' and failing to investigate carefully whether the proposed transaction is in the best investors' interest. See *AP Services, LLP v. Lobell, et al.* (N.Y. Supreme Court, 19 June 2015).
14 For a discussion on how these procedural protections should be considered in identifying the correct standard of review of the board's conduct in possible fiduciary duty lawsuits, see Jeffrey Crough, Bryan Gividen and Michael Holmes, 'SPACs & Entire Fairness: What Standard of Review Applies to the de-SPACing Transaction' (*JD Supra*, 14 December 2020) <https://www.jdsupra.com/legalnews/spacs-entire-fairness-what-standard-of-40324/> accessed 15 September 2021.
15 Alex Moeller, *Alternative Initial Public Offering Models* (Mohr Siebeck 2016) 52.
16 Vincenzo Donativi and Piero Corigliano, 'Le SPAC (Special Purpose Acquisition Companies): il modello internazionale e la sua compatibilità col diritto italiano' (2010) 29 *Società* 17.
17 Nilsson (n 1) 254.
18 Filippo Garramone, 'Una panoramica in tema di Special Purpose Acquisition Companies (SPAC)' (2020) *Banca Impresa Società* 131, 159.
19 Rodrigues and Stegemoller (n 3) 870. In the text, I use the words 'contract' and 'company' in a technical sense as a way of contrasting an inter-individual exchange relationship with a form of organization of business activity set by the law, without any implication as to the possibility of qualifying the company itself as a *nexus of contracts*. However, the SPAC may be a good example to reveal both the main merit and conceptual limitations of this approach: the company is indeed a mercantile phenomenon, but it requires some form of cooperation on the part of the legal system. For further remarks see Carlo Marchetti, *La 'Nexus of Contracts Theory': teorie e visioni del diritto societario* (Giuffrè 2000).
20 Because of a change in the business purpose and/or duration of the company. See Section 2437 of the Italian Civil Code.
21 De Biasi (n 5) 729.
22 Nilsson (n 1) 262 (observing that 'Thanks to the trust account, redemption rights and warrants, investing in a SPAC until the completion of the business combination is seen as a risk-free investment with an option').
23 Moeller (n 15) 12.
24 Ibid., 44.

25 Daniele D'Alvia, 'SPACs: limiti e prospettive tra hard law e soft law' (2017) *Rivista del Diritto Societario* 1167.

26 Filippo Annunziata, 'Le società di gestione dei mercati regolamentati' in Mario Cera and Gaetano Presti (eds), *Il Testo Unico finanziario*, vol II (Zanichelli 2020) 1107.

27 Antonio Di Ciommo Andrea Palazzolo and Gustavo Visentini, 'Special Purpose Acquisition Company' (*Iurisprudentes*, 10 July 2020) <https://www.iurisprudentes.it/2020/07/10/special-purpose-acquisition-company-analisi-del-veicolo-dinvestimento-e-della-sua-dinamica-applicativa-nellordinamento-interno-ed-eurounitario/> accessed 15 September 2021.

28 Barcellona (n 4) 92. See also, in France, Annie Maudouit-Ridde and Stéphane Sabatier, 'SPAC: les clés d'une opération réussie' (2021) 313 *Fusions & Acquisitions*. A different view is expressed by D'Alvia (n 25) 1186 and in this edited collection see Part I, Chapters 1 and 2.

29 Translated from *Borsa Italiana* S.p.A., *Avviso n. 3584* (12 March 2015) 3.

30 *See* section 1 (1) (k) and (n) of the TUF.

31 De Biasi (n 5) 734.

32 After all, until the business combination is approved, the SPAC is a 'piggybank company' listing a trust account with no assets but the deposited cash. See also Tasca and Giacometti (n 10) 74.

33 Barcellona (n 4) 52.

34 For similar remarks under French law, see Jean-Baptiste Bourbier and Gersende Renard, 'Le SPAC: un véhicule d'investissement susceptible de réconcilier marchés financiers et capital investissement?' (2018) *Revue OFIS* <https://droit-master-ofis.pantheonsorbonne.fr/revue-ofis> accessed 15 September 2021.

35 *See* section 2 (2) (36) of the Market Rules by *Borsa Italiana* S.p.A., and Section 8 of the AIM Market Rules for Companies.

36 Giuseppe Ferri jr. and Mario Stella Richter jr., 'L'oggetto sociale statutario' (2002) 52(11) *Giustizia civile* 483, 488.

37 Daniele D'Alvia, 'SPAC: A Comparative Study Under US, Asian and Italian Corporate Framework. Soft Law vs. Hard Law' (*SSRN*, August 2014) <http://ssrn.com/abstract=2476867> accessed 15 September 2021.

38 Giuseppe Ferri, *Manuale di diritto commerciale* (13th edn, Utet 2010) 230.

39 Barcellona (n 4) 94.

40 Sections 2082 and 2195 ICC. See Giusppe Ferri jr., *Investimento e conferimento* (Giuffrè 2001) 73.

41 Under German law, some doubts have been raised by David Günther, *Special Purpose Acquisition Companies Und Die Ineffizienz Des Kapitalsystems* (De Gruyter 2021) 148 (asserting that the SPAC corporate purpose would result in an 'artificial division').

42 Mario Porzio, '. . . allo scopo di dividerne gli utili' (2014) 41(4) *Giurisprudenza Commerciale* 661.

43 See Section 1 (1) (i), (i-*bis*), (l) and (m-*ter*) TUF. Apart from the contractual model represented by the mutual fund, these are the two specific organizational forms that an Italian alternative UCI to be set up in the corporate form must adopt considering that, in the field of collective investment management, a principle of typicality still applies. Giuseppe Spolaore, 'La gestione collettiva del risparmio' in Mario Cera and Gaetano Presti (eds), *Il Testo Unico finanziario*, vol. I (Zanichelli 2020) 590.

44 Enrico Gabrielli, *'Operazione economica' e teoria del contratto* (Giuffrè 2013) 159.

45 Michael Klausner, Michael Ohlrogge and Emily Ruan, 'A Sober Look at SPACs' (*SSRN*, 28 October 2020) <https://papers.ssrn.com/sol3/papers.cfm?abstract_id=3720919> accessed 15 September 2021, and forthcoming on Yale Journal on Regulation (2022).

46 The paper by Klausner, Ohlrogge and Ruan, has since 2020 started an animated discussion. See also, under the same title, the debate brought forward on the Harvard Law School Forum on Corporate governance (<https://corpgov.law.harvard.edu/>).

47 De Biasi (n 5) 726. Normally, in Italian SPACs, such sums amount to more than 90% of the post-IPO share capital of the company.

48 Donativi and Corigliano (n 16) 19; D'Alvia (n 37) 21.

49 Carlo Angelici, 'A proposito di 'interessi primordiali" dei soci e "gestione esclusiva" degli amministratori' in Maurizio Irrera (ed), *La società a responsabilità limitata: un modello trans-tipico alla luce del Codice della crisi* (Giappichelli 2020) 456.

50 G.B. Portale, 'Rapporti fra assemblea e organo gestorio nei sistemi di amministrazione' in Pietro Abbadessa and G.B. Portale (eds), *Il nuovo diritto delle società*, vol. 2 (Utet 2006) 25; Angelici (n 50) 351.

51 Luigi Ardizzone, 'Il rapporto tra soci gestori e soci investitori nelle Sicaf' (2016) 61 *Rivista delle Società* 1094, 1099.

52 This is also in accordance with the changed function of the purpose clause with the eclipse of the *ultra vires* doctrine. The purpose clause now mainly serves to define the scope of management's authority rather than the corporation's capacity. This is clear in Section 2380-*bis* (1) ICC too, where the directors' exclusive task of managing the firm is expressly justified within the limits of the corporate purpose. Massimo Miola, 'L'oggetto sociale tra autonomia statutaria ed autonomia gestoria' (2008) 13 *Rivista di Diritto Privato* 703.

53 Angelici (n 50) 220.

54 Ideally, this situation is opposite to that arising from the general commerce clause allowed under English company law, where that dialectic will entirely take place at the level of ordinary business management rather than involving the power to amend the by-laws. See Massimo Bianca, 'Le società con oggetto sociale "unrestricted": un esempio da imitare?' (2009) 36 *Giurisprudenza Commerciale* 293. Still on the conceptual level, it could also be argued that the SPAC relies upon a considerable expansion of the logic underlying Section 2361 ICC, stipulating that '[t]he acquisition of holdings in other companies, although generically admitted in the company by-laws, is not permitted if, by reason of the size and the subject of such purchase, the company's purpose, as described in the by-laws, would become materially changed.' See Angelici (n 50) 460.

55 See for instance the by-laws of *Industrial Star of Italy 3 S.p.A.* (§ 4) and *Spactiv S.p.A.* (§ 3). Similar conclusions are reached by German scholars in the face of the doubtful applicability of the *Holzmüller/Gelatine* doctrine to SPAC merger transactions. See Moeller (n 15) 49; Günther (n 41) 139.

56 Moeller (n 15) 52.

57 Cristofaro (n 7) 275.

58 These sums will be invested in safe assets, mainly short-term treasury bills. It must be stressed that while it is sometimes provided that the trust value also extends to the proceeds of the reinvestment of the sums therein (this is the case in the US), in Italy the prevailing solution is for accrued interests to be used by the directors as working capital. Hence, if the acquisition is not finalized, the investor will only suffer a limited loss on the sums locked up for a couple of years. See Tasca and Giacometti (n 10) 67.

59 De Biasi (n 5) 726.

60 Sections 2331 (4) and 2342 (2) ICC. See M.S. Spolidoro, 'I conferimenti in denaro' in G.E. Colombo and G.B. Portale (eds), *Trattato delle società per azioni*, vol. 1 (Utet 2004) 289.

61 Cristofaro (n 7) 276.

62 See Michele Sandulli, 'Articolo 2380-*bis*' in Michele Sandulli and Vittorio Santoro (eds), *La riforma delle società*, vol. 2/I (Giappichelli 2004) 398.
63 Consider that in Italy the obligation to set up the escrow account is only required by the stock exchange rules governing the MIV market (see Section 2 (2) (37) (9) of the Market Rules cited in note 36). No similar provision can be traced for the AIM, so that for SPACs listed on that system the 'source' of the segregation is simply anchored in the by-laws.
64 See Section 2439 (1) ICC.
65 This problem has been particularly discussed within the German doctrine, and recently reiterated by some Italian scholars. See Moeller (n 15) 44; Günther (n 41) 128; Di Ciommo et al. (n 27).
66 Di Ciommo et al. (n 27) speculate that the presence of the trust account might alter the system governing the liquidation of the company's assets, as the resulting investors' redemption claims would circumvent the seniority of debt within the company's capital structure.
67 Kay-Michael Schanz, 'SPACs – Neue Finanzierungsform und deutsches Recht' (2011) 36 *Neue Zeitschrift für Gesellschaftsrecht* 1407, 1411.
68 De Biasi (n 5) 714, who is asserting that it cannot derogate from the general principle of Section 2740 ICC on the unity of the debtor's assets.
69 Ibid., 735.
70 About this contract, Italian scholars speak of a type of '*fiducia legale*' (legal trust), meaning that it amounts to a fiduciary transaction whose effects are directly predetermined by dedicated statutory provisions (Law n. 1966/1939 and Ministerial Decree of 16 January 1995). See Aurelio Gentili, 'La fiducia: tipi, problemi (e una proposta di soluzione)', in Enrico Ginevra (ed), *La fiducia e i rapporti fiduciari* (Giuffrè 2012) 51.
71 Elisabetta Righini, 'Le società fiduciarie e la fiducia nell'ambito del diritto dei mercati finanziari' (2015) 66 *Studi urbinati* 393.
72 See for instance the admission document of *Innova Italy 1 S.p.A.* and the prospectus of *Space S.p.A.*
73 Similarly, an authorising resolution of the shareholders is required when it comes to converting part of the escrow fund into additional working capital of the SPAC, should the promoters' initial contributions prove insufficient to continue the scouting of the target.
74 Section 1773 ICC. See Arturo Dalmartello, G.B. Portale, 'Deposito (diritto vigente)' in *Enciclopedia del diritto*, vol. 12 (Giuffre 1964) 266.
75 On such distinction see Maurizio Lupoi, 'La realizzazione della funzione di garanzia mediante il deposito a favore e nell'interesse del terzo' (1970) 68 *Rivista del Diritto Commerciale* 441, 459.
76 In Italian SPACs, in the event of liquidation, public investors' common stock will have repayment priority over founders/managers' special shares only. See, e.g., the by-laws of *Space S.p.A.* (§ 21), *Crescita S.p.A.* (§ 23), *Spactiv S.p.A.* (§ 28), and *Industrial Star of Italy 3 S.p.A.* (§ 29).
77 Klausner et al. (n 45); Minmo Gahng, J.R. Ritter and Donghang Zhang, 'SPACs' (*SSRN*, 29 January 2021) <https://papers.ssrn.com/sol3/papers.cfm?abstract_id=3775847> accessed 4 October 2021.
78 Jessica Bai, Angela Ma and Miles Zheng, 'Segmented Going-Public Markets and the Demand for SPACs' (*SSRN*, 1 January 2021) <https://papers.ssrn.com/sol3/papers.cfm?abstract_id=3746490> accessed 4 October 2021.
79 D'Alvia (n 25) 1184.
80 Rodrigues and Stegemoller (n 3) 906; Nilsson (n 1) 259; Günther (n 41) 16.

81 Daniele D'Alvia, 'Come guidare la SPAC Revolution in Italia' (*Norme&Tributi Plus*, 30 October 2020) <https://ntplusdiritto.ilsole24ore.com/art/come-guidare-spac-revolution-italia-ADVTLFz> accessed 4 October 2021.
82 See also Georges Ugeux, 'Regulating SPACs – Before It's Too Late' (*CLS Sky Blog*, 31 March 2021) <https://clsbluesky.law.columbia.edu/2021/03/31/regulating-spacs-before-its-too-late/> accessed 4 October 2021.
83 See Heather Perlberg, 'How the SPAC Era Will End' (*Bloomberg Businessweek*, New York, 15 March 2021) 10.

Part III
Experiments in SPACs

7 Shadow Banking and the Special Purpose Acquisition Company

Yochanan Shachmurove

7.1 Introduction

Shadow banking has changed the nature of financial intermediations. However, the name has a negative connotation of murkiness and uncertainty. "Shadow banking" is an umbrella term that describes non-commercial bank financial activities, which are not subject to financial regulatory oversights. Specifically, its activities, such as credit, maturity, and liquidity transformation, occur with no direct or transparent access to public liquidity sources, insurance from central banks, or credit guarantees from the public sector. This kind of undertaking, an alternate route to creating credit, is conducted by financial intermediaries, a group of institutions called "shadow banks," confined together along a mediation chain known as the shadow banking system.[1]

Non-bank financial institutions, or shadow banks, operate by intermediating credit across an array of different securitization and secured funding practices such as asset-backed securities (ABS), commercial paper (CP), collateralized debt obligations (CDOs), and repurchase agreements (repos) to provide short- and long-term financing. Examples of intermediaries include investment banks, insurance companies, mutual funds, hedge funds, pension funds, private equity funds, mortgage companies, payday lenders, unlisted derivatives traders, and various unlisted instrument corporations.[2]

Remarkably, the official website of the International Monetary Fund (IMF) uses a thought-provoking proverb to introduce the complicated nature of the shadow banking system. "If it looks like a duck, quacks like a duck, and acts like a duck, then it is a duck – or so the saying goes. However, what about an institution that looks like a bank and acts as a bank? Often it is not a bank – it is a shadow bank."[3] The shadow banking system's complexity is recognized and revealed in this seemingly playful manner.

When people think of banks, traditional commercial "big name" banks, such as Citibank, Wells Fargo, Bank of China, or Deutsche Bank, often come to mind. Banks operate by managing the flow of money between people and businesses by channeling money from deposit accounts and extending loans to customers in mortgages, constructions, and other types of debt. It

DOI: 10.4324/9781003169079-11

is important to note that these financial institutions are strictly regulated, supervised by institutions such as central banks designed to safeguard their financial stability and the saver's interest. For example, in the United States, the Federal Reserve Bank serves as the federal regulator of bank-holding corporations.

Shadow banks operate in a similar way to traditional banks, in that one of their main objectives is to rely on and raise short-term money funds using those funds to buy assets with long-term maturities.[4] However, the difference between traditional banks and these novel non-banks is that shadow banks are not subject to the financial regulations that traditional banks face. Consequently, they cannot borrow from a central bank and do not have traditional depositors whose funds are covered by insurance.[5] Moreover, since shadow banks are not categorized as depository institutions, they cannot lend deposits to borrowers. Instead, they rely on money from investors to extend loans.

For stability and shared certainty in the governmental financial system, commercial, traditional banks use secured institutions, such as the Federal Deposit Insurance Corporation (FDIC) in the United States, or other governmental institutions. These organizations protect deposits; examine and supervise financial institutions for safety, soundness, and consumer protection; and manage receiverships. However, users of shadow banks are not protected by these safeguards.

Shadow banks have developed into one of the most significant, growing sources of credit, increasing economic efficiency by moving underutilized resources to better uses, thus significantly contributing to overall global economic activity and growth. However, the increase in the size of the shadow banking system and, therefore, its risk may contribute to its downfall.[6] Moreover, compared with the regulated banking system, shadow banking transforms risk and maturities without direct access to public liquidity or deposit insurance sources, indicating that shadow banking is fundamentally fragile (Pozsar et al., 2012).

Figure 7.1 presents data from the Federal Reserve Bank of the United States on non-bank financial institutions' assets to gross domestic product (GDP) for the world (series DDDI031WA156NWDB) since 1960. Unfortunately, this series has been discontinued since January 2015. Nevertheless, the figure shows the importance of the ratio of the non-bank financial institutions (NBFI) assets to the world's GDP. Interestingly, this ratio reached its peak during the reported period in 1984, when the ratio stood at a staggering 11.28 percent. In the 1990s, the ratio was 4.13, and in the last reported date of 2015, this ratio increased to 6.14.

The following monitoring aggregates are referred to throughout this chapter: (i) The non-bank financial intermediation (NBFI) sector is a broad measure of all non-bank financial entities. It comprises all financial institutions that are, not central banks, banks, or public financial institutions. (ii) Other financial intermediaries (OFIs) comprise the NBFI sector, comprising all financial institutions, not central banks, banks, public financial

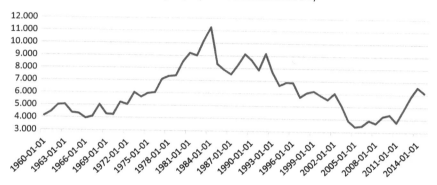

Figure 7.1 Non-bank financial institution assets to gross domestic product (GDP) for world.

Source: FRED https://fred.stlouisfed.org/series/DDDI031WA156NWDB

institutions, insurance corporations, pension funds, or financial auxiliaries. OFIs include, for example, investment funds, captive financial institutions and money lenders (CFIMLs), central counterparties (CCPs), broker-dealers, finance companies, trust companies, and structured finance vehicles. (iii) The narrow measure of NBFI (or "narrow measure of non-bank financial intermediation") comprises a subset of entities of the NBFI sector that authorities have assessed as being involved in credit intermediation activities that may pose bank-like financial stability risks (i.e., credit intermediation that involves maturity/liquidity transformation, leverage or imperfect credit risk transfer) or regulatory arbitrage, according to the methodology and classification guidance used by the Financial Stability Board.

Figure 7.2 presents some data based on the total global financial assets. The data span from 2002 until 2019. The size of the NBFI sector as a percent of total global financial assets stood at 41 percent in 2002, reaching 49.53 percent in 2019.

Figure 7.3 uses the same data source as Figure 7.2. It postulates the global sizes of non-banking Financial Institutions (NBFI) versus banks expressed in US dollars. One can easily observe the increased divergence of global NBFI versus international banks, especially after 2011. In 2019, Banks had US$155.4 trillion versus US$200.15 trillion for the NBFI, a gap of about US$45 trillion.

Shadow banking has been explored in much of the current literature. Earlier, Pozsar et al. (2012) differentiate and categorize shadow banking institutions. They define shadow banking as a group of financial intermediaries that "conduct credit intermediation into a chain of wholesale-funded,

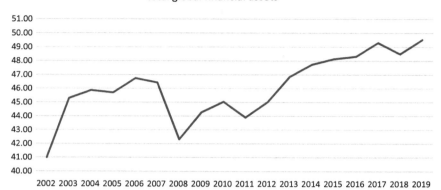

Figure 7.2 Total global financial assets, the NBFI sector as a percentage of total global financial assets.

Source: Jurisdictions' 2020 submissions, Financial Stability Board (FSB) calculations available at: https://www.fsb.org/2020/12/global-monitoring-report-on-non-bank-financial-intermediation-2020/

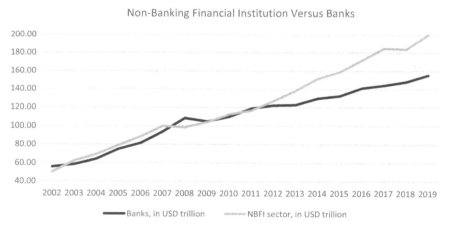

Figure 7.3 The global sizes of non-banking financial institution (NBFI) versus banks in US dollars (trillions).

Source: Jurisdictions' 2020 submissions, Financial Stability Board (FSB) calculations available at: https://www.fsb.org/2020/12/global-monitoring-report-on-non-bank-financial-intermediation-2020

securitization-based lending" (Pozsar et al., 2012). The authors identify four categories of shadow banking. The first category is *internal shadow banking*. These financial intermediaries are branches of banking holding corporations, such as insurance companies, broker-dealers, hedge funds, and money market funds (MMFs). They provide securitization and wholesale funding.

The second category of shadow banking is *external shadow banking*. Although it is not their primary business endeavor, these independent and regulated institutions exercise shadow banking activities.

The third group is labeled as *independent shadow banking*. Financial intermediaries specialized in utilizing structured investment vehicles within the shadow banking sector, stand-alone MMFs, and other asset-backed securities.

The final category is *government-sponsored shadow banking*. These are government-sponsored enterprises (GSEs), which are quasi-governmental entities, or organizations with both private and public features formed to further improve the flow of credit to specific sectors of the economy. Thus, these institutions, although private, provide public financial services. For example, GSEs enable borrowing for customers such as students, farmers, and homeowners. Notable examples in the United States are Fannie Mae and Freddie Mac. Again, it is important to note that these categories may intersect with one another.[7]

"Shadow banking" as a phrase incorporates risky investment products, pawnshop, loan-shark operations, credit default swaps, and peer-to-peer lending between individuals and businesses. The common denominator of these intermediaries is that their practices operate outside the traditional banking system, beyond the supervision of regulators.

Figure 7.4 presents non-bank financial institutions' assets to GDP for the United States. The data are for the period 1996 – 2017. This ratio stood at 108 percent in January 1996; it stands at above 160 percent by January 2017,

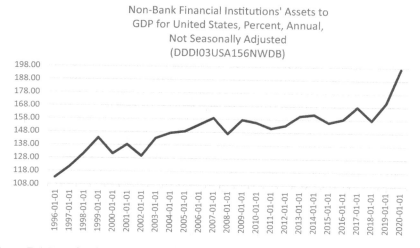

Figure 7.4 Non-bank financial institution assets to GDP for the US.

Source: FRED Graph Observations; Non-Bank Financial Institutions' Assets to GDP for the United States, Percent, Annual, Not Seasonally Adjusted. Original Data: The World Bank. https://fred.stlouisfed.org/series/DDDI03USA156NWDB

and at 197 percent, three years later, that is, January 2020, indicating the sharp rise in the non-bank financial institutions' (NBFI) assets to GDP.

The spread of shadow banking epitomizes the financial system's failure, which led to the Global Financial Crisis 2007–2010. Notably, contrary to the era of the Great Depression, one of the most devastating runs of the Global Financial Crisis 2007–2010 did not stem from commercial, regulated bank deposits. Instead, the recent Global Financial Crisis 2007–2010 originated from non-bank financial institutions, such as the Lehman Brothers and MMFs.[8]

7.2 Non-bank Financial Institutions

Non-bank financial institutions (NBFIs) are broadly defined as institutions other than banks that offer financial services. The US Patriot Act defines a variety of entities as financial institutions. Common examples of NBFIs include, but are not limited to

  I. casinos and card clubs,
  II. airline loyalty programs,
  III. securities and commodities firms (e.g., brokers/dealers, investment advisers, mutual funds, hedge funds, or commodity traders),
  IV. money services businesses (MSB),
  V. insurance companies,
  VI. loan or finance companies,
  VII. credit card rewards programs, and
  VIII. other financial institutions (e.g., dealers in precious metals, stones, or jewels; pawnbrokers).

The policy of low-interest rates by the Federal Reserve System and the spread of non-bank financial institutions decreases the cost of borrowing, destabilizing the cost of credit, and fuels appreciation in real estate and residential market prices. Furthermore, before the crisis, NBFIs relied on creating credit by using short-term, liquid liabilities to fund risky, long-term illiquid assets. This highly volatile activity contributed to the financial system's vulnerability to a run. When this finally happened, the world witnessed one of the most profound financial crises since the Great Depression. All in all, the surfacing of the shadow banking system shifted the systemic risk-return tradeoff toward cheaper credit intermediation at the expense of higher severity of the crisis and costlier intermediation during the following downturns.

Using history as a precautionary measure, governments worldwide chose to protect the traditional banking system by granting them access to backstop liquidity through discount lending and deposit insurance. Before the financial crisis, shadow banking was believed to be a safe practice, with liquidity and credit insurance provided by the private sector, specifically commercial banks and insurance companies, allowing these financial institutions to issue highly liquid short-term liabilities. However, when the private sector failed to support the shadow banking system, credit rating agencies, investors, and regulators lost confidence in the stability of this novel practice. As a result, all underestimated the aggregate risk of shadow banking operations. Thus, this significant structural change in how non-bank financial institutions would continue to operate – replacing the private sector with credit and liquidity guarantees. In 2008, the fall of Lehman Brothers caused most of the shadow banking system to collapse altogether.[9]

Figure 7.5 presents the global sizes of equity and fixed-income funds expressed in US dollars (trillions). Again, the figure illustrates the increased sizes of the two funds, with the equity fund far exceeding the fixed-income fund.

Table 7.1 shows the time series data for credit assets in trillions of US dollars, held by selected OFIs, for 21+ Advanced economies (E.A.)-Group; in trillions of US dollars. The data include broker-dealers, finance companies, hedge funds, MMFs, other investment funds, SFVs, and trust companies.

The remainder of the chapter is organized as follows. Section 7.3 describes shadow banking as it is related to the home-mortgage markets. Section 7.4 elaborates on the MMFs financial institutions. Section 7.5 discusses the fintech sector. Section 7.6 offers a discussion on Special Purpose Acquisition Companies (SPACs). Section 7.7 extends the analysis to the development of shadow banking in the fast-growing economy of China. Section 7.8 concludes.

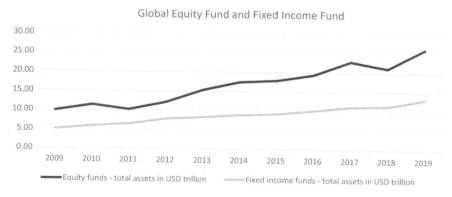

Figure 7.5 Global sizes of equity and fixed-income funds expressed in US dollars (trillions).

Source: Jurisdictions' 2020 submissions, Financial Stability Board (FSB) calculations available at: https://www.fsb.org/2020/12/global-monitoring-report-on-non-bank-financial-intermediation-2020

Table 7.1 Credit assets held by selected OFIs (21+EA-Group; in USD [trillions])

Year	Broker-dealers	Finance companies	Hedge funds	Money market funds	Other investment funds	SFVs	Trust companies
2002	2.33	2.21	0.00	2.96	2.27	2.33	0.04
2003	2.75	2.44	0.00	2.78	2.52	2.63	0.05
2004	3.26	2.62	0.00	2.63	2.76	3.15	0.05
2005	3.52	2.70	0.00	2.87	3.25	4.06	0.07
2006	3.80	2.87	0.00	4.32	3.60	4.96	0.08
2007	4.55	2.94	0.00	5.31	4.12	5.48	0.21
2008	3.85	3.13	0.07	6.29	4.71	5.40	0.21
2009	3.55	2.87	0.09	5.69	6.59	7.43	0.29
2010	4.80	3.38	0.14	4.93	7.33	6.44	0.38
2011	5.00	3.40	0.91	5.00	7.95	6.24	0.56
2012	5.27	3.35	1.27	4.81	9.21	5.70	0.86
2013	4.85	3.36	1.34	4.70	10.02	5.17	1.21
2014	4.84	3.41	1.92	5.03	10.76	5.06	1.45
2015	4.67	3.34	1.87	5.34	11.25	4.97	1.59
2016	4.83	3.41	2.01	5.47	12.22	4.89	1.80
2017	4.94	3.53	2.47	5.64	13.51	4.85	2.31
2018	5.43	3.76	2.93	5.85	13.77	5.01	2.14
2019	5.57	3.99	3.45	6.72	15.77	5.37	1.93

Source: Total global financial assets, the NBFI sector as percent of total global financial assets. Source: Jurisdictions' 2020 submissions, Financial Stability Board (FSB) calculations available at: https://www.fsb.org/2020/12/global-monitoring-report-on-non-bank-financial-intermediation-2020/.

7.3 Home Mortgage

Shadow banking first piqued the curiosity of economists because of its ability to turn home mortgages into securities. The securitization process began with creating a mortgage that was bought and sold by financial agencies to become part of a mortgage loan package used to back securities sold to investors. The value of mortgage-backed securities was associated with the other loans in the package. Any payouts were from the interest and principal customers paid on their mortgage loans. All in all, nearly every step of the "securitization chain," from the creation of the mortgage to the sale of the security, took place beyond the oversight of financial regulatory entities.[10]

As a result, the US home mortgage market structure is highly segmented, with traditional banks affecting an increasingly smaller part of it. In the last few decades, financial institutions have challenged traditional banking, which does not take deposits and typically does not have brick-and-mortar branches but issues mortgage loans. After the global economic crisis of 2007–2009, the predatory lending to low-income households, and the bursting of the housing bubble with mortgage-backed securities collapsing in value, the world has become aware of the risks involved in home funding and banking, with one severe risk being a phenomenon called "shadow banking."

During the years leading up to the financial crisis, the government-sponsored institutions – Freddie Mac and Fannie Mae – as well as commercial banks, were, in practice, active in the unregulated lending sector.[11]

In the last forty years, the worldwide banking sector has experienced three significant trends: the continual decline in real interest rates, the shift of bank investments from corporate loans to real estate loans (mortgages), and the rise of unregulated banking or "shadow banking" in comparison to traditional regulated banking. In this manner, Pool (2018) outlines a framework that connects all these three trends in his paper "Mortgage debt and shadow banks," explaining the correlation between the growth of shadow bank liabilities and mortgage loans.

The causal relationship among these trends is attributable to the consistent decline in interest rates, which led to increases in the share of real estate investments, causing the interbank market for mortgage securities to become more liquid. The rise in funding liquidity consequentially gives shadow banks a comparative advantage in the supply of mortgage loans compared to traditional banks, causing an increase in the shadow banking sector. The growth in the shadow banking sector, which led to many uninsured deposits, exposes the entire financial market to risk.

Pool (2018) differentiates between two types of assets that function as collateral for loans: physical capital for corporate loans and real estate for mortgages. These assets have different supply elasticities, with the supply of physical capital being more elastic than the supply of houses. The lower the supply elasticity of the collateral, the higher the fluctuations in price and credit. With the inflow of deposits onto bank balance sheets lowering interest rates, individuals are prompted to demand more credit for assets, houses, and physical capital. However, since the housing supply is relatively inelastic compared to physical capital, the collateral value for mortgage loans increases.

Therefore, banks must increase the capacity for mortgage lending relative to that corporate lending. This correlation between the deposit inflow and the subsequent increase in mortgage lending establishes the cause of growth in the shadow banking sector. Both types of financial institutions – banks, and non-banks – can grant loans or deposits to households, with the main difference being that banks must purchase insurance to safeguard their deposits. Because of mortgage lending growth, the interbank market for mortgage loans has become more prevalent and liquid.

The increase in funding liquidity by non-bank financial institutions led shadow banks to lower their liquidity risk exposure, allowing them to use regulatory arbitrage to their advantage concerning the supply of mortgage loans. Consequently, the shadow banking system experienced growth compared to the traditional banking system since the mortgage loan market grew relatively faster than the corporate loan market.[12]

Nevertheless, it is critical to denote the risks that the financial stability of the global economy faces since the shift of loans directed at housing investment rather than physical capital formation might harm the economy's production capacity, making it harder to repay the mortgage debt.[13] Furthermore, the rise of shadow banking may also be a sign of mounting risk since it increases asset price volatility, increasing the likelihood of fire sales and bank runs.

As mentioned earlier, the growing shadow banking sector is exposed to another financial crisis, considering that many uninsured deposits are created. This growth further strengthens the dependency of banks on the Central Bank for liquidity support. Pool (2018) analyzes how deposit inflows reduce interest rates and increase mortgage demand. This, in turn, fosters the growth of the shadow banking sector, reducing financial stability since shadow banks create more uninsured deposits compared with the socially optimal allocation of credit supply.[14]

The American residential mortgage market represents the largest customer finance market. In 2020, the size of the US mortgage market was $11.05 trillion as measured by outstanding mortgages, with $1.91 trillion in new mortgages funded in 2020.[15,16] The mortgage market has a unique structure, with the federal government playing a critical role in regulating home loans. To make the process of issuing mortgages more accessible, the federal government created two private GSEs, Fannie Mae and Freddie Mac. Since 2004, in an attempt to be more profitable, the two companies have been increasing the riskiness of their loan portfolios.

With the fall in housing prices, the fate of these mortgage companies became apparent. By allocating loans to different financial entities, the GSEs expanded the mortgage market, increased the availability, and lowered the credit price, one of the leading causes of why the US homeownership rate rises.

The question becomes, "Why do Financial Entities and Investors prefer Shadow Banking when it comes to mortgages?" The structural breakdown of banking and non-banking institutions is crucial for correctly recognizing the corresponding positions of traditional and shadow banks in the mortgage market. Mainly, these structural differences between traditional and shadow banks lead to two types of division in the mortgage market, as Greg Buchak of the University of Chicago, Gregor Matvos of the University of Texas, Tomasz Piskorski of Columbia University, and Amit Seru of Stanford University, outline in their 2018 policy brief titled "Regulation of the Mortgage Market Must Consider Shadow Banks." First, the heavier regulations and stricter compliance requests that traditional banks are burdened with certainly positioned them at a competitive disadvantage in the mortgage market. Buchak et al. (2018) describe a period from 2008 until 2017 when bank capital requirements became stricter. As a result, shadow banks grew their share of compliant mortgage originations from around 25 percent to almost 60 percent.

Another critical aspect of market segmentation is a balance sheet capacity to hold mortgages. Banks with more owners' capital are more prone to holding mortgages on their balance sheets than inadequately capitalized banks,

which will inexorably start behaving more like shadow banks and begin selling the mortgages they create. Overall, the shadow banking sector has a more
significant advantage in the mortgage market, primarily because of the lack
of regulations.[17]

7.4 Money Market Funds

In current literature, shadow banking has been introduced as one of the primary sources for the recent financial crises. Even though shadow banking has
been a well-studied topic, particularly after the Global Financial Crisis 2007–
2010, there is still a feeling of unfamiliarity connected to this unregulated
banking method. One of the distinguishing features of the concept of shadow
banking is the so-called MMFs that have been thought to contribute a large
part to the spread of systematic risk. Kodres (2015) points out that during
the financial crisis, experts noticed that some of the wholesale funding runs
were on MMFs, which had previously worked with US and European commercial and universal banks.[18] Endrejat and Thiemann (2020) explore how
asset-backed commercial papers and money market mutual funds develop
following a financial crisis.[19]

MMFs can be defined as independent shadow banking entities that
invest in low-risk "money market" instruments, such as short-term credit
or liquid debt instruments, government treasury bills, securities – backed
by company debt or trade receivable – CDs, in the end, to provide repurchase (repo) financing.[20,21] MMFs have an increasingly important role in the
shadow banking sector, primarily because of their direct involvement in risk
and maturity transformation. This implies that they are potentially the leading causes of the systematic risk perpetuated by the non-bank institutions.
However, Pellegrini, Meoli, and Urga (2017) pinpoint that MMFs are typically perceived to have negligible risk because their asset does not carry the
possibility of the so-called maturity mismatch. Therefore, the authors adopt
the Conditional Value-at-Risk (CoVaR) measure introduced by Adrian and
Brunnermaier (2016), which calculates a financial institution's contribution
to systematic risk, quantifying the MMF contribution as a different sector of
the financial industry.

It is essential to highlight that within the shadow banking system, the
wholesale funding structure is the reason for generating the systematic risk,
a concept that Paltalidis et al. (2015) explore in their study "Transmission
Channels of Systemic Risk and Contagion in the European Financial Network."[22] That is why MMFs are essential to the wholesale funding structure and one of the most important suppliers of credit. Therefore, they have
been thought of as posing high risks for the structure of shadow banking.
However, the question is whether MMFs have been the reason for generating
systematic risk. In that case, it is not vital to consider the liquidity mismatch
since they finance their asset through investors' shares, not liabilities, as traditional banks do. The concern with liquidity mismatch is that MMFs may have

trouble returning an investor's deposits if they do not receive cash immediately available. This led Pellegrini, Meoli, and Urga (2017) to offer two hypotheses that directly tackles the question of liquidity mismatch and MMFs:

Hypothesis 1: The higher is the liquidity mismatch of an MMF, the higher will be the contribution to systemic risk.
Hypothesis 2: During a financial crisis, the higher the liquidity mismatch of an MMF is, the lower the contribution to systemic risk will be. (Pellegrini, Meoli and Urga, 2017)[23]

Figure 7.6 presents retail and institutional MMFs in billions of dollars using weekly, not seasonally adjusted data from FRED (series WRMFSL and WIMFNS). As a result of the Global Financial Crisis 2007–2010, the US Securities and Exchange Commission (SEC) took steps to stabilize the industry. A fundamental change was directed at institutional prime MMFs sold to institutional investors and financial firms rather than individual investors. They are now required to let the share price of the fund float to reflect price changes in the market prices of the assets they hold. This change allows for *breaking the buck*, that is, redeeming shares for less than $1. Retail prime MMFs were allowed to keep their price per share at $1 but were authorized to charge investors redemption fees when selling shares and limit redemption volume during a given time period.

Figure 7.6 Retail and institutional money market funds in US dollars (billions) using weekly, not seasonally, adjusted data from FRED (the series WRMFSL and WIMFNS at https://fred.stlouisfed.org/series/WIMFNS and https://fred.stlouisfed.org/series/WRMFSL).

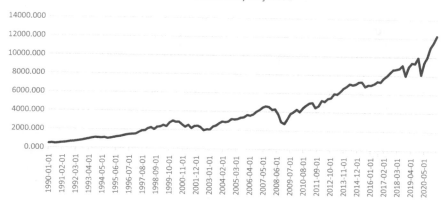

Figure 7.7 Mutual fund shares held by households and nonprofit organizations in US dollars (billions), not seasonally adjusted data from FRED (the series WRMFSL and WIMFNS at https://fred.stlouisfed.org/series/HNOMFSA).

This regulatory change did not help in March 2020, during the COVID-19 pandemic, when investors started redeeming money market mutual fund shares, forcing the funds to sell their commercial paper. On the buyers' side of the market, the 2008 regulations intended to reduce risk. Large banks such as JPMorgan Chase and Goldman Sachs could only buy a limited amount of the commercial paper the funds were attempting to sell. The regulation dovetailed the results of 2008, causing the commercial paper market to freeze. Once again, the US Federal Reserve Bank stepped in, reviving its Commercial Paper Funding Facility and directly purchasing CP, restoring liquidity to the financial markets. Figure 7.6 clearly shows the effects of this in both 2008 and 2020.

Figure 7.7 shows the explosion in the use of mutual fund shares held by households and nonprofit organizations in US dollars (billions). It increased from about $462 billion in 1990 to $12,290 billion in the second quarter of 2021.

7.5 Fintech

Throughout this chapter, the focal point is that financial intermediation has shifted from the traditional banking sector to shadow banking. Although up until this point in time, there has yet to be a significant systematic analysis behind this drastic shift to shadow banking. Two leading hypotheses have tried to explain the rise of shadow banking: the regulatory burden and more significant capital constraints associated with traditional banking causing higher regulatory costs and changing the price of their funding services.

According to Buchak et al. (2017), the other hypothesis is a disruptive technology. In this case, the novelty of 21st-century technological change, or the recent rise of the fintech industry, created a new market and value network for cheaper and higher quality products that eventually displaced established market-leading firms and products.

The fintech industry boomed by 2015 due to shadow banking loans, which accounted for a third of all the loans. This suggests that the rise of fintech had a considerable impact on the decline of traditional banking. Furthermore, technological innovation is also an indicator of the decline of traditional banking, since the rapid pace at which it is changing and evolving suggests the dexterity of the business model that is shadow banking and its ability to cooperate and partner with other institutions, something that traditional banks are relatively weak in doing. Also, according to Buchak et al. (2017), if fintech lenders experience reduced costs because they offer better and newer products to customers, fintech lenders will pass those cost savings to borrowers and offer more convenience.[24]

Overall, the fintech industry has improved the core of financial services. However, it has yet to succeed in acquiring a dominant position in the market. For reference, fintech credit accounts make up only a tiny share of the total credit of countries. Furthermore, fintech hubs are only found in countries with higher average annual incomes per capita and less competitive financial systems, such as the U.K., the United States, and China. Moreover, most countries still need to build an ecosystem infrastructure and rely on traditional financial infrastructure to build their businesses. Although nevertheless, according to the Organisation for Economic Co-operation and Development (OECD), they still need to alter the competitive scene in finance and business. They have serious potential in the realm of disruptive technology and the unprecedented speed of innovation change.[25]

Wang et al. (2021) describe how the development of FinTech impacts risk-taking with banks. They use Chinese unbalanced bank-level panel data for the years 2011 through 2018. The development of fintech is evaluated by obtaining information about fintech from media sources. Their findings indicate that bank risk is worsened due to increased fintech development. Declining asset quality due to fintech development is prominent in larger banks, shadow banks, and thus the lower overall efficiency of financial markets. While fintech initially escalates bank risk, it is expected to reduce risks by traditional banks over time.

7.6 Special Purpose Acquisition Companies and Shadow Banking

SPACs have been at the current forefront of venture capital. These are alternative investment vehicles that provide private companies access to the public market through a reverse merger rather than a traditional initial public offering (IPO). They mainly acquire private companies or startups looking for an easier path to "going public," completely reinventing the conventional IPO route. The formation of these investment vehicles dates to 18th-century

England, where blank check companies were first mentioned as "blind pools" during the South Sea Bubble (see, for example, Shachmurove and Vulanovic (2015, 2016, 2017)).

Since being introduced to US markets, SPACs have become very popular, from the number of SPAC IPOs only 1 in 2009 to 248 by 2020, which amounts to a 320% increase. This results from SPACs outperforming traditional IPOs, accounting for raising $79.87 billion in gross proceeds from 237 counts with an average IPO size of $337 million.[26] In addition, 2021 even surpassed the amount of capital that SPACs raised, accounting for $88.5 billion in capital.[27]

Table 7.2 shows total US IPOs and SPAC-IPOs. Whereas in 2003, the percent of SPAC IPO out of total IPOs was almost zero, in the year 2020, it increased dramatically to 46 percent. Furthermore, in 2021 this statistic stands at 59 percent.

Table 7.2 SPAC IPOs and US IPOs activities[28]

Year	SPAC IPOs	Total US IPOs	%	SPAC proceeds $M	TOTAL US IPO proceeds $M	2%
2021	368	525	70	112,804	190,689	59
2020	248	450	55	83,361	179,364	46
2019	59	213	28	13,600	72,200	19
2018	46	225	20	10,750	63,890	17
2017	34	189	18	10,048	50,268	20
2016	13	111	12	3,499	25,779	14
2015	20	173	12	3,902	39,232	10
2014	12	258	5	1,750	93,040	2
2013	10	220	5	1,447	70,777	2
2012	9	147	6	490	50,131	1
2011	16	144	11	1,110	43,240	3
2010	7	166	4	503	50,583	1
2009	1	70	1	36	21,676	0
2008	17	47	36	3,842	30,092	13
2007	66	299	22	12,094	87,204	14
2006	37	214	17	3,384	55,754	6
2005	28	252	11	2,113	61,893	3
2004	12	268	4	485	72,865	1
2003	1	127	1	24	49,954	0
TOTAL	1004			265,242		

Source: SPAC Analytics, SPAC Analytics – Home, n.d. https://www.spacanalytics.com/

The rise of SPACs can be related to shadow banking since the recent boom in the SPACs market is also causing an increase in the shadow banking system. This increase is connected to SPACs being very active in fintech. SoFi, the Neo-bank, and digital lenders are examples of Fintech companies taking the SPACs route to access the public market. SoFi raised more than $3 billion in capital, positioning itself in lending, investments, a mortgage, and wealth management business. A similar situation occurred with Chime and Robinhood when they reached a valuation worth DecaBillions (or $14 billion for Chime). SPACS gives firms, especially startups, a cheaper, more sustainable route to an IPO. SPACs are revolutionizing current worldwide financial institutions. They are on the way to becoming a serious actor on the global finance stage since they can reshape financial markets and the traditional business model.

7.7 China and Shadow Banking

The COVID-19 pandemic has affected governments, financial markets, and societies worldwide. The Chinese economy was hit, impacting its foreign trade, resulting in foreign demand slumps and disruption in supply chains, labor markets, and the overall economy's monetary and fiscal aspects.[29] Nevertheless, although the People's Republic of China's government has implemented strict measures, the economy has almost normalized and is back on track.

However, Chinese financial regulators are concerned about risks as the economy opens. Because of an increase in property prices, Chinese household debt reached 150 percent of its disposable income in December 2020, with a significant portion financed by shadow banking. The People's Bank of China (PBC) defines Chinese shadow banking as "credit intermediation involving entities and activities outside the regular banking system." As mentioned earlier, since shadow banking processes operate outside the reach of financial regulation, that is, outside of the traditional banking sector, they lack the safety insurance guaranteed by the government in the form of credit insurance or lender of last resort services by the Chinese Central Bank.[30]

The shadow banking system represents a vital source of finance in China. Dissimilar to the case in other economies, Chinese shadow banking is mainly dominated by commercial banks due to the bank-dominated financial system. Lee (2013) describes how China draws more attention to shadow banking-based risk. This is due to the issues that began in June 2013 in China. Shadow banking in China has been a worry for many years. Banks use wealth management products to provide investors with securitized deposits informally.

Overall, shadow banking in developed markets operates parallel to traditional banks through the securitization of loans, mortgages, and wholesale funding. Resources are raised through capital markets, using unique purpose entities and repossession agreements. As described earlier, regulatory arbitrage is a critical factor in the global emergence of shadow banking. However, China has a history of the emergence of its shadow banking system.

In 2010, credit tightening and the imposition of unique banking regulations triggered the rapid growth of the Chinese shadow banking system.

The Global Financial Crisis 2007–2010 did not severely impact China as it did other advanced economies. However, the decline in capital inputs from foreign direct investment still resulted in the government providing a "booster" for the economy in the form of a $586 billion stimulus package. The most considerable portion of the package, almost 75 percent, was utilized for infrastructure building. The rest had to be financed by local governments, which were already facing a significant structural burden since they could not borrow funds themselves and faced restrictions on lending. This turned out to be a substantial reason for shadow banking to grow in the first place, along with an increase in fixed investment, driving economic growth but at a high cost.

Bell et al. (2021) describe Chinese changes and responses to the Global Financial Crisis 2007–2010. This includes a significant increase in the spread of Chinese shadow banking. They use historical institutional theory to analyze these changes. After the Global Financial Crisis 2007–2010, Chinese development is analyzed to investigate how the overall banking and financial sectors have changed. Bell et al. (2021) use this institutional approach to find a link between the different theories they postulate. Shadow banking in China has much in common with other countries, such as credit creation and regulatory arbitrage. However, some of its features are products of the Chinese financial and regulatory systems.[31]

Zhu (2021) explores the increasing number of Chinese shadow banks since 2009. He argues that this trend is not a result of the Global Financial Crisis 2007–2010 but has been part of the Chinese financial system since the 1980s. This stems from the desire to bypass requirements and directives for lending that the central government issues to banks. Two types of shadow banking are in the foreground, influenced by either banks or state-owned enterprises. Zhu (2021) concludes that shadow banking positively impacts real estate investments. However, shadow banking negatively impacts investments outside real estate by private firms.[32]

China operates through a so-called bank-based financial system, and securities financing (debt and equity) presents only approximately one-fifth of the total credit to non-financial institutions. It is also important to note that banks and the financial sector are predominately state-owned. Therefore, the primary function of Chinese commercial banks is taking deposits and making loans.

At the beginning of the reformation of the Chinese economy, the relaxation of the financial discipline in the form of softening budget constraints was quite alarming for the banking sector. As a result, the state-owned banks experienced corporatization transformations like privatizing state-owned enterprises (SOEs), making them far more autonomous and profit-driven. However, in 1995, banks and their day-to-day operations became more regulated with the passing of the PBC and the law of commercial bank.

This reform was further reinforced by establishing the China Banking Regulatory Commission agency in 2003, a state council-authorized entity that regulates and supervises Chinese banking, insurance institutions, and the public listing of all the central commercial banks in the 2000s. These events heightened the competition in the Chinese banking sector, promoting financial innovations and eventually leading to increases in the shadow banking sector.[33]

This competition among banks for issuing deposits induces a rise in wealth management products (WMPs), a saving instrument with no imposed ceiling on the deposit rate. As a result, at the beginning of the 21st century, banks began to issue wealth management products with higher returns.[34] Moreover, the imposition of a stricter loan-to-deposit relationship in the 2010s increased the number of non-guaranteed wealth management products. This off-loading led to exuberant shadow banking activities.[35]

This type of banking can be defined from the perspective of the credit money-creation process while showcasing the main differences between traditional and non-traditional banking practices in China. Sun (2019) presents an in-depth analysis of the critical role of Chinese shadow banks in the money creation process and their effects on monetary policy operations and financial risk management. He analyzes the Chinese shadow banking sector's money-creation mechanisms in detail, investigating its impact on financial risk based on surveys of recent regulations.

Sun (2019) defines the difference between banks' shadow and shadow banking in China as follows: "*Banks' shadow* is defined as banks' money creation through accounting treatments that generate liabilities from assets, whereas *traditional shadow banking* refers to credit creation by non-bank financial intermediaries through money transfer." It is important to note that even though shadow banking in China operates in the same way as it does in other economies, banks' shadows are loans that take the form of different types of assets, challenging the monetary policy and its efficiency by hindering its ability to influence money creation and therefore causing financial stability risks. It also disrupts banking regulations regarding lending and exacerbates the accumulation of systemic risk.

Due to the rapid growth of the Chinese shadow banking system, many studies have recently concentrated on analyzing shadow banking as a relatively unique feature of the country's financial system. Dang et al. (2015) explore the phenomenon from a bank-centric perspective, underlining an asymmetrical perception of the risks which stem from shadow banking activities. Wang et al. (2016) emphasize the role of credit controls and the liberalization of interest rates in contributing to the rapid rise of Chinese shadow banking. Chen, Ren, and Zha (2018) examine the impact of shadow banks on the effectiveness of monetary policy by analyzing entrusted loans. Ehlers et al. (2018) provide a comprehensive and structured view of Chinese shadow banking. They introduce a shadow banking map for the PRC, emphasizing commercial banks and their role. Although their structural map of Chinese shadow banking is informative, it is too complex to convey an accurate picture of the substance of activities of this sector.

Sun (2019) is the first to systematically emphasize the role of money creation by the shadow banking sector, primarily focusing on its effect on financial risks and monetary policy. He provides a measurement of the Chinese shadow banking system using the deduction approach introduced by Sun and Jia (2015). This approach measures the banks' shadow from the banks' liability side by deducing all "non-shadow assets" from the possible liabilities. With this, Sun (2019) induces that banks' shadow amounts to a large share of the credit money creation process, thus amounting to substantially more financial risk. Additionally, the paper empirically analyzes the effect of shadow banking on financial risk at both the macro and micro levels, summarizes, evaluates the regulations implemented by the Chinese government on shadow banking, and provides solutions to the related issues.[36]

7.8 Conclusion

This chapter on shadow banking thoroughly investigates vital aspects of this critical phenomenon in the contemporary global economy. By presenting different definitions of the term, this chapter also explores its resulting categorization, an in-depth historical overview of the development of shadow banking, and a focus on the Global Financial Crisis 2007–2010. By discussing topics such as home mortgages, MMFs, Fintech, the SPACs industry, and the Chinese shadow banking system, the emphasis is put on the growing global reach of shadow banking and its overall contribution to the future of financial intermediations.

Shadow banking is defined under an umbrella term that includes all non-commercial bank financial activities not subject to financial regulatory oversight. More precisely, shadow banking creates an alternate route to creating credit, which entails that its main actions of credit, maturity and liquidity transformation occur with no direct access to public sources from central banks nor credit guarantees from the public sector. It is also explained that these non-bank financial institutions intermediate credit across an array of different securitization and secured funding practices such as asset-backed securities, commercial paper, collateralized debt obligations, and repurchase agreements to provide short and long-term financing.

One of the most critical issues discussed in this chapter is the nature of the shadow banking industry in that it develops an in-depth compare and contrast overview of shadow banking and traditional banking, through which the distinctive form of the shadow banking system is put forth. Shadow banks operate similarly to conventional banks by relying on and raising short-term money funds and then utilizing those funds to buy assets with long-term maturities. However, throughout this chapter, the emphasis is also on the difference between traditional and non-banking financial instructions – traditional banks rely on heavy and strict regulations. In contrast, shadow banks are not subject to the financial restrictions that conventional banks are. This is also why shadow banks rely on investors' money to extend loans. In addition, commercial (traditional) banks use secured institutions, such as the FDIC in the United States or other governmental institutions, to uphold stability.

Before the Global Financial Crisis 2007–2010, it is essential to note that non-bank financial instructions created credit by using short-term liquid liabilities to fund risky, long-term illiquid assets, a very unpredictable activity in and of itself. This eventually led to the financial system having its first run, and the world finally witnessed one of the biggest financial crises since the Great Depression. All in all, the emergence of the shadow banking system shifted the systemic risk-return tradeoff toward cheaper credit intermediation at the expense of higher severity of the crisis and costlier intermediation during the following downturns.

Shadow banking has also played a significant part in the global financial system because it turned home mortgages into securities. This is seen in the notion that the US home mortgage market structure is highly segmented, with traditional banks affecting an increasingly smaller part. The main reason for this decrease is that in the last few decades, traditional banking has been challenged by shadow banking financial institutions since they do not take deposits and typically do not have brick-and-mortar branches. Overall, this chapter concludes that the global banking sector has undergone three significant trends in the last forty years: the continued decline in real interest rates, the shift of bank investments from corporate loans to real estate loans (mortgages), and the rise of unregulated banking or "shadow banking" in comparison to traditional regulated banking. The chapter helps to explain the correlation between the growth of shadow bank liabilities and mortgages.

One of the main questions this chapter aims to answer is "why do financial entities and investors prefer the shadow banking route relative to the traditional banks when it comes to conforming to the mortgage market?" This is further explained in the structural breakdown of both bank and non-bank institutions that this chapter tries to present, which is vital for recognizing the corresponding standings of both types of institutions in the mortgage market. With traditional banks having the burden of stricter compliance requests, and capital requirements, shadow banks had the opportunity to grow their stake in mortgage originations. As a result, the shadow banking sector has a more significant advantage in the mortgage market, primarily because of the lack of regulations.

This chapter also develops another look at the importance of shadow banking in the contemporary global economy by looking at the effect non-bank financial entities had on the fintech industry shadow banking lending. The fintech industry exploded in 2015. The sector had grown to the point where the sort of loans now accounted for a third of all loans. The expansion in the SPACs market is also fueling an increase in the shadow banking system. Therefore, the growth of SPACs can be attributed to the rise in the shadow banking sector. Finally, this chapter examines the shadow banking sector's increasing presence in one of the most developed and rapidly growing economies of the 21st century – China. This chapter uncovers the growing importance of the Chinese shadow banking system as a vital source of finance.

Interestingly, Chinese shadow banking is mainly dominated by commercial banks. Shadow banking in developed markets operates parallel to traditional banks through the securitization of loans, mortgages, and wholesale funding. Resources are raised through capital markets, using unique purpose entities and repossession agreements. As described earlier, regulatory arbitrage is a critical factor in the global emergence of shadow banking.

One of the most important conclusions from this chapter is that nowadays, shadow banks have developed into one of the most significant, growing sources of credit, increasing economic efficiency by moving underutilized resources to better uses and thus significantly contributing to overall global economic activity and growth. However, this continuing growth of the shadow banking system is also one of the many reasons for its associated risk and its consequent potential failure. As explained earlier, the shadow banking system's fragility stems from its practice of transforming risk and maturities with no direct access to public liquidity or deposit insurance sources.

Appendix

The data for Table 7.1 is from the Financial Stability Board, 2020. Here are the definitions of each category.

The 29-Group includes Belgium, France, Germany, Ireland, Italy, Luxembourg, the Netherlands, Spain, Argentina, Australia, Brazil, Canada, the Cayman Islands, Chile, China, Hong Kong, India, Indonesia, Japan, Korea, Mexico, Russia, Saudi Arabia, Singapore, South Africa, Switzerland, Turkey, the United Kingdom, and the United States.

The 21+EA Group includes Argentina, Australia, Brazil, Canada, the Cayman Islands, Chile, China, Hong Kong, India, Indonesia, Japan, Korea, Mexico, Russia, Saudi Arabia, Singapore, South Africa, Switzerland, Turkey, the United Kingdom, the United States, and the Euro area.

The advanced Economy Group includes Belgium, France, Germany, Ireland, Italy, Luxembourg, the Netherlands, Spain, Australia, Canada, the Cayman Islands, Hong Kong, Japan, Korea, Singapore, Switzerland, the United Kingdom, the United States, and the Euro area.

The Emerging Market Economy Group includes Argentina, Brazil, Chile, China, India, Indonesia, Mexico, Russia, Saudi Arabia, and South Africa.

Notes

1 'Regulation of the Mortgage Market Must Consider Shadow Banks' (*SIEPR*, 1 December 2018) <https://siepr.stanford.edu/research/publications/regulation-mortgage-market-shadow-banks>.

2 Emmanuel Farhi and Jean Tirole, 'Shadow Banking and the Four Pillars of Traditional Financial Intermediation' (2021) 88(6) *The Review of Economic Studies* 2622–2653.
3 Laura E. Kodres, 'What Is Shadow Banking? – Back to Basics – Finance & Development' (June 2013) *International Monetary Fund* <https://www.imf.org/external/pubs/ft/fandd/2013/06/basics.htm>.
4 Craig Kirsner, *Investment Adviser Representative. "What You Need to Know About the Shadow Banking System Now."* (Kiplinger, 21 June 2019) <https://www.kiplinger.com/article/credit/t040-c032-s014-what-you-need-to-know-about-shadow-banking-system.html>.
5 Kodres (n 3).
6 Global Monitoring Report on Non-Bank Financial Intermediation. Financial Stability Board, 2020 <https://www.fsb.org/wp-content/uploads/P161220.pdf>
7 Z. Pozsar, T. Adrian, A. Ashcraft and H. Boesky, 'Shadow Banking' (2012) *Federal Reserve Bank of New York Staff Report No. 458.*
8 Jun Luo, 'Shadow Banking' (*Bloomberg.com*, 24 September 2018) <https://www.bloomberg.com/quicktake/shadow-banking>.
9 Zoltan Pozsar, Tobias Adrian, Adam Ashcraft and Hayley Boesky, 'Shadow Banking' (December 2013) *FRBNY Economic Policy Review* <https://doi.org/https://www.newyorkfed.org/medialibrary/media/research/epr/2013/0713adri.pdf>.
10 Laura E. Kodres, 'Shadow Banks: Out of the Eyes of Regulators' *F&D Article* <https://www.imf.org/external/pubs/ft/fandd/basics/52-shadow-banking.htm> accessed 13 August 2021.
11 'Still Lurking in the Shadows: A Look at Home Mortgages and Shadow Banking' (*Mark Weinstein Law*, 28 October 2020) <https://markweinsteinlaw.com/still-lurking-in-the-shadows-a-look-at-home-mortgages-and-shadow-banking/>.
12 Sebastiaan Pool, 'Mortgage Debt and Shadow Banks' DNB Working Paper PDF <https://www.dnb.nl/media/phbaxba2/working-paper-no-588_tcm47-373438.pdf> accessed 13 August 2021.
13 B. Bernanke, *The Global Saving Glut and the U.S. Current Account Deficit. Sandridge Lecture* (Virginia Association of Economics, 10 March 2005).
14 Pool (n 12).
15 J. Hebron, 'Size of U.S. Mortgage Market in 2020 (January edition)' (*Yahoo! Finance*, 8 January 2020) <https://finance.yahoo.com/news/size-u-mortgage-market-2020-154148225.html?guccounter=1&guce_referrer=aHR0cHM6Ly93d3cuZ29vZ2xlL&...>.
16 'Research and Economics: Mortgage Bankers Association' *MBA* <https://www.mba.org/news-research-and-resources/research-and-economics> accessed 13 August 2021.
17 Amit Seru, 'Regulation of the Mortgage Market Must Consider Shadow Banks' <https://siepr.stanford.edu/research/publications/regulation-mortgage-market-shadow-banks> accessed December 2018.
18 L.E. Kodres, 'Shadow Banking – What Are We Really Worried About?' in S. Claessens, D. Evanoff, G. Kaufman and L. Laeven (eds), *Shadow Banking Within and Across National Borders, World Scientific* (World Scientific Publishing Company 2015) 229–37.
19 Vanessa Endrejat and Matthias Thiemann, 'When Brussels Meets Shadow Banking – Technical Complexity, Regulatory Agency and the Reconstruction of the Shadow Banking Chain' (2020) 24(4, 6) *Competition and Change* 225–47 <http://proxy.library.nyu.edu/login?url=https://www.proquest.com/scholarly-journals/when-brussels-meets-shadow-banking-technical/docview/2510588953/se-2?accountid=12768>
20 'Cheat Sheet: What Are Shadow Banking & Money Market Funds (MMFs)?' (*Finance Watch*, 20 February 2019) <https://www.finance-watch.org/publication/cheat-sheet-what-are-shadow-banking-money-market-funds-mmfs/>.

21 Carlo Bellavite Pellegrini, Michele Meoli and Giovanni Urga, 'Money Market Funds, Shadow Banking and Systemic Risk in United Kingdom' (2017) 21 *Finance Research Letters* 163–71, ISSN 1544–6123 <https://www.sciencedirect.com/science/article/pii/S1544612317300697>.
22 N. Paltalidis, D. Gounopoulos, R. Kizys and Y. Koutelidakis, 'Transmission Channels of Systemic Risk and Contagion in the European Financial Network' (2015) 61 *Journal of Banking Finance* S36–S52.
23 Pellegrini et al. (n 21).
24 Greg Buchak, Gregor Matvos, Tomasz Piskorski and Amit Seru, 'Fintech, Regulatory Arbitrage, and the Rise of Shadow Banks' (2018) 130(3) *Journal of Financial Economics*, Elsevier 453–83.
25 Organization for Economic Co-operation and Development (OECD) OECD (2020), Digital Disruption in Banking and its Impact on Competition <http://www.oecd.org/daf/competition/digital-disruption-in-financial-markets.htm>.
26 Z, '2020 Has Been the Year of SPAC IPOs: Here Are the Prominent 4' (*Nasdaq*, 28 December 2020) <https://www.nasdaq.com/articles/2020-has-been-the-year-of-spac-ipos%3A-here-are-the-prominent-4-2020-12-28>.
27 R. Corales, *Q1 2021 Global Capital Markets Activity: SPAC IPOs, Issuance in Consumer Discretionary Sector Surge* (S&P Global Market Intelligence, 3 May 2021).
28 SPAC Analytics, SPAC Analytics – Home, n.d. <https://www.spacanalytics.com/>
29 Kerry Liu, 'COVID-19 and the Chinese Economy: Impacts, Policy Responses and Implications' (2021) 35(2) *International Review of Applied Economics* 308–30. doi:10.1080/02692171.2021.1876641.
30 A. Maheshwari, 'Shadow Banking and the Real Estate Bubble: Is Financial Crisis a Real Possibility in China?' (20 July 2021) <https://icsin.org/blogs/2021/07/20/shadow-banking-and-the-real-estate-bubble-is-financial-crisis-a-real-possibility-in-china/>.
31 Stephen Bell and Hui Feng, 'Rethinking Critical Juncture Analysis: Institutional Change in Chinese Banking and Finance' (2021) 28(1) *Review of International Political Economy* 36–58 <http://dx.doi.org/10.1080/09692290.2019.1655083>. http://proxy.library.nyu.edu/login?url=https://www.proquest.com/scholarly-journals/rethinking-critical-juncture-analysis/docview/2500885212/se-2?accountid=12768>
32 Xiaodong Zhu, 'The Varying Shadow of China's Banking System' (2021) 49(1/3) *Journal of Comparative Economics* 135–46.
33 Zheng (Michael) Song and Wei Xiong, 'Risks in China's Financial System' (2018) 10(1) *Annual Review of Financial Economics* 261–86.
34 Viral V. Acharya, Jun Qian, Yang Su and Zhishu Yang, 'In the Shadow of Banks: Wealth Management Products and Issuing Banks' Risk in China' (28 February 2021) <https://ssrn.com/abstract=3401597 or http://dx.doi.org/10.2139/ssrn.3401597>.
35 Song and Xiong (n 33).
36 Guofeng Sun, *China's Shadow Banking: Bank's Shadow and Traditional Shadow Banking* BIS Working Papers 822 (Bank for International Settlements 2019).

8 Special Purpose Acquisition Companies as Venture Companies

Giorgio Tosetti Dardanelli

8.1 Introduction

The Special Purpose Acquisition Company (SPAC) is undeniably a new financial product of Wall Street. However, further questions emerge as SPACs have climbed the chart of the entire initial public offerings (IPOs) market in the United States between 2020 and 2021. According to D'Alvia,[1] under a multilevel definition of SPACs, those investment vehicles are flexible and dynamic and can take as many forms as the markets demand. However, what happens when SPACs are venture companies or non-bank lenders in distressed companies? This chapter aims to provide preliminary remarks on those important and open-ended questions as the SPAC market evolves. A key feature of SPACs is clear: SPACs are based on equity instruments (common shares, preference shares, and warrants) rather than debt securities.[2]

The regulation of the loan market matters, at least since the global credit crisis of 2008–2010, later defined as the Global Financial Crisis (GFC). Specifically, it has been seen that the growth of private debt has significantly contributed to a 'credit bubble.' When it arose out of the 2007 financial crisis, governments consolidated international banking regulation. Think of the Basel III agreements published in December 2010. Since then, banking regulators worldwide have tightened laws to strengthen financial systems to prevent another crash. Essentially, the primordial idea was to connect the crisis to the growth of excessive bank financing. Regulators concluded that restrictions on certain types of financing were the way to limit systemic risk. Since then, banks have been required to keep more cash in reserve to lend to businesses rather than government loans. This means that some businesses have less access to credit or no access at all. Even if a company has positive earnings before interest, taxes, depreciation, and amortization, this does not guarantee that the business can be accredited to receive bank financing.[3]

This has opened up an ideal opportunity for institutional and private investors to fill the vacuum. Private debt instruments might have some advantages for investors' portfolios, namely higher yield and the absence of a direct connection to market volatility. However, investing in private debt

DOI: 10.4324/9781003169079-12

means scarifying liquidity for a higher return and capital stability. This, in turn, has given rise to the acknowledgment that the level of private debt cannot be ignored. It is destined to play a central role in contemporary financial markets regarding access to finance and as a great sign of the intrinsic nature of financial systems to fail to systemic risk and moral hazard. The money is bypassing the traditional and heavily regulated banking system and flowing through a growing network of businesses that finance high-risk businesses and investments. This is not coming for free. Indeed, a spotlight was shone on the vulnerabilities of the shadow banking sector when Archegos Capital Management (Archegos) collapsed in March 2021. Archegos was a family office capital management firm. They controlled some $5.9 trillion in assets. That is more than the total assets of hedge funds. The successive headline-making blow-ups of Greensill Capital and Archegos have sobering effects on money managers and risk investors across the globe.

SPACs do not have much in common with family offices. However, family offices can be involved either on the SPAC sponsor side or in de-SPAC transactions as targets to become listed entities. The fact that a family office can act as a sponsor or as the final public entity does not imply that SPACs shall be considered financing instruments. However, SPACs might act as venture companies providing new financing to business entities. In section 8.2, I introduce the topic of distressed finance and the importance of having priority rules in corporate restructuring and financing provided by third parties. This paves the way to the discourse of what can be defined as a 'white-knight' or 'financier' SPAC, namely an SPAC that has as a primary objective the acquisition of distressed businesses and that is targeting distressed markets in geographically distressed areas and in so doing it can rescue those companies and restructure their finances. I outline that establishing specific rules to protect new financing is critical and can also influence the geographical area.

As we all know, shadow banks, as non-bank lenders are called, have been a source of unpleasant surprises for markets across the globe over the years. Think of failed experiments in crypto banks such as the collapse of Celsius Network LLC in July 2022 or the failure of FTX Trading Ltd in November 2022, commonly known as FTX (short for 'Futures Exchange'), is a bankrupt company that formerly operated a cryptocurrency exchange and crypto hedge fund. In SPACs, it still seems premature to speak about shadow banking because of the lack of practical instances even when real examples have emerged, as I illustrate in section 8.3, and also because the typical function of non-bank lending is mainly based on providing access to finance for consumer credit, mortgages, and company financing, especially in those areas where there is a lower-income people such as in Latin America or China.[4] SPACs targeting distressed businesses do not necessarily follow such objectives; instead, they aim to acquire the seller's control. Consolidating remarks are provided in section 8.4.

8.2 Distressed Businesses in Times of Crisis

Insolvency systems can contribute to the recovery of a distressed economy by targeting the overhand debt problem and encouraging bridge financing.[5] Debt overhang refers to a condition where existing debt hinders the raising of new debt, potentially depriving businesses of financial difficulty from new finance. The overhang can characterize economies hit by a systemic shock, be it liquidity, supply or demand shock, or other types of shocks, for example, shocks fuelled by a global health crisis.

New finance can be vital in various stages during the rehabilitation of businesses, from financing immediate liquidity needs to funding a business model change. Interim finance is necessary for a business to continue operating until a reorganization plan is formed. The availability of additional finance reinforcing a reorganization plan can be decisive in securing adequate creditor support for such plans.[6] A systemic crisis amplifies the importance of rescuing economically viable businesses suffering under temporary financial pressures to preserve employment and thus reduce the social cost of economic shocks.[7] At the same time, rescue efforts should be optimized to prevent supporting unhealthy businesses, diverting scarce financial resources away from viable businesses, and reducing the chances of the latter recovering.

In the context of the COVID-19-induced crisis, the World Bank has pointed to the need for complementing fiscal and regulator measures with insolvency-related measures. As the World Bank advocates, bridge financing can help solvent companies alleviate the detrimental effects of economic shock, and insolvency laws can play a role in encouraging pre-insolvency financing by protecting such financing from avoidance actions and prioritizing related claims in the event of a failed rescue attempt.

The possibility of providing new financing and prioritization, amongst other elements, can characterize an insolvency regime. The lack of priority afforded to new finance has been identified as a potential obstacle to reorganization.[8] It is suggested that insolvency regimes with fewer impediments to restructuring are better prepared to tackle inefficient capital reallocation, that is, the wasteful use of capital in non-viable 'zombie' firms.[9]

National insolvency regimes vary concerning the treatment of new finance. While Organisation for Economic Co-operation and Development (OECD) focuses on the positive effects of prioritizing new finance over unsecured creditors,[10] certain jurisdictions permit the prioritization of new finance over administrative expenses (super-priority) or secured creditors (priming). For example, super-priority and priming are distinguishing features of the US's debtor-in-possession finance scheme in Chapter 11 bankruptcy proceedings.[11] However, certain jurisdictions remain skeptical toward similar prioritizing rules. For example, in the UK, although legislators recognize the importance of rescue finance, the government rejected the super-priority rule in administration. Moreover, it excluded it from legislative reforms regulating a preventive restructuring framework.[12]

The COVID-19-induced economic crisis has placed priority and avoidance actions on the agenda of various countries. For example, the Covid Insolvency Suspension Act protected new finance from avoidance actions in Germany and excluded lender liability. While the new rules safeguard new third-party rescue financiers, they do not protect the novation or extension of loans.[13] New shareholder loans that support liquidity (excluding extensions or new advances under existing subordinated shareholder loans or new security granted to shareholder loans) enjoy similar protection. However, these temporary measures may not be available in the long term. By contrast, for instance, Poland introduced a new, simplified restructuring procedure to respond to the economic crisis. Under the new rules, should the simplified proceedings fail, new finance is safeguarded in subsequent restructuring proceedings or liquidation.[14] On the other hand, the new rules do not protect new finance if the restructuring arrangement is disapproved.

The UK legislator has adopted a different view during the recent crisis. New priority-related rules were introduced in the preventive framework under the Corporate Insolvency and Governance Act 2020. The rules permit granting security subject to the monitor's consent (and a statement about rescue potential) during the standalone moratorium.[15] Moreover, they accord priority to debt arising in the moratorium or stemming from undertakings thereunder ('moratorium debt') or debts existing prior to the moratorium, provided neither payment-holiday nor acceleration is attached to them ('priority pre-moratorium debt'). Where liquidation follows, priority is established over all claims except the receiver's, and where administration follows, over the administrator's expenses, preferential claims subscribed part, and existing floating charge holders. As practitioners pointed out, new moratorium lenders thus enjoy high priority and are ranked ahead of pre-existing floating charge claims.

International standards generally promote the prioritization of new finance and its exemption from avoidance actions. As demonstrated, some jurisdictions have already followed the lead even though they are under the duress of the recent recession. Despite apparent consensus at the supranational level and acknowledged global best practices, there seems to be a disagreement about whether new finance should be protected and, if so, to what extent. Proponents primarily argue that protecting new finance helps overcome the debt overhang problem. Opponents mostly hold that safeguarding new finance may result in opportunistic behavior and should be avoided.[16] Furthermore, it is argued that prioritization and exemption from avoidance actions may complement each other. However, it may not be necessary to introduce both.

Priority means the superior status of a claim in ranking against more junior claims. Statutory priority rules are generally set out in liquidation proceedings. However, priority may also be created by a contractual agreement outside of insolvency proceedings (ex-ante priority) or a bargain between creditors in reorganization-type insolvency proceedings (ex-post priority).

From the prioritization perspective, there is tension between the existing creditors of the distressed debtor and its potential rescue financiers. On the one hand, existing creditors may reasonably insist on the order of priority established pre-insolvency, as this ensures predictability and confidence.

On the other hand, however, this may result in biases in the event of financial distress. As the 'New Bargain Theory proposed,' the unforeseen consequences of financial stress are 'not contractible.' Therefore, the purpose of reorganization-type insolvency proceedings is to provide a framework for renegotiating imperfect contracts.

On the other hand, new finance is frequently needed to reorganize the distressed debtor. Distressed debt financiers generally seek enhanced protection through payment priority and security, while existing secured creditors are interested in protecting pre-insolvency security interests.[17] Thus, one indicator of the efficiency of priority rules may be how effectively they can tackle the conflict between existing and new creditors in reorganization.

Ex-post priority will likely incentivize new finance as it promises a relatively low-risk investment. However, ill-placed capital injections can further distort operational and financial capacity. New finance may be used unproductively, that is, non-profitable projects may be financed (often referred to as 'overinvestment'), or opportunities to finance profitable projects may be missed without incentives (often referred to as 'underinvestment'). New finance may be essential in assessing profitable investment opportunities and business volatility. This role may be even more critical where insolvency courts face the severe pressure of mass bankruptcies with limited capacity to assess the viability of reorganization plans.[18] It may indicate whether the priority rules adequately incentivize new finance to support value generation.

As pointed out earlier, international organizations generally advocate prioritizing new finance. The flagship legislation on the global stage has traditionally been the United States' Chapter 11 procedure with its concept of debtor-in-possession finance. The underlining concept of debtor-in-possession financing is that, in bankruptcy proceedings, a security right granted to new investors can be ranked ahead of (or rank equally to) the claims of creditors that secured 'first-in-time-priority' outside of bankruptcy (priming). Where priming is not an option, financiers can secure automatic administrative expensive status (for unsecured finance in the ordinary course of business); or, with the court's approval, can obtain administrative expense status for unsecured finance (outside the ordinary course of business), or for secured finance (i) super-priority status overall administrative expenses; (ii) first lien in uncharged assets, or (iii) second lien in charged assets. These features present debtor-in-possession financing in a positive light.

By contrast, the UK legislator, as I have briefly outlined before, refused super-priority because providing super-priority to new finance, which increases return prospects of new financiers without guaranteeing a commercially sound rescue plan, may be so detrimental that it is safer to avoid.[19] Sometimes it is argued that incumbent creditors may withhold additional credits or increase interest rates as a deterrent against reallocating priorities to new super-priority financers. Furthermore, protecting new finance is opposed because it invites opportunistic behavior.[20] Opportunistic use of new finance may occur on the lender's side through (i) cross-collateralization and roll-up or (ii) 'loan-to-own' financing. Cross-collateralization is a form of 'defensive financing' where an existing lender provides interim financing to obtain security for earlier unsecured loans or higher-rank security for secured loans. Indeed, pre-petition lenders' willingness to provide new finance may be enhanced by the prospect of converting pre-existing junior claims into senior claims and thereby substantially reducing the overall lending risk.

Similarly, new finance may be conditional upon repaying earlier debts (roll-up). However, unsecured creditors may contest such opportunistic moves, and the court may scrutinize the ratio of funds used for roll-up versus funds injected into the business. By contrast, the loan-to-own arrangement is an 'offensive financing' strategy, as the lender's intention is frequently to finance businesses destined to default where the lender's ultimate goal is to acquire shareholding or assets.[21] However, with these financing structures, the debtor may secure more favorable terms than it would otherwise be able to obtain from a third-party lender.

The borrower can also be opportunistic. For example, the management or shareholders of the debtor company often engage in 'conduit pipe finance.' This refers to the phenomenon when instead of dedicating raised funds to business improvement, it is spent on repaying debts guaranteed by the management or shareholders, thus decreasing their financial exposure.

In our case, the SPAC is a versatile investment vehicle, and sometimes it cannot be excluded that upon the occurrence of the right circumstance, it might be used as a bridge finance vehicle or even as a venture company or financier providing new financing to distressed business entities or new emerging companies.

8.3 Broadstone Acquisition Corp.: A Case Study

In August 2020, a new possible trend emerged with the incorporation of Broadstone Acquisition Corp. (Broadstone): an SPAC sponsored by Sun Capital Partners. Broadstone was incorporated as a Cayman Islands company, listed in New York and headquartered in London. It has been a swift change in the purpose of SPACs: distressed opportunities.

In September 2020, Broadstone announced the closing of an IPO of 30,000,000 units for $10 per unit on the New York Stock Exchange, targeting companies either in the UK or in Europe that are in distress. This is evidenced by the S-1 form filed with the SEC on 13 August 2020, which reads that the main focus of the SPAC is on "sound but stressed businesses." This is because the management of Broadstone believes that the pandemic is creating an unusually large number of undervalued acquisition opportunities as target businesses suffer from financial indebtedness and a lack of equity funding alternatives. Specifically, Broadstone can be an ideal liquidity solution for vendors that lack alternative equity sources available for private companies. At the same time, shareholders may get share exchange deals.

In the second quarter of 2021, Broadstone announced the business combination with Vertical Aerospace (Vertical), a global aerospace and technology company pioneering zero-emissions aviation. Vertical is a leading UK-headquartered engineering and aeronautical business developing electric Vertical Take-Off and landing (eVTOL) aircraft. The transaction makes Vertical a publicly-traded company with a pro forma equity value of approximately $2.2 billion. Vertical will be listed on the New York Stock Exchange following the combination that has been eventually approved in December 2021. Vertical was founded in 2016 by Stephen Fitzpatrick, an established entrepreneur best known as the founder of the Ovo Group, a leading energy company determined to create a world without carbon and which includes Ovo Energy, the UK's second-biggest energy retailer with revenues of $6.5 billion.

8.3.1 Remarks on White-Knight or Financier SPACs

As it can be seen, Broadstone started as an example of a white-knight or financier SPAC by providing finance to distressed companies and ended up acquiring a start-up or zero-revenue company in aviation instead. SPACs are traditionally used to target private operating companies. Then the trend swiftly to positive EBITDA companies, and last but not least, pre-revenue companies (think of Arrival or Cazoo in the UK or super app Grab in Singapore). This shows that when a sponsor sets up an SPAC in the United States, it is genuinely free to pursue the business combination that mostly fulfills its business objectives. Moreover, there is no specific prohibition of pursuing a different business combination if the economic circumstances during the two-year life span of the SPAC might impose a reconsideration of the initial targets stated in the S-1 form. This example directly shows the SPAC model's dynamicity, and it provides us with a direct instance that an SPAC whose objective is to provide new financing to distressed businesses is a real possibility. Specifically, a white knight or financier SPAC will look at national corporate provisions on protecting new financing in terms of priority and avoidance actions (see section 8.2). This will be essential in determining the geographical area and the applicable law of the de-SPAC transaction. In other words, a white-knight SPAC will tend to acquire targets based in jurisdictions that protect new financing, especially if the SPAC is acting as an injection of new liquidity or in terms of shares' purchase and, therefore, the provision of new assets in a restructuring procedure of a distressed company. This phenomenon's importance is new, mainly due to the current pandemic and hyperinflation, where companies saw their balance sheets squeezed on the side of assets with a growing and exponential increase of their current liabilities to establish an insolvency state.

Finally, it is interesting to highlight that providing new financing is not new. The most critical example of financing new vessels can be seen in the shipping industry in the United States between 2004 and 2013.[22] According to Shachmurove and Vulanovic, the SPAC was used as a financing tool and corporate model for the shipping industry. Shipping companies merged into SPACs to acquire a public listing status and receive the SPAC's cash in the form of new financing.

8.4 SPACs: From 'Back-Door Listing' to Venture Companies

The SPAC is a well-known form of accelerated listing in the United States that is mainly used for high-speed exits by tech investors. Many Swiss investors are familiar with SPACs, as these vehicles have bought and listed many start-ups (the example I have provided in section 8.3 is just one of many others). For instance, Adam Said, owner of Geneva-based investment firm Ace & Company, exited in 2020 at several return multiples from three US start-ups he held in his portfolio (ChargePoint, Eos Energy, and Momentus Space) where three different SPACs took them over. SPACs have become a common way to list start-ups with few or no questions asked. This might raise concerns from a regulatory point of view (see Part I of this edited collection). However, defenders of SPACs praise them for providing liquidity to innovative ventures and for being flexible conduits for money cashing out of private equity and rushing into IPOs. Indeed, as long as the Federal Reserve supports the market and rates are so low, there is a market for SPAC creators. Indeed, high-risk assets have become the investments of choice as global markets swim in liquidity while interest rates remain at historic lows, spurring worries about another financial crash.

However, the SPAC remains a risky investment, at least from a de-SPAC transaction point of view and with a specific reference to the quality of the target companies and SPAC sponsors. There are as many critics of the lack of regulations for those listings as there are 'fans' of the effectiveness of these transactions. This edited book provides many instances in this regard.

Nonetheless, beyond those traditional and classic disputes on SPACs as an alternative to traditional IPOs, the SPACs are evolving toward a new frontier: to become venture companies, namely company vessels that, by raising money on the capital market, are then ready to canalize that money into new 'business adventures' of promising target companies by financing their dreams.[23] The following section provides a recent example that emerged on a recognized investment exchange in London by the end of 2021. It raises further remarks on whether those investment vehicles, namely the SPACs, are ready to perform additional duties beyond a classic 'back-door' listing appearance.

8.4.1 AQSE: SPACs as Venture Companies

In the face of Brexit, as shown in Part I of this edited collection, it is essential to design competitive regulatory frameworks to attract new capital inflows into the country. Moreover, when entrepreneurs need capital injection and liquidity, SPACs can play a pivotal role. In light of this, in December 2020, the Aquis Stock Exchange (AQSE) in London introduced new eligibility criteria to the Access Rulebook for Special Purpose Acquisition Companies. However, before analyzing these new listing rules, it is important to trace back a short history and background of AQSE in London.

Historically smaller companies have sought to list on the Alternative Investment Market (AIM) of the London Stock Exchange. However, the pace of such listings slowed following a change to the AIM Rules implemented in 2016, by which the fundraising threshold, at the time of listing, was increased from £3 million to the current threshold of £6 million. As a result, companies turned their attention toward listing SPACs on the standard segment of the main market of the London Stock Exchange, given that this only required a minimum capitalization of £700,000 to secure a listing on this market.

However, following the changes to the Listing Rules in July 2021, SPACs must now raise a minimum of £100 million to list on this market (see Chapter 1 of this edited collection for further remarks). This means that smaller SPACs that cannot meet these minimum fundraising thresholds will now need to look elsewhere for a suitable listing venue in the UK. One suitable exchange may be the Aquis Growth Market of the Aquis Stock Exchange, as this only requires fundraising of £2 million for SPACs.

AQSE is a recognized investment exchange and operates two primary markets: the AQSE Main Market and the AQSE Growth Market. Listing on AQSE Main Market also requires the publication of a prospectus. Companies listing on AQSE Main Market must comply with a two-stage application process:

I. Apply to the FCA for admission to the official list
II. Apply to the AQSE to join the AQSE Main Market

The requirements for admission to the AQSE Main Market are set out in the AQSE Main Market Admission and Disclosure Standards and the Listing Rules. In addition, listing on AQSE might benefit companies with a positive social and environmental impact, as they will be listed in the Impact Segment, distinguishing them from impact-conscious investor audiences.

The AQSE Growth Market is a multilateral trading facility more suitable for smaller companies seeking access to investment than the AQSE Main Market. The eligibility criteria and regulatory requirements are less onerous than for the AQSE Main Market, especially since no prospectus is required. Companies are still required to complete an AQSE Exchange Admission document, but this task is more manageable than producing a prospectus.

Many of the eligibility criteria for the Growth Market are simple to fulfill, for instance, twenty-four months audited accounts, at least ten percent free float, and the appointment of one non-executive director. These features enable entrepreneurial companies seeking a faster listing with lower ongoing obligations to gain access to investors at a lower price. The AQSE Growth Market is also a Recognized Growth Market by the HMRC, which means that trades executed by UK companies on this market are exempt from the UK Stamp Duty and Stamp Duty Reserve Tax.

In 2020 – as said – after the Hill Report in March 2020, AQSE has defined SPACs as companies whose assets consist solely/mostly of cash or whose predominant objective is to identify/acquire/merge with other businesses within specific parameters. After the changes to AQSE rules in December 2020, AQSE comprises two main market segments: the Access and the Apex segments. The Apex segment is aimed at more significant, more established companies. It requires applicants to have a minimum market capitalization of £10 million and prepare a UK Growth Prospectus to list. In contrast, the Access segment of the AQSE Growth Market is designed for early-stage companies and SPACs.

As part of the IPO process, Aquis makes sure that the board of directors of the prospective SPAC has the appropriate skills and experience to execute the strategy and that the strategy is sufficiently specific – rather than a woolly 'invest in interesting companies with growth potential' that is sometimes stated by shell companies. So part of the application process will see the Aquis arrange a meeting with the board to discuss the strategy and how they intend to implement its ad to ensure they have clear plans. Aquis wants to attract SPACs that offer a genuine and credible investment proposition.

The Admission Document is required for listing on the Access segment of AQSE, and it must be published and contain the required information set out in Appendix I of the AQSE Rules. In addition, this document must contain such information as required to enable investors to make an informed assessment of the assets and liabilities, financial position, profits and losses, and prospects of the company and the rights attached to its securities. Alongside the Admission Document, various ancillary documents will be prepared as required by applicable law or the AQSE Rules. In particular, should funds be raised at the time of listing by an appointed adviser, then separate agreements will need to be drafted that set out the terms on which any fundraiser is conducted on behalf of the company.

Once the SPAC has been listed and it prepares to make its acquisition, the acquisition itself will be treated as a 'reverse takeover.' Upon the announcement of the reverse takeover, trading in the company's securities will be suspended until the publication of an Admission Document in respect of the issuer as enlarged by the reverse takeover; or AQSE is satisfied that sufficient information is publicly available about the reverse takeover such that an informed assessment can be made as to the financial positions and prospects of the company as enlarged by the reverse takeover.

The acquisition must be conditional upon shareholder approval, and therefore this must be factored as part of the acquisition process and the overall timetable. In addition, the company's admission will be canceled once it completes the reverse takeover. Therefore, it must re-apply to AQSE for admission to the enlarged group to the AQSE once again. As such, this necessitates drafting another Admission Document to include information about the enlarged group, which can usually be drafted while the acquisition is being negotiated. This allows for listing as soon as possible after the acquisition is completed.

8.5 Conclusion

In this chapter, I have discussed new emerging features of SPACs. One of them is their possible role as white-knight and financiers of distressed companies. This role can inevitably give rise to the issues I have outlined in sections 8.2 and 8.3, namely the potential undermining of unsecured and secured creditors' positions whose priorities were already established pre-insolvency. Furthermore, SPACs that target distressed entities should also be concerned about the applicable law and the geographical area of the target company in distress because different rules can allow either a priority or super-priority of new financing lenders.

Finally, SPACs today in the UK have specific listing requirements, and as has been shown in Chapter 1 of this edited collection, the UK is the first harmonized for SPACs in Europe. Specifically, in this chapter, I have examined the listing requirements of the AQSE. Here SPACs are defined as 'Enterprise Companies that can provide finance or carry out acquisitions or takeovers.' This is a direct instance of a multi-level SPAC definition as first theorized by D'Alvia, which I have explained in this chapter's introduction. SPACs are enterprise companies, and they are constantly becoming more a specification of private equity, as the emergence of new financing techniques at the de-SPAC phase in the United States also shows.[24] To this end, SPACs constitute a unique alternative acquisition model. They are correctly identified as venture companies capable of obtaining financing and new equity for distressed companies and smaller private entities by performing reverse takeovers on the AQSE.

Notes

1 Daniele D'Alvia, 'From Darkness to Light: A Comparative Study of Special Purpose Acquisition Companies in the European Union, the UK, and the US' (2022) 23 *Cambridge Yearbook of European Legal Studies* <https://www.cambridge.org/core/journals/cambridge-yearbook-of-european-legal-studies> accessed 10 January 2023; Daniele D'Alvia, 'The International Financial Regulation of SPACs between Legal Standardised Regulation and Standardisation of Market Practices' (2020) 21(2) *Journal of Banking Regulation* 107.
2 Nonetheless, please refer to Part I and to Introduction and Conclusion of this edited collection.
3 The US, for example, developed the Volcker Rule, which prohibits banks from using customers' money to make their own bets on the markets, under the Dodd-Frank Financial Reform framework, as sweeping regulatory act that subjects financial firms to stricter government oversight.
4 Please refer to Chapter 7 of this edited collection.
5 World Bank Group, 'Covid-19 Outbreak: Implications on Corporate and Individual Insolvency' (13 April 2020) <https://pubdocs.worldbank.org/

en/912121588018942884/COVID-19-Outbreak-Implications-on-Corporate-and-Individual-Insolvency.pdf> accessed 10 September 2021.

6 Directive (EU) 2019/1023 of the European Parliament and of the Council of 20 June 2019 on preventive restructuring frameworks, on discharge of debt and disqualifications, and on measures to increase the efficiency of procedures concerning restructuring, insolvency and discharge of debt, and amending Directive (EU) 2017/1132 (Directive on Restructuring and Insolvency) [2019] OJ L 172/18 (66).

7 World Bank Group (n 5).

8 Müge Adalet McGowan, Dan Andrews and Valentine Millot, 'Insolvency Regimes, Zombie Firms and Capital Reallocation' (2017) 39 *ECO/WKP*.

9 Ibid., 32.

10 Ibid.

11 US Bankruptcy Code 1978. Chapter 11 of the Bankruptcy Code of the US provides for reorganization of a corporation or partnership. The proceedings entail the preparation of a reorganization plan which shall be approved by the bankruptcy court.

12 House of Commons, 'Corporate Insolvency Framework: Proposed Major Reforms, Briefing Paper' (2019) 32 <https://commonslibrary.parliament.uk/research-briefings/cbp-8291/> accessed 23 October 2021.

13 Hengeler Mueller, 'Insolvency Law' <https://www.hengeler.com/en/covid-19/restrukturierung/insolvency-law> accessed 3 November 2021.

14 Jakub Kokowski, 'Simplified Restructuring Procedure: A New Tool for Businesses in Crisis' (25 June 2020) <https://codozasady.pl/en/authors/jakub-kokowski> accessed 10 January 2023.

15 Cathryn Williams and Paul Muscutt, 'The Corporate Insolvency and Governance Act: The Moratorium and Just How "Super" Is Super Priority?' (*Crowell & Morning*, 13 July 2020).

16 See for example, Rolef de Weijs and Meren Baltjes, 'Operating the Door for Opportunistic Use of Interim Financing: A Critical Assessment of the EU Draft Directive on Preventive Restructuring Frameworks' (2018) 27 *International Insolvency Review* 223.

17 Lijie Qi, 'Availability of Continuing Financing in Corporate Reorganisations: The UK and US Prospective' (2008) 20 *Comparative Law* 162, 163–4.

18 David Skeel, 'Bankruptcy and the Coronavirus' (*Brookings*, April 2020) 10 <https://www.brookings.edu/research/bankruptcy-and-the-coronavirus/> accessed 10 January 2023.

19 Gerard McCormack, 'Super-priority New Financing and Corporate Rescue' (2007) *Journal of Business Law* 701, 707.

20 De Weijs and Baltjes (n 16).

21 Ibid., 228–30.

22 Yochanan Shachmurove and Milos Vulanovic, 'Specified Purpose Acquisition Companies in Shipping' (2015) *Global Finance Journal* 64–79.

23 Daniele D'Alvia, 'Are SPACs the Second Coming of the IPO – or a Flash in the Pan?' (*Fortune*, 22 May 2021) <https://fortune.com/2021/05/22/spacs-ipo-stock-grab-arrival-deliveroo/> accessed 15 October 2021.

24 For further arguments, please see Introduction and Conclusion sections of this edited collection.

Conclusion

Special Purpose Acquisition Companies (SPACs) have earned much attention lately on Wall Street and in the media. This edited collection has shown that SPACs have been around in various forms for decades in the United States, but they have only taken off in the US between 2020 and 2022 as the following Figure C.1 is showing:

Starting from 30 July 2020 with Michael Klein's SPAC Churchill Capital Corp IV, which announced the pricing of a $1.80 billion initial public offering (IPO) on the New York Stock Exchange. Klein's other SPACs include Churchill Capital Corp. III, which raised $1 billion in February 2020, and an announced $11 billion merger deal with MultiPlan, a healthcare management service. July 2020 saw a very active SPAC market, with proceeds reaching $1.9, without considering Klein's fourth SPAC.

Recent years have witnessed a dramatic increase in the number of SPAC deals. Their numbers are storytelling. For instance, 2019 was the record year when 59 SPACs went public, attracting $13.6 billion in funding from the investor base. While some observers already called the peak of the SPAC market, at the end of July 2020, fifty-five new SPACs entered the space obtaining

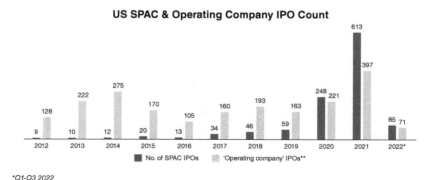

*Q1-Q3 2022
**'Operating company' IPO: IPOs & direct listings with market cap > US$50m (excludes closed-end funds, unit offerings, & SPACs)
Source: SPACInsider.com (SPAC statistics); Renaissance Capital (Operating Company IPO statistics)

Figure C.1 US SPAC and operating company IPO count.

DOI: 10.4324/9781003169079-13

$22.5 billion in financing and continuing the revolution in the equity issuance market. However, more SPACs came with the astonishing results of 2020: more than 240 SPACs listed on the New York Stock Exchange (NYSE) and National Association of Securities Dealers Automated Quotations (NASDAQ), raising a record $83 billion. SPACs overtook 2020's record in 2021 with over $115.6 billion raised via more than 400 SPACs, but in the first quarter of 2022, the SPACs market saw 54 SPACs raise $9.9 billion in proceeds similar to the 2019's data.

This edited collection has clearly shown that the decreasing numbers of SPAC offerings can be associated with something other than a lack of interest in the product or with malfunctioning their regulation and structures. By contrast, the regulatory uncertainty created by the SEC has been paramount in determining such a negative trend. As a result, the Biden administration has thought of substituting itself for the market. Indeed, if in 2009, the economy's recovery was slowed by the Obama-era regulatory policy, then 2022 is certainly coming with regulatory activism that also brings more issues to the table. As stated in an opinion written by Phil Gramn and Hester Peirce in January 2023 on the *Wall Street Journal*, the Securities and Exchange Commission is in an excess regulatory mode and tends

to substitute its own judgement for that of investors, corporate directors and managers. Its recent set of proposed rules, many of which go beyond any statutory remit, have little to do with preventing abuse or fostering transparency. The SEC has taken on the role of telling companies how to run themselves and investors how to invest. In the process, the SEC is eviscerating the vital barrier in our market-driven economy between the limited and legally constrained responsibilities of the public sector and the primacy of the private sector as the driver of American prosperity.[1]

The proposal of the new SPAC Reform in the United States in March 2022 is a clear symptom of such an approach. In a recent research paper published in Cambridge, D'Alvia defines this approach as regulation by enforcement.[2] Where the SEC has shown destructive activism, and it is over-regulating SPACs with no legal grounds to justify such intervention and sometimes issuing warnings that are signed without an implementation date and legal force (think of the accounting and reporting considerations for warrants issued by SPACs in April 2021 suggesting their inclusion as liabilities rather than equity or assets of the company).

The regulation by enforcement is also going a step forward by initiating pretentious high-profile enforcement actions and concerning, among others, Momentus Inc. and Nikola Corporation. Additionally, the SPAC litigation has also been triggered by profitable opportunities that sometimes have been put forward by short sellers in an attempt to fabricate misleading information to profit from trading by selling short.

On 3 January 2022, the Delaware Court of Chancery issued a long-awaited decision in the MultiPlan Stockholder Litigation case relating to the de-SPAC transaction between Churchill Capital Corp. III, an SPAC founded by Michael Klein, and MultiPlan, Inc.

The claim in the MultiPlan case asserted that the structure of the SPAC created divergent interests between the Class A shareholders (public investors) and Class B shareholders (the sponsor) and alleged that the defendants (including the directors of the SPAC) prioritised their personal interests above the Class A shareholders interests in completing the merger and issued a false proxy statement that deprived Class A holders of the right to make an informed decision as to whether to redeem their shares. In this respect, the complaint asserted a breach of fiduciary duty claims against the directors of the SPAC.

Specifically, the claim of Class A holders was based on a report issued by Muddy Waters Research LLC (Muddy Waters) in November 2020, about a month after the Churchill SPAC closed its $11 billion acquisition of Multi-Plan, asserting that MultiPlan was on the verge of losing its biggest customer, United Healthcare Services Inc. (United Healthcare). It was stated that United Healthcare had created a competing product to siphon off 35% of Multi-plan's revenue by the end of 2022. Hence, the valuation of the merger made by Churchill SPAC was 'ridiculous' per the Muddy Waters Chief Executive Officer (CEO) Cason Block. Because Churchill did not disclose such circumstances, this could be detrimental to the SPAC's investors (Class A holders).

The Court concluded that the claimant's allegations were sufficient to survive the defendant's motion to dismiss, principally because of the potential conflicts of interest between the public shareholders (who would profit if the stock were to trade above the redemption price of US$10.04 per share) and the defendants (who would profit from their Class B shares even if the stock were to trade substantially below that price). Accordingly, in November 2022, MultiPlan announced that the case had been resolved with claimants for $33.75 million.

It is worth noting that many SPACs do not have the same alleged conflicts as witnessed in the MultiPlan case. Indeed, the MultiPlan case is an isolated case because the sponsor could elect all directors prior to the de-SPAC closing, the directors had a substantial amount of Class B shares, and there was a longstanding relationship between Klein and the other directors.

Since then, claimants have looked at the MultiPlan case as a precedent to rely on and to claim a breach of fiduciary duty allegations in subsequent lawsuits. However, we believe that the MultiPlan case cannot constitute a legal precedent. In fact, in January 2023, Klein was successful in another litigation concerning the merger between Churchill Capital Corp. IV and Lucid Motors in July 2021. Specifically, Lucid Group Inc. won the dismissal of a lawsuit accusing the luxury electric car maker of defrauding investors in the SPAC that helped take it public, by significantly overstating its production outlook on 5 February 2021 on CNBC's 'Squawk on the Street'. US District Judge Rogers in Oakland, California, said that despite media speculation, Churchill Capital Corp. IV shareholders, who brought the proposed class action, had no reason to know in early 2021 that the SPAC would merge into Lucid. As a result, the allegedly misleading statements could not have been material to public investors' decisions to invest in the SPAC.

In addition, cases have been filed in Delaware and in the US District Court for the Southern District of New York against SPACs that received termination fees stemming from failed mergers and subsequently liquidated. These cases focus on whether the Class A holders are entitled to receive additional distributions above and beyond their pro rata share of the trust account if the SPAC liquidates. The Delaware courts have yet to issue a dispositive decision on any of these cases, and this – we believe – will be an area to watch in 2023.

Finally, it is worth mentioning the decision upheld in January 2023 by the Vice-Chancellor Lori Will of the Delaware Court of Chancery, who had another opportunity to weigh in on SPAC's breach of fiduciary duty claims. In Delman v GigAcquisitions3, the court went well beyond her earlier MultiPlan decision in finding that breach of fiduciary duty claims survived a motion to dismiss. Among the novel rulings making, this a 'must-read' for anyone involved with SPACs or SPAC transactions are the court's holdings:

I. The SPAC's redemption feature is a 'bespoke check on the sponsor's self-interest' and the 'primary means protecting stockholders from a forced investment in a transaction they believe is ill-conceived' (making disclosure relating to the redemption option essential).
II. The SPAC sponsor, even though it controlled less than 25% of the SPAC's voting power, could be considered a controlling stockholder based solely on the SPAC's structure.
III. The Corwin doctrine does not apply to SPAC mergers because stockholders' voting interests were decoupled from their economic interests as a result of the redemption feature.

GigCapital3, Inc. (Gig3 or the Company)– now Lightning eMotors Inc.– was a Delaware SPAC. Gig3's sponsor GigAcquisition3 (the Sponsor), was issued 'founder shares' for $25,000 (amounting to about 20% of Gig3's post IPO equity), which could not be redeemed, lacked liquidation rights and were also subject to a lock-up. The Company's Sponsor was controlled by the defendant and alleged 'serial founder of SPACs' Avi Katz. According to the court, Mr. Katz, via the Sponsor, effectively ran Gig3, including serving as its executive chairman secretary, president and CEO. He also appointed Gig3's initial directors and officers, which included his wife and four other directors with ties to himself and other Gig3 entities.

Following the IPO, Gig3's officers and directors identified Lightning eMotors Inc. an electric vehicle manufacturer, as the merger target. According to the court, Nomura and Oppenheimer, Gig3-s IPO bookrunners, were also hired to serve as Gig3's financial advisors, but they were not asked to provide a fairness opinion on the merger.

The Company issued a proxy statement in connection with Gig3 stockholder vote on the merger. Approximately 98% voted in favour, with 28% redeeming.

After closing, New Lightning saw its stock price crater, and litigation followed. In particular, the Court held that the de-SPAC merger with Old Lightning was a conflicted transaction. Even though the Sponsor had less than 25% of Gig3's pre-merger equity and voting power, the Court concluded that the sponsor controlled Gig3 because – as it is typical of SPAC sponsors – it controlled all aspects of the Company from creation until the de-SPAC merger. Additionally, the Court determined that the Sponsor was conflicted because the SPAC's economic structure allowed the Sponsor to extract unique value at the expense of the public stockholders in two ways: (i) the Sponsor's interest diverged from the public stockholders in the choice between a 'bad deal' and a liquidation and (ii) the Sponsor had an interest in minimising post-merger redemptions because the merger was conditioned on Gig3 contributing $150 million in cash, $50 million of which was required to come from the trust account. The Court stated 'by minimising redemption the Sponsor reduced the risk that the merger would fail and increased the value of the Sponsor's interest if it closed'. Finally, a majority of the board was not disinterested or independent, the Court held. It determined that Mr. Katz, through his ownership and control of the Sponsor, had a material conflict based on the 155.900% return on its initial $25,0000 investment, and his wife (also a director) shared these interests.

It is important to highlight that like MultiPlan, Gig3 was a pleading stage decision where the court is required to accept the plaintiff's allegations as true. Moreover, the Delaware Supreme Court has not yet had an opportunity to weigh in on the issues addressed in either MultiPlan or Gig3. Gig3's legal analysis clearly illustrates the court's skepticism of the current SPAC structure that fuelled some of its novel decisions. However, we believe that many aspects of the opinion in Gig3 appear to have been driven by the fact that the board was not independent of the SPAC sponsor. This emphasises the need for SPACs to have independent directors, and for such directors to thoroughly evaluate any potential SPAC target, with advice from unconflicted advisors. Finally, as with MultiPlan, Gig3 highlights that adequate proxy disclosures remain paramount.

As can be seen, SPACs have been the subject of securities litigation in 2022 in the United States. We predict that this trend will continue into 2023 and 2024. However, the securities class action will be likely to diminish. For instance, in 2021, there were 199 closed de-SPAC transactions, a number that is almost double the 102 de-SPACs closed in 2022. In addition, in 2021, 33 securities class actions were filed following 2020, a year with only 64 de-SPACs. Based on the average time after the merger or the SPAC IPO that it takes for a securities class action to materialise, we could expect a much higher number of securities class actions. However, only 24 were filed in 2022 – a 27% decline from 2021.

A reason for this decline is based on the fact that in 2022 there was a recession in the United States. Many companies have been experiencing disappointing performance. Hence, it is difficult for plaintiff's lawyers to claim that one particular team or merger did particularly bad. The second reason is the proposed SEC rules regarding SPACs, which came out in March 2022. Even though those rules still needed to be finalised, many adopted them as a playbook and quickly adjusted their disclosures and transactions to comply. As we have claimed in this edited collection, the SEC can enforce and encourage disclosure regarding SPAC and its target company. However, one main point that should be clear is that such pre-IPO disclosures can only be illustrative rather than definitive.

Furthermore, we assert that the benefits of SPACs are not eventually undermined, and SPAC will still be seen as a viable method of reaching public markets. They give private companies access to growth capital and investors a means of getting into one of the ground floors to back high-potential companies (see Introduction). Nonetheless, the regulatory uncertainty in the US and the volatile markets influenced by inflation in both the US and Europe will need to be addressed in order to stage a proper comeback.

The same risks in securities litigation and securities class actions are not to be seen in Europe, which traditionally relies less on judges and more on investors' judgments. As a result, European investors are more risk-averse than US investors, and the financial industry is more conservative. This is also why Europe is currently a preferred destination for SPAC sponsors, especially in dynamic jurisdictions such as the Netherlands and the UK.

Furthermore, the quality of investors differs between the United States and Europe. On the one hand, the United States has seen an increase of private retail investors, whereas European SPACs have been always highly influenced and invested mainly by qualified and institutional investors. However, the European Union has taken a clear stance in support of retail investors in any case since the ESMA public statement issued in July 2021. Efforts to protect retail investors are surely important, but we believe that retail investors represent a minority in comparison to the universe of institutional investors, who gravitate around SPACs both in Europe and in the United States.

Specifically, early investors in SPACs – often hedge funds – obtain warrants that allow them to buy more shares at a pre-set price in the future. They also typically sell their SPAC's shares before deals are completed to limit their risk. Hence, hedge funds usually profit from SPACs as early investors in the United States. Indeed, even if the SPAC shares fall, early investors are protected by the right to withdraw. Throughout the whole process, they can sell warrants or hold onto them. As a result, when SPACs shares surge, warrants become more valuable.

On the other hand, small investors or retail investors buy at market price and tend to hold shares after the merger, exposing themselves to the risk of a subpar deal. Markets evolve, and investors can determine their risk appetite for investments and price them accordingly, or not invest at all. For instance, a retail investor who does not redeem shares when these are trading below their net asset value is surely negligent and should avoid investing. It is self-evident that SPACs are a new financial product where financial literacy is remarkably important. Financial regulators in Europe and the United States might consider adopting specific non-binding guidelines to provide investors with acumen in financial knowledge of SPACs. This is a preferable and more reasonable choice rather than over-burdening SPAC sponsors with excessive disclosures that in relation to the de-SPAC phase – in any case – might necessarily be more illustrative (as we said) than definitive.

The edited collection has shown that European sponsors buy equity and avoid warrants. In Europe, founder shares are assigned under preference shares, although in Amsterdam, a sponsor is free to replicate the full US-style features with the founder warrants if he wishes to do so. Furthermore, in Europe, new structures align founder shares to the SPAC's performance (e.g. Ian Osborne's Hedosophia on Euronext Amsterdam, or Arietti's Industrial Stars of Italy four on Euronext Growth in Italy), and they try to mitigate criticalities of SPAC investors' dilution. This confirms the importance of market practices in SPACs, and market practices in the European Union are likely to be the future of SPACs, rather than strictly imposed rules. Italy is a good instance of innovative practices in SPACs from the sponsor side. For example, in 2018, the first SPAC in Insurtech, named Archimede S.p.A., and promoted by Andrea Battista, Gianpiero Rosmarini and Matteo Carbone raised €47 million on the Alternative Investment Market (AIM). Specifically, Archimede S.p.A. acquired the target company Net Insurance, and this gave rise to a new business combination model: the merger had already been agreed and planned before an IPO functional to raising funds useful for the merger. This was the implementation of a successful plan. In May 2018, investors rewarded with €47 million for the successful collection of the IPO of the SPAC Archimede. In June, in fact, the first official act of the business combination between Archimede was marked with Net Insurance. The administrative bodies of the two joint-stock companies have approved and signed the binding framework agreement relating to the project of merger by reverse incorporation of Archimede into Net Insurance. This can give rise to an 'instant SPAC'. Something that Italy has pioneered, and that Revo S.p.A. always in Insurtech has followed in 2021.

One of the last innovations on the sponsor side is always coming from Italy, and it has been pioneered by Arietti in summer 2021 with the definition of 'rechargeable SPAC'. The SPAC Industrial Stars of Italy 4 listed on AIM Italia in July 2021, which raised €138 million to invest in medium-sized Italian private companies characterised by a strong competitive positioning in their field of activity and a significant international presence or international development plans. In particular, Attilio Arietti worked on the issue of redemption, which was the root of the problems of many SPACs in Italy. In fact, as this edited collection has shown, the Italian Civil Code provides for a series of cases in which shareholders have the right to redeem, but a company can in turn establish other possibilities of redemption for its shareholders (the so-called conventional withdrawal). Industrial Stars of Italy 4 opted for this solution. The SPAC has reserved the right of withdrawal or redemption only to the original or early investors (i.e. those who bought shares of the SPAC during the IPO and who will keep those shares in their portfolio). Those investors are the only ones allowed to vote on the business combination proposal. In light of this, moral hazard is reduced by avoiding that secondary markets' investors can enter the SPAC when the share price is below the IPO price of €10 per share. Indeed, those investors are usually following opportunistic behaviours by intending to redeem their shares when the business combination occurs to obtain the redemption price, which is obviously higher than the initial purchase price. In this way, they do make a profit on the difference without even evaluating the proposed business combination.

This solution, however, entails the fact that the SPAC will not merge with the target company, as it usually happens. In fact, when the merger occurs, the law on the redemption right of the shareholders who disagree with the transaction would apply; therefore, all the shareholders, regardless of whether they are original investors in the SPAC or investors who entered the secondary market will have the possibility to obtain the redemption price. Furthermore, in the case of a merger the shareholders' resolution would have had to be voted in an extraordinary assembly and, therefore, with the majorities required for the extraordinary assembly.

For this reason, the SPAC of Arietti planned a new structure. It was envisaged that the target company at the moment of the business combination will launch a capital increase that the SPAC will subscribe to with the capitals raised during the IPO. The SPAC once the target shares have been obtained will pass them on to its shareholders as a distribution of extraordinary reserves without tax effect, and admission to listing on *Borsa Italiana* S.p.A. will be requested. This solution has also the advantage of not requiring the resolution of an extraordinary shareholders' meeting. In fact, the ordinary shareholders' meeting is sufficient, which means that it is easier to reach the decision-making quorum, which has proved to be another of the problems of Italian SPACs in recent times. Finally, the timing of the operation will also be significantly reduced, because without the merger, the 60 days period provided by the Italian Civil Code for creditors to oppose the merger will not have to pass (which in the case of the SPACs is nonsense). And also the withdrawal or redemption right periods will be much shorter than those provided by the law: instead of waiting for 15 days from the registration of the shareholders' resolution, a certified e-mail within 48 hours from the meeting is enough. This prevents the outcome of the operation from being suspended for 20 or 30 days.

From this new structure also derives the fact that essentially the SPAC will be, as anticipated earlier, a 'rechargeable SPAC', because once freed from the actions of the first target, it will be able to raise other capitals to be allocated to a new operation or, if it finds an interesting target larger than expected, for which the necessary investment should be more important than the initial capital raised in the IPO. Indeed, before the SPAC's IPO, a capital increase of up to 500 million will be approved with the delegation to the Board of Directors to implement it when appropriate within five years. This makes it possible to obtain additional funds from the market or, in case of non-interest, from a third party, according to a logic similar to that of the PIPE widely used in the United States, if the capital raised in the IPO of the SPAC would not be sufficient for the proposed business combination.

Finally, to provide an incentive to original investors to vote on the proposed business combination, the sponsor has set up a very generous mechanism for assigning warrants. The original investors will get two warrants for every ten SPAC shares at the time of the IPO and another eight warrants for every ten shares at the time of the operation's success. On the other hand, investors who have purchased the shares on the secondary market and who have not exercised the withdrawal or redemption right will obtain six warrants for every ten shares at the time of the transaction. As for the warrants of the shares that will be subject to withdrawal, they will not disappear, but they will be redistributed among the original shareholders. The same for the two additional warrants of the original shareholders who will have sold the shares on the secondary market. If a simulation is made, assuming 20% of withdrawals and 20% of shares sold on the secondary market, then the original shareholders who did not sell and did not withdraw would have 14.7 warrants for every ten shares.

It is obvious that all this will have the effect of reducing trading on the secondary market and therefore making the sale of the shares by the original shareholders more complicated. To overcome this problem, the sponsor has created three 'put options' windows at pre-established prices (at 6th, 12th and 18th month, respectively, at €9.6, €9.7 and €9.8). When these windows occur, those who want can sell their shares to the SPAC itself. All for a maximum amount of 20% of the shares in circulation.

We believe that the corporate structure of this SPAC might be too complex sometimes to be understood by public investors. Indeed, the proposed structure of Arietti is not even an SPAC in the traditional and common understanding of this concept. Nonetheless, this example is paramount in order to highlight the importance of being competitive on the sponsor side and propose new structures to market participants in order for the sponsor to distinguish itself. Eventually, the answer of the Italian market to this proposal was positive and successful with over €100 million raised on the AIM.

The edited collection has shown how the Italian financial market has a great potential for SPACs. Back in 2017–2019, Italy has led the SPAC revolution in Europe. However, such initial enthusiasm and openness of the Italian financial markets has been superseded by a sceptic aptitude towards SPACs that was not and it is not connected to the lower numbers of SPAC listings in the United States between 2022 and 2023. By contrast, this negative approach towards SPACs in Italy has been especially influenced by complex company law provisions (see Chapter 3, and Part II in general), and a lack of a proper financial literacy of SPACs that can be seen in market operators from accountancy firms until investment banks in Italy. For these reasons, we do believe that the Italian Exchange, namely *Borsa Italiana* S.p.A., shall further take into account the implementation of soft law guidelines to enhance financial literacy of SPACs to benefit investors as well as market operators, including investment banks and bankers. *Borsa Italiana* S.p.A. should work possibly with Consob (the Italian financial regulator) in consultation with scholars and market participants to achieve such objective, and agree on a common text that can serve as a guidance to any SPAC stakeholders.

Finally, the Italian legal system in terms of SPACs still has a preconception. The preferred SPAC structure in Italy is based on an SPAC incorporated under Italian law possibly by a famous and serial SPAC sponsor from Italy that wishes to target an Italian company to get listed in Italy. In other words, there is a strong emphasis on the domestic environment based on the idea that domestic investors, namely Italian investors would like to support a domestic target company. This is because an Italian investor is more familiar with Italian companies and Italian markets, and being the SPAC listed in Milan, it seems like the natural consequence to target an Italian company. The same idea of SPAC is more or less followed by the financial industry in the UK, Germany, Spain, France and so forth. The true exception in the European Union might be the Netherlands where foreign sponsors can easily list without any preference reserved to national sponsor by investment banks, and where they can target companies beyond the borders of the Netherlands. Indeed, as this edited collection has shown, the United States has portrayed an idea of SPAC that is universal and transnational (see Grab, Cazoo, Arrival, Zegna etc.). In this feature rests one of the most important characteristic of the SPAC, namely its international vocation and the ability to move capital within and across borders. The European Union and the UK are still new to the concept of SPAC, and they still have to fully understand the great potentials that a full implementation of the SPAC concept can produce because – as we have outlined – the SPAC can generate a political issue. In other words, national companies can be the target of foreign SPACs, and they can eventually list on foreign markets. Consequently, this can cause an in-flow and out-flow of capital within and across national borders. Probably the most recent and significant evidence that confirms the need of having an accommodating and flexible traditional IPO framework in addition to evolved SPAC-friendly market rules is the London IPO of Arm that in March 2023 preferred New York to London. Since then the Financial Conduct Authority has been blamed by some UK officials and SoftBank staff for London losing out to New York the Cambridge-based semiconductor company owned by SoftBank.[3] This also constitutes a direct evidence to the arguments we highlighted in Introduction of this edited collection when we commented on the reasons of existence of the SPAC, namely an inefficient IPO listing process that seems a constant of many legal systems of the world.

For these reasons, we urge *Borsa Italiana* S.p.A. and the Italian government to promote a competitive environment in Italy and to educate the financial industry in becoming more SPAC-friendly. This is also to avoid that national companies in Italy might follow the example of Zegna in trading their shares on foreign exchanges contributing to an outflow of capital from Italy and Europe more generally. This effort should also be followed by a specific modification of Italian company law in order to design dedicated legal provisions for SPACs (see Chapter 3 on this point too). This is to consent the SPAC to be incorporated under a more flexible company law framework that could be based on the model of the Netherlands or Belgium company laws. Indeed, those two jurisdictions could serve as a possible legal transplant for the Italian legal system. Spain also is an example that might be useful to confirm once more the understanding that company law provisions are more important that listing requirements in SPACs (see Chapter 1). Additionally, another example can be seen in Amsterdam where in the absence of pre-established market rules for SPACs, the flexibility of its company law framework is sufficient to lure the interest of SPAC sponsors and investors alike. Such modification in Italy would also prevent more complex structures such as Arietti's rechargeable SPAC.

To this end, we believe that the future of SPACs in the United States, the European Union or the UK is within their market practices, and in the creativity of sponsors to propose innovative structures in SPACs that can benefit public investors and stakeholders. Only flexible corporate law frameworks rather than strict financial regulation can make the difference in attracting more SPAC sponsors within domestic borders or providing national investors with more enthusiasm and possibilities in sponsoring SPACs within their own jurisdiction.

Notes

1 Phil Gramm and Hester Peirce, 'The SEC Seeks to Supplant the Market' (*Wall Street Journal*, 19 January 2023).
2 Daniele D'Alvia, 'From Darkness to Light: A Comparative Study of Special Purpose Acquisition Companies in the European Union, the UK, and the US' (2022) 23 *Cambridge Yearbook of European Legal Studies* <https://www.cambridge. org/core/journals/cambridge-yearbook-of-european-legal-studies> accessed 10 January 2023.
3 Anna Gross et al., 'FCA Regulator Blamed for Arm's Decision to Shun London Listing' (*Financial Times*, 3 March 2023).

Index

Note: Page numbers in *italics* indicate a figure and page numbers in **bold** indicate a table on the corresponding page.